Smart Chicks on Screen

D1607569

Smart Chicks on Screen

Representing Women's Intellect in Film and Television

Edited by
Laura Mattoon D'Amore

ROWMAN & LITTLEFIELD
Lanham • Boulder • New York • London

Published by Rowman & Littlefield
A wholly owned subsidiary of The Rowman & Littlefield Publishing Group, Inc.
4501 Forbes Boulevard, Suite 200, Lanham, Maryland 20706
www.rowman.com

Unit A, Whitacre Mews, 26-34 Stannary Street, London SE11 4AB

Copyright © 2014 by Rowman & Littlefield
First paperback edition 2016

British Library Cataloguing in Publication Information Available

Library of Congress Cataloging-in-Publication Data
The hardback edition of this book was previously published by the Library of Congress as follows:

Smart chicks on screen : representing women's intellect in film and television / edited by Laura Mattoon D'Amore.
pages cm. — (Film and history)
Includes bibliographical references and index.
1. Gifted women in motion pictures. 2. Gifted women on television. I. D'Amore, Laura Mattoon, editor.
PN1995.9.W6S63 2014
791.43'6522—dc23
2014025507

ISBN 978-1-4422-3747-6 (cloth : alk. paper)
ISBN 978-1-4422-7562-1 (pbk : alk. paper)
ISBN 978-1-4422-3748-3 (electronic)

♾ ™ The paper used in this publication meets the minimum requirements of American National Standard for Information Sciences Permanence of Paper for Printed Library Materials, ANSI/NISO Z39.48-1992.

Printed in the United States of America

I have been extremely lucky to have colleagues in the field who believe that what I have to contribute is valuable, and who have given me the opportunity to write and publish. I am also indebted to the love and support of my family, who are always proud of what I do.

Sophie, Lola, and Ben—you are my rock stars.

Contents

Acknowledgments

This project has allowed me to cross paths with many wonderful people. For me, edited volumes are inspired by the excellent work that I see in other scholars, and I grow excited about bringing them into a dialogue with one another that offers them the space to flourish. I am grateful to the Film and History series editor, Cindy Miller, for her interest in the work that the authors and I were doing. It was through her encouragement and expertise that I was able to craft what has turned out to be an interesting and thought-provoking book. As well, I am thankful for the authors who found the book topic interesting and wrote chapters for this final product. The Film and History conference in Milwaukee in 2012 introduced me to many of the people featured here, and is always a fantastic space to vet ideas. Finally, I want to give special thanks to the Roger Williams University Foundation for the Promotion of Scholarship and Teaching, which gave me invaluable resources that allowed me to pull this project together.

Introduction

Laura Mattoon D'Amore

In the cover image, actress Barbara Feldon (as Agent 99 from the 1960s television series *Get Smart*) looks coy, a smirk on her face as she reads a book titled *How to Get Smart*. The star of the show was its namesake, Maxwell Smart (played by Don Adams), who is a bumbling, incompetent American spy. Agent 99 is his more competent partner; she is an award-winning spy who speaks four languages and is accomplished in dance, violin, and singing. She is clearly qualified for her job, and given her position as an "intelligence agent," it can be assumed that she is already "smart." However, Agent 99 is secretly in love with Smart, which makes her identity as a smart intelligence agent less crucial to her storyline than her potential romantic connection with the male lead. Therefore, the cover image embodies ironic tension. Is Agent 99 reading the book to "get smart," to get ahead and perhaps show the world what she can do? Or is she reading the book to discover how to "get Smart," as in Maxwell Smart, to win him as her own? This dual potential is perfectly emblematic of the complexities of representations of women's intellect in film and television, where women often find their potential as smart and independent overshadowed by plotlines about their beauty, madness, or romantic interest.

Since the Second Wave feminist movement, Hollywood has slowly begun to give prominent and leading roles to women. However, the intellectual representations of women are out of line with reality, in many cases failing to reflect the successes and struggles that women have faced in a resistant social and political environment. In contemporary America, more women go to college than men, get better grades than their male classmates, and still, as a demographic, go on to less-prestigious jobs where pay equity is still elusive. Whereas fifty years ago we could shrug this off by making the claim that women earn less because they work less, that is no longer the case.

One of the repercussions of these facts is that intellect, which is the imagined standard by which work output is measured, is still considered a masculine trait. We imagine that men belong in the paid workforce because they are competitive and aggressive, and we are still inclined to believe that women "belong in the home because of their 'natural' focus

1

on relationships, children, and an ethic of care."[1] And while 73 percent of American adults believe that more women in the workforce is a trend for the better,[2] a 2012 Pew Research study found that the vast majority believes mothers who work part time (47 percent) or not at all (33 percent) are ideal for the well-being of children; in our cultural heart, we still want women in the home rather than the workplace. Interestingly, in that same survey, 70 percent of the public believed that fathers should work full time, reaffirming men's "natural" place outside the home.[3] This is because men's sense of manhood and social identity has historically derived from their relationship to their work; women's identity, conversely, has historically been tied to domesticity.[4]

Despite the reality of women's successes in traditionally male-dominated fields like medicine, law, finance, and academia, there is still a vast disparity in how we imagine the intellect of women compared to men. We imagine women as more emotional, and we encourage them to move into careers that can capitalize on that, in jobs that require a high ethic of care or knowledge of domestic duties, such as nursing, teaching, secretarial work, social work, childcare, and housecleaning. Conversely, we encourage men to take on heavy hitting, high-powered, or highly skilled careers in fields where women's emotions could be a liability. Intellect, therefore, gets intertwined with the strict regulation of gender roles and fosters the belief that women are differently intellectual, and less financially and politically valuable, than men.

Of course, this definition of women's intellect is extremely reductive. Women's intellect cannot be measured by a direct comparison to fields of work that have been historically dominated by men (smart or not). We need to reevaluate what intelligence looks like for women, and revalue the work that women do. After all, it is not that women are inherently less intelligent, but rather, that society devalues the work—and the intellectual output—that has historically been done by women. For example, there are 7.2 million teachers in the United States, and more than 75 percent of them are women. Seventy-seven million students are directly affected by our (mostly female) teachers each day.[5] We rely on them for the production of our own futures, through the successes and failures of our children, and yet teaching is not coded as intelligent or skilled work. We need to shift the way we value work in order to shift our ways of thinking about women's intellect.

Another problem that arises when we link intellect with the male-dominated sectors of the workforce is that it fails to account for what women want to do with their intelligence. One misconception of the notion of women's equality is that women must be allowed to raise themselves to the bar set by men—but what if they don't want what men have? Equality is not about lifting women up to the men's level, but rather equally valuing work regardless of gender. This means we have to allow men to do work that has historically been coded as feminine (such as childcare, teaching, nursing); allow women to do work that has historically been coded as male (such as carpentry and the military); and also respect women's choices to do work that has been traditionally designated as feminine (such as mothering, sewing, and baking) without tying that to her intellectual value.

All of these nuances are missing in our popular culture, where we continue to find women marginalized for their choices, overshadowed by men, and judged by their bodies. In fact, women's intellect is rarely the center point of television or film narratives, and when it is, those women are often represented as socially awkward—such as Dr. Temperance Brennan (*Bones*), the women of *The Big Bang Theory*, and Jess on *New Girl*—or doomed to perpetual failure in their intimate relationships, such as Olivia Pope (*Scandal*), Sydney Bristow (*Alias*), and Kalinda Sharma (*The Good Wife*).[6] In "TV's New Wave of Women: Smart, Strong, and Borderline Insane," Heather Havrilesky writes in the *New York Times* about the contemporary trend of making smart, confident female characters "completely nuts," specifically naming Carrie Mathison (the bipolar and brilliant heroine of *Homeland*) and Jackie Peyton (the skilled yet drug addled nurse on *Nurse Jackie*). To this list could be added (among many) Lisbeth Salander (*The Girl with the Dragon Tattoo*), whose high intellect and severe social ineptitude is coded as mental illness; and Maggie Jordan (*The Newsroom*), who has an extreme anxiety disorder that manifests in debilitating panic attacks often triggered by her intense fears of her own perceived shortcomings.[7]

As for those smart women who are not "crazy," Havrilesky argues that they are fixated on men, like Mindy on *The Mindy Project*, who is "a highly paid ob-gyn who's obsessed with being too old and not pretty enough to land a husband."[8] To this example could be added Meredith Grey of *Grey's Anatomy*, who regularly puts the needs of her handsome husband ahead of her own. Alternatively, smart women whose careers are more important to them than men, like Cristina Yang (also from *Grey's Anatomy*), are coded as emotionally frigid and incapable of maintaining intimate relationships.[9] Referring to the old adage that women can be "too smart for their own good," an idea that seems relevant to the punishment that smart women endure, Havrilesky concludes, "Many so-called crazy women are just smart, that's all. They aren't too smart for their own good, or for ours."

In addition to the social marginalization of smart women on film and television, there is also a deeply ingrained connection between women's intellect and women's beauty. If smart women on film and television are attractive, they are often neutralized in such a way that their intellect becomes subjugated to their beauty, as with Dr. Jane Foster in *Thor*, whose role as a scientist is significantly less noteworthy than her role as the love interest of an Asgardian King. Or, if they are average looking, or nerdy, they are often forced to trade their intellect for desirability, like

Laney Boggs in *She's All That*. Notably, characters who actively defy these norms, such as Dr. Pamela Isley/Poison Ivy in *Batman & Robin*—who insists on maintaining brilliant scientific intellect and extreme sex appeal—are often characterized as evil or aberrant, a threat to the social order. As such we find that classically blonde bombshells like Sugar Kane (*Some Like It Hot*), and Billie Dawn (*Born Yesterday*)—both beautiful Hollywood starlets—are, on the surface, ignorant dupes, to hide the threat of their subliminal wit.[10] And, highly intelligent actresses like Natalie Portman, a graduate of Harvard University, and Hedy Lamar, who invented early technology that led eventually to wireless communication, find that their intellect is completely overshadowed by their physical beauty.[11]

This book brings together an impressive array of scholarship that interrogates representations of women's intellect in film and television. The interdisciplinary, international contributions consider the multiple complexities in such readings. For example, in what ways are women in film and television limited or ostracized by their intelligence? Are there cases in which women are set free, or live better, as a result of intellectual growth? How do female roles in film reinforce standards of beauty, submissiveness, and silence, over intellect, problem solving, or leadership? In what ways are smart women infantilized, or commodified, by their intelligence? How does an actress's personal standards of intellect in her real life affect the way she is given roles or seen on screen? Are there women in film and television who are intelligent, without also being objectified?

In chapter 1, "Not Just *Born Yesterday*: Judy Holliday, the Red Scare, and the (Miss-)Uses of Hollywood's Dumb Blonde Image," Stephen R. Duncan argues that actress Judy Holliday utilized the "dumb blonde" image, which she had perfected as Billie Dawn in *Born Yesterday*, to her advantage when called to testify before the anticommunist Senate Judiciary Committee in the 1950s. Able to hide behind gendered assumptions about her body as a blonde woman, and knowing that her stardom was at least in part predicated on the public's conflation of her personal life with her movie roles, Holliday was able to defuse criticism of her potentially unsavory dealings with communism. Duncan deals here with the blurred lines between reality and fantasy, and considers ways that oppositional readings can uncover intentionality in gender performance. Similarly, in chapter 2, "The Fuzzy End of the Lollypop: Protofeminism and Collective Subjectivity in *Some Like It Hot*," Melissa Meade rereads Marilyn Monroe as Sugar Kane. Monroe is usually reduced to her image as a blonde bombshell, and Meade argues that it is precisely this forced dichotomy between smart and naïve that influences a feminist politics in the following decades that demands new respect for the female subject.

In chapter 3, "Brainy Broads: Images of Women's Intellect in Film Noir," Sheri Chinen Biesen argues that rather than being presented as thoughtful, multifaceted, intelligent individuals, women in 1940s film noir were often reduced to simplistic stereotypes—either lethal sexual temptresses or naïve victims, thus undermining their intellect in screen portrayals as the toxic blonde femme fatale or gullible innocent redeemer. Her investigation considers how intelligent women were channeled from professional careers back into the home from 1945 to 1950. As an interesting comparison, chapter 4, "Troubling Binaries: Women Scientists in 1950s B-Movies," considers how B-movies gave female characters the opportunity to explore careers that were not otherwise available to them—in reality or in film and television. Author Linda Levitt notes that these female roles offered viewers the chance to see women in careers that were taken seriously, even though other stereotypical behaviors—such as the beautiful damsel in distress—still emerged. Leaping ahead in time, but still considering the representation of female scientists, is chapter 5, "'The High Priestess of the Desert': Female Intellect and Subjectivity in *Contact*," by Allison Whitney. Here, Whitney explores Jodie Foster's intellectual and psychological journey in the film, allowing the tensions between them to become apparent as she struggles to be taken seriously as a scientist and as a woman.

In chapter 6, "*Mad Men*'s Peggy Olson: A Prefeminist Champion in a Postfeminist TV Landscape," Stefania Marghitu articulates that *Mad Men*'s Peggy Olson is an unusually intellectual woman in the prefeminist 1960s, but is written as a contemporary postfeminist heroine because she does not suffer from her choice to flout prescribed gender roles. Her character hides feminism beneath a cloak of women's success, making it appear, ahistorically, that feminism was not (and is not) necessary to ensure equality. Similarly, in chapter 7, "A Deeper Cut: Enlightened Sexism and *Grey's Anatomy*," Mikaela Feroli argues that highly successful women on television dramas like *Grey's Anatomy* entice audiences into believing that feminism is done, because women's workplace achievements seem to come without struggle.

In chapter 8, "'There Is No Genius': Dr. Joan Watson and the Rewriting of Gender and Intelligence on CBS's *Elementary*," Helen Kang and Natasha Patterson consider what is at stake when a traditionally white male character is reimagined as an Asian American woman. Joan Watson challenges the definition of intelligence and its raced and gendered construction, and also challenges sexism and misogyny in science. In chapter 9, "Stories Worth Telling: How Kerry Washington Balances Brains, Beauty, and Power in Hollywood," De Anna J. Reese considers how Kerry Washington, as an actress and activist, as well as in her role as Olivia Pope on *Scandal*, deepens our understanding of the diversity of black women. In believing that her value comes from her intellect rather than her beauty, Washington has been able to leverage her personal commitment to issues that matter through the roles she has taken on as an actress. Importantly, both of these chapters consider the critical importance of the intersections of race and gender on screen, since role models for women of color are scarce in the media.

In chapter 10, Margaret Tally considers the popular television show *Girls*, in "Postfeminism, Sexuality, and the Question of Millennial Identity on HBO's *Girls*." Here she argues that above all, the women on the show are "thinking women," and their intellectual commitments to their work as artists, writers, and students is what informs all of their actions in the world, including their actions with young men. In chapter 11, "I Can't Believe I Fell for Muppet Man! Female Nerds and the Order of Discourse," Raewyn Campbell considers the role of nerdom in narratives about contemporary gender roles, noting that males are more culturally credible as nerds than are women. As male nerds are largely validated through conforming to notions of hegemonic masculinity, female nerds are unable to sit comfortably within this paradigm. In chapter 12, "Brains, Beauty, and Feminist Television: The Women of *The Big Bang Theory*," Amanda Stone further considers the role of the female nerd in the new television canon. She articulates that there is a potential feminism to be read through the highly intelligent yet socially awkward women on the show, which gives them space to redefine successful intimate relationships and laws of attraction. Whereas smart women have traditionally been read as either beautiful or smart, and are rarely sexualized, the women of *The Big Bang Theory* navigate all three terrains. In these three chapters, authors consider ways in which intellectual representation challenges the hegemonic tradition of the sexualization of the female subject.

Finally, in chapter 13, Rachel Shaina Bernstein discusses Jewish women on television in "Too Smart for Their Own Good? Images of Young Jewish Women in Television and Film." Here, Bernstein posits that smart, young Jewish women are depicted as failures at relationships, mirroring a deep cultural ambivalence about the role of Jewish women in the home and family. As more Jewish women put off starting families in favor of building careers, their film and television counterparts face romances that fail and find themselves punished for making independent choices.

The chapters in this book consider the intersections of women's intellect, beauty, relationships, and work, because as the authors considered the representations of women's intellect in film and television, they found that our cultural ideologies necessitate such a connection. Women have made great strides in work and education, especially since the 1970s, though equality is still elusive. Our popular culture seems to accept those gains, as represented by many of the successful women explored herein, but in most cases actually rejects them, by forcing audiences to view them through their bodies and their relationships rather than through their intellect.

NOTES

1. Joan Williams, *Unbending Gender: Why Work and Family Conflict and What to Do about It* (Oxford: Oxford University Press, 2000), 1.
2. Kim Parker, "Women, Work and Motherhood," *Pew Research Center*, April 13, 2012, http://www.pewsocialtrends.org/2012/04/13/women-work-and-motherhood (accessed 8 March 2014).
3. Wendy Wang, "Mothers and Work: What's 'Ideal'?" Pew Research Center, August 19, 2013, http://www.pewresearch.org/fact-tank/2013/08/19/mothers-and-work-whats-ideal (accessed 8 March 2014).
4. Williams, *Unbending Gender*, 25.
5. "Education: Elementary and Secondary Education: Staff and Finances," United States Census Bureau, 27 June 2011, http://www.census.gov/compendia/statab/cats/education/elementary_and_secondary_education_staff_and_finances.html (accessed 22 February 2014).
6. Dr. Temperance Brennan (*Bones*) is played by actress Emily Deschanel; the women of *The Big Bang Theory* are played by actresses Kaley Cuoco, Melissa Rauch, and Mayim Bialik; Jess (*New Girl*) is played by actress Zooey Deschanel; Olivia Pope (*Scandal*) is played by actress Kerry Washington; Sydney Bristow (*Alias*) is played by actress Jennifer Garner; and Kalinda Sharma (*The Good Wife*) is played by actress Archie Panjabi.
7. Carrie Mathison (Homeland) is played by actress Claire Danes; Jackie Peyton (*Nurse Jackie*) is played by actress Edie Falco; Lisbeth Salander (*The Girl with the Dragon Tattoo*) is played by actress Rooney Mara; Maggie Jordan (*The Newsroom*) is played by actress Alison Pill.
8. Heather Havrilesky. "TV's New Wave of Women: Smart, Strong, Borderline Insane," *New York Times*, March 12, 2013, http://www.nytimes.com/2013/03/17/magazine/tvs-new-wave-of-women-smart-strong-borderline-insane.html?pagewanted=all&_r=0 (accessed 4 March 2014).
9. Mindy (*The Mindy Project*) is played by actress Mindy Kaling; Meredith Grey (*Grey's Anatomy*) is played by actress Ellen Pompeo; Cristina Yang (*Grey's Anatomy*) is played by actress Sandra Oh.
10. Dr. Jane Foster (*Thor*) is played by actress Natalie Portman; Laney Boggs (*She's All That*) is played by actress Rachel Leigh Cook; Dr. Pamela Isley/Poison Ivy (*Batman & Robin*) is played by actress Uma Thurman; Sugar Kane (*Some Like It Hot*) is played by actress Marilyn Monroe; Billie Dawn (*Born Yesterday*) is played by actress Judy Holliday.
11. Thank you to Cindy Miller for pointing out this comparison.

BIBLIOGRAPHY

Alias. Television Series. Performed by Jennifer Garner. Los Angeles: ABC Studies, 2001–2006.

Bacon, Lauren. "The Tech Industry's Women Problem: Statistics Show It's Worse Than You Think." *Quartz.* November 7, 2013. http://qz.com/143967/the-tech-industrys-woman-problem-statistics-show-its-worse-than-you-think (accessed 22 February 2014).

Batman & Robin. Directed by Joel Schumacher. Performed by Uma Thurman. Los Angeles: Warner Bros., 1997. DVD.

The Big Bang Theory. Television Series. Performed by Kaley Cuoco, Melissa Rauch, and Mayim Bialik. Los Angeles: Warner Bros., 2007–.

Bones. Television Series. Performed by Emily Deschanel. Los Angeles: Fox Studios, 2005–.

Get Smart. Television Series. Performed by Barbara Feldon. Los Angeles: CBS Studios, 1965–1970.

The Girl with the Dragon Tattoo. Directed by David Fincher. Performed by Mara Rooney. Los Angeles: Columbia Pictures, 2011. DVD.

The Good Wife. Television Series. Performed by Archie Panjabi. Los Angeles: CBS Studios, 2009–.

Grey's Anatomy. Television Series. Performed by Ellen Pompeo and Sandra Oh. Los Angeles: ABC Television Center, 2005–.

Homeland. Television Series. Performed by Claire Danes. Los Angeles: Showtime Networks, Inc., 2011–.

The Mindy Project. Television Series. Mindy Kaling. Los Angeles: Kaling International, 2012–.

National Foundation for Women Legislators. "Facts about Women Legislators." http://www.womenlegislators.org/women-legislator-facts.php (accessed 22 February 2014).

New Girl. Television Series. Performed by Zooey Deschanel. Los Angeles: Elizabeth Meriwether Pictures, 2011–.

The Newsroom. Television Series. Performed by Alison Pill. New York: HBO Entertainment, 2012–.

Nurse Jackie. Television Series. Performed by Edie Falco. Los Angeles: Showtime Networks, Inc, 2009–2013.

Parker, Kim. "Women, Work and Motherhood," Pew Research Social & Demographic Trends, 13 April 2012. http://www.pewsocialtrends.org/2012/04/13/women-work-and-motherhood (accessed 8 March 2014).

Pomerantz, Dorothy. "Robert Downey, Jr. Tops Forbes List of Hollywood's Highest Paying Actors." *Forbes*, 7 July 2013. http://www.forbes.com/sites/dorothypomerantz/2013/07/16/robert-downey-jr-tops-forbes-list-of-hollywoods-highest-paid-actors (accessed 22 February 2014).

Scandal. Television Series. Performed by Kerry Washington. Los Angeles: ABC Studios, 2012–.

She's All That. Directed by Robert Iscove. Performed by Rachel Leigh Cook. Los Angeles: Miramax, 1999. DVD.

Thor. Directed by Kenneth Branagh. Los Angeles: Paramount Pictures, 2011. DVD.

United States Census Bureau. "Education: Elementary and Secondary Education: Staff and Finances." 27 June 2011. http://www.census.gov/compendia/statab/cats/education/elementary_and_secondary_education_staff_and_finances.html (accessed 22 February 2014).

Wang, Wendy. "Mothers and Work: What's 'Ideal'?" Pew Research Center. August 19, 2013. http://www.pewresearch.org/fact-tank/2013/08/19/mothers-and-work-whats-ideal (accessed 8 March 2014).

Williams, Joan. *Unbending Gender: Why Work and Family Conflict and What to Do about It*. Oxford: Oxford University Press, 2000.

Women Make Movies. "Film Facts." http://www.wmm.com/resources/film_facts.shtml (accessed 22 February 2014).

ONE

Not Just *Born Yesterday*

Judy Holliday, the Red Scare, and the (Miss-)Uses of Hollywood's Dumb Blonde Image

Stephen R. Duncan

On March 29, 1951, Judy Holliday sat in New York's La Zambra night-club on 52nd Street, listening anxiously as the club's loudspeaker, transmitting the Academy Awards ceremony from Los Angeles, crackled out the news that she had won the award for Best Actress.[1] Holliday's winning role was in the comedy *Born Yesterday* (1950), playing Billie Dawn, a racketeer's chorus-girl moll who went from bubble-headed bimbo to political sophisticate under the tutelage of a Washington reporter. One year later, Holliday's career was upended when the anticommunist Senate Judiciary Committee called her to testify about her left-wing political activism. Like many during the Red Scare, Holliday's reputation suffered from innuendoes of communism, which jeopardized her cinematic success. Yet she was able to sidestep contempt charges and avoid implicating compatriots by mobilizing her Billie Dawn persona before the Senate committee—playing dumb, despite her famously high IQ. Holliday's story has since become a cautionary tale about the excesses of McCarthyism, her promising career cut short by the fervor to root out subversion as the conflict in Korea heated up and Soviet spies were rounded up. She is portrayed as "a woman unfinished," borrowing a phrase from fellow traveler Lillian Hellman, a portrait intensified by Holliday's untimely death from cancer in 1965.[2]

Yet this portrayal is not quite right, historically or metaphorically. Holliday's "dumb blonde" Senate committee performance actually saved

9

her career from Hollywood's anticommunist blacklist. She completed all seven of her contracted films with Columbia Pictures, each with some box office success, before becoming too ill to work in 1961. And although conservative protests from 1950 to 1953 temporarily threatened her work in film and television, a deft public relations campaign revived her big- and small-screen popularity. What was lost, however, was Holliday's public image as an intelligent, independent woman—an image she had deliberately developed by contrasting her colorful offscreen sophistica- tion to the bauble-laden blankness of Billie Dawn. Her successful tactic against the committee required her to sink back beneath the surface of a dumb blonde image that left the Cold War status quo undisturbed. As a symbol of the progressive postwar American woman, Judy Holliday was not "unfinished"; she was submerged.

Billie Dawn's intellectual awakening in *Born Yesterday* had represent- ed postwar American idealism, a symbol of democracy in action that both relied on and subverted traditional gender norms. Her political edu- cation embodied themes of visibility and autonomy, defining freedom as the ability to see and be seen. Alongside this came a figuration of national conscience that posited the woman's sphere as democracy's moral bas- tion, which the film underscored by containing Billie's social agency within domesticity and marriage. Yet Holliday's performance simultane- ously undermined patriarchal norms of power and masculine force, in- sisting that knowledge trumped muscular might, redefining *dumb* not as silence or absence, but as a failure to reject the politics of violence. Holli- day's onscreen feminism was reinforced intertextually by publicity that spurned Tinseltown glitz and emphasized her cultivated life off screen. The result was a discourse that undercut conservative figurations of the "American girl," which equated beauty and obeisance, with a kind of progressive patriotism, suggesting that women's democratic participa- tion was indeed "smart."

Having started out in left-wing satirical cabaret, Holliday was entirely comfortable with this kind of subversion. It also made her a clear target for red-baiters. The Senate committee's tactic to expose Holliday's alleged disloyalty relied on two kinds of naming. As they did with all such depo- nents, the committee pressed her to identify political compatriots. But they also interrogated her identity, focusing on her Jewish given name and questioning her status as a married yet independent professional woman, signaled by the moniker "Miss Holliday." Holliday defended herself by claiming that her political activism had been "stupid," while using social norms of beauty to deflect the committee's antifeminist con- cerns. The resultant publicity reduced her previous multidimensionality to a Billie Dawn stereotype. Her story therefore eclipsed straightforward issues of Left versus Right. Judy Holliday's performances, in *Born Yester- day* and before the committee, exemplified interwoven Cold War dis- courses of gender and national belonging that converged in Hollywood's figure of the dumb blonde—an image that ultimately engulfed Holliday's liberated persona.

A brief comparison with the decade's other eminent dumb blonde, Marilyn Monroe, further highlights the depth of this submersion. Monroe died tragically and was enshrined in national collective memory, while Holliday has been largely forgotten. In 1950, however, Holliday first fully entrenched the dumb blonde as a Hollywood trope. Blondeness had long been multivalent, evoking everything from ingénues to witches, from the ancient sun goddess to liberated flappers and the assertive sexuality of stars like Marlene Dietrich and Mae West.[3] There were literary precedents for blondeness as a sign of vacuity, but the modern advent of chemical hair dyes and mass consumerism crystallized this image in the public mind—most prominently in Anita Loos's Lorelei Lee character in the 1925 novel, *Gentlemen Prefer Blondes*. Holliday was originally tapped for the film version in 1951, an appropriate choice since her talent for satire matched the tone of Loos's prose. Yet the part instead went to Monroe. By 1953, Monroe became America's archetypal sex symbol, perfectly suited for the decade's dominant male fantasies: a nonthreatening baby-boom-and-bust spectacle that simultaneously suggested sexuality and the matronly safety of matrimony. Onscreen beauty dominated Monroe's public image, even as she demonstrated behind-the-scenes career savvy and labored to establish artistic credibility by studying at the Actor's Studio in New York—a real-life analogue to the multifaceted Billie Dawn. It took Monroe's drug-induced death to finally confirm her as a tormented artist, an introspective woman hounded by her inability to transcend the spectacle.[4]

Such complexity had to contend with Cold War concerns about the lines between public and private, manifested in calls for nuclear-family "togetherness" amid fears of communist subversion "from within." These trends polarized the 1950s into an era that demanded outward conformity on one end and pursued inward authenticity on the other, layering American culture with a patina of sitcom domesticity over the subterranean sensibilities of rebels in search of a cause. When anticommunists associated Holliday's literate and liberated personal life with her left-wing politics, she found shelter in a dumbed-down projection of her onscreen persona. This placid exterior placated the Senate committee by suggesting she was too shallow for the intricacies of "communist front" subversion. But by submerging her intelligence, Holliday also acquiesced to an artificial calm in the waves of feminism. Afterward, she seldom broke the surface of the dumb blonde image.

JUDY TUVIM TAKES A "HOLLIDAY"

Born Judith Tuvim on June 21, 1921, Holliday's progressive bona fides ran in her blood. Her parents had immigrated from Russia in the late nineteenth century and, like many Jews who settled in New York's Lower East Side, had multiple left-wing ties. Her father, Abraham Tuvim, was a socialist organizer with labor leader Eugene Debs and a member of the "Yiddish intelligentsia" who hung out in the bohemian "Edna St. Vincent Millay" atmosphere of Greenwich Village. Holliday's mother, Helen Gollomb, was interested in the labor movement through the influence of her brother, Joe. Another uncle, Joseph Tuvim, was also a labor leader; Holliday's aunt, Mary Tuvim, was a Communist Party member who worked in Gotham cabarets as a bookkeeper. Holliday's own introduction to show business was performing at the communist Tamiment resort, and as a teenager she worked the switchboard at Orson Welles's left-wing Mercury Theatre.[5] Having grown up in a left-leaning bohemian milieu, Holliday often had her performances shot through with social criticism.

Judy Tuvim's real show-business rise began in a satirical troupe, with Adolph Green, Betty Comden, Alvin Hammer, and John Frank, who dubbed themselves the Revuers in 1939.[6] The Revuers first appeared at the Village Vanguard, a cabaret with links to the cultural wing of the Popular Front (an alliance of communists and left liberals formed in the 1930s to combat fascism and the Great Depression). Performing "topical skits," the troupe was in the vein of "sophisticated," politically tinged entertainment that historian Michael Denning has termed the "Cultural Front."[7]

As the Revuers' popularity rose, however, Judy Tuvim started swimming toward the mainstream. By the mid-1940s, the troupe had moved from nightclubs to the radio show *Duffy's Tavern*. With the show slotted for a film adaptation, the Revuers headed for Hollywood, only to be disappointed when the project was canceled. But the studio singled out Judy as the most beguiling of the group, and with her film debut in 1944 came a name change. Pressed to drop "Tuvim" as too ethnic, she adopted its rough English translation, "Holliday," adding the extra *l* to avoid confusion with singer Billie Holiday. When her small part failed to make a splash, she returned to familiar terrain on the New York stage, disenchanted with Hollywood but determined to make a name for herself.[8]

Holliday's breakthrough came with the 1946 Broadway production of *Born Yesterday*. Written by Garson Kanin, who mingled on the fringes of the Cultural Front, the play immediately garnered praise as a smart comedy that demonstrated "what a democracy is about." Raves focused on the empathetic humor of Billie Dawn, as well as the acumen that clearly lurked beneath Holliday's cleverly crafted dumb blonde veneer. By the end of the play, the *New York Times* proclaimed, she "clearly is headed for an intellectual salon of her own."[9]

Equally important was press coverage on Holliday herself. Journalists depicted her as a strong, independent, quirky woman not afraid to reverse gender roles with her partner, musician David Oppenheim. "Miss Holliday lives in a Greenwich Village apartment which has been mostly built by her own hands," confided the *Los Angeles Times*, "assisted by her husband." Holliday continuously resisted Hollywood's standards of glamour, insisting that she was overweight, with "bad ankles and a prizefighter's jaw." *Life* reported that she often traipsed around the Village "impenetrably disguised as a housewife." Significantly, many articles spotlighted the dichotomy between Billie Dawn and Holliday's quick wits. "With the IQ of a Genius, She Plays a Dumb Blonde," declared one headline, noting that at age ten she had scored 172 on the Otis intelligence test. Similarly, *Life* headed its five-page spread in terms that captured both her sophistication and dramatic ambitions: "'Born Yesterday's' Not So Dumb Blonde Prefers Slacks to Mink, Likes Proust, Hates Hollywood, Hopes Someday to Play Ophelia."[10]

When Hollywood once again came calling, Holliday insisted that she return only on her own terms. "A few days ago Leo McCarey telephoned about a movie role for her," one reporter wrote, setting a scene between actress and producer:

> "Is it a big, important role?" asked Miss Holliday. . . . "It couldn't be a bigger or more important role," said McCarey. "It's a two-character movie to be called 'Adam and Eve.'" . . . "It could be a bigger and more important role," corrected Miss Holliday, . . . "it could be called 'Eve and Adam.'"[11]

Holliday refused several offers before agreeing to another Garson Kanin vehicle, *Adam's Rib*, which Kanin co-wrote with his wife, Ruth Gordon. Holliday appeared with another tenacious actress, Katherine Hepburn, who became something of a mentor. When Columbia's Harry Cohn optioned *Born Yesterday*, Hepburn, Kanin, and Gordon mounted a campaign to convince the prickly producer that Holliday should reprise her Billie Dawn role. Cohn resisted, failing to see the bankability of a "fat Jewish broad" when svelte starlets were so plentiful, but he relented under Hepburn's star-powered pressure. Veteran George Cukor was hired to direct. Cukor shared Kanin and Gordon's Cultural Front sensibilities, had worked well with the couple on *Adam's Rib*, and was determined to maintain the integrity of *Born Yesterday*'s stage production.[12] The parts were in place for Holliday's most strident cinematic statement.

GIRLS WITH GLASSES: DOMESTICITY AND VISION IN
BORN YESTERDAY

Billie Dawn is a walking spectacle. The first scene in *Born Yesterday* tracks her arrival at a Washington DC luxury hotel, and she is a classic object of the gaze. Both the audience and the hotel's bellboys follow her with their eyes from car to lobby, and into a private elevator to the penthouse suite. She is extravagant in a black gown topped with mink, sparkling with diamond jewelry, a small flowered hat perched atop a curly pile of platinum blonde—the outsized reflection of her wealthy companion's desire. Billie is a goddess of conspicuous consumption, a Botticelli embodied, a Venus on display for the voracious "junkyard king" Harry Brock (Broderick Crawford). Harry barks orders to the hotel staff as Billie walks silently through the scene. She doesn't say a word until three minutes into the film.

As soon as Billie speaks, the spell is broken. She shouts monosyllabic responses to Harry across the penthouse in a New York yawp peppered with Yiddish, her voice nasal and cracked. Holliday's performance was both comic and subversive. Billie's harsh, piercing tones jolt the senses, colliding with her previous sensuality. As Laura Mulvey and E. Ann Kaplan have argued, the predominant cinematic gaze is subjectively male, upheld by both social norms and the patriarchal structures of Hollywood production. Even when feminine authority replaces the masculine "power of action," Kaplan continues, this structural logic is ultimately maintained, inverted rather than disrupted.[13] Yet Billie's voice is just such a disruption, the abrasion of sound cracking the pristine facade of sight, satirizing the snowy blonde goddess.

Her reappearance on screen, however, quickly restores order. Summoned by Harry, Billie is told to keep quiet and get dressed in preparation for the arrival of distinguished guests. Her crestfallen look is offset by her preposterously wiggling walk as she leaves the room, a mocking anatomical acknowledgment of her status as a "kept woman." Although this subtle humor foreshadows Billie's later feminist awakening, the scene's overarching motif demands the dumb blonde's return to silence.[14] The film's male gaze now includes "liberal" journalist Paul Verrall (William Holden), sent to interview Harry for a feature story. Having watched bemusedly as Billie strolled through the hotel's lobby, Paul now looks concerned, signaling his obvious paternalist affection for the verbally abused Billie. Harry soon heeds the warning of his dissipated but well-connected lawyer (Howard St. John) that dealings in DC call for "judgment and intelligence" and hires Paul to educate Billie in capital-city etiquette. The dawn of Billie's intellect is clearly peeking over the horizon, but, as ever in such Pygmalion-like plots, her fate is held firmly in manly hands as she passes from paramour to protégé.

Born Yesterday's themes of domesticity and political autonomy were partly the product of its historical period following World War II. Harry's shady business dealings—including bribing a congressman to award him exclusive access to European scrap steel—reflected concerns about the consolidation of production and power amid public-private wartime cooperation. This behemoth corporate liberalism continued into postwar conversion, which was fraught with gender conflicts as male troops returned home and women war workers fought to maintain the independence that good pay had purchased. The desires of homeward-bound men were further shaped by propaganda that proffered pinup girls and prosperity as their eventual reward for service—what George Lipsitz has termed a "rainbow at midnight" image of almost mystical comfort: domesticity lighting the darkness of uncertainty and impending cold war.[15] This sense of domestic protection was captured in Harry's need to marry Billie, who was unwittingly embroiled in his misdoings, as a tactic to gain spousal privilege against her potential testimony in court. This represented the kind of discursive "containment" of women noted by historians such as Elaine Tyler May as a parallel to America's Cold War policies against the Soviet Union.[16]

Born Yesterday simultaneously resisted and reinforced such containment, positing Billie as a voice for independence and liberation, but always within prescribed gender norms. In each of the first two acts, before her bookish transformation, she sloughs off Harry and his cohorts' attempts to determine her behavior, declaring, "It's a free country." To Paul's pedagogical advances, however, Billie insists that she likes being "stupid," cheerfully proclaiming, "As long as I know how to get what I want, that's all I want to know." She then propositions him, suggesting, "It's only fair, we'll educate each other." Paul demurs, undercutting the notion that her sexual and intellectual fulfillment are compatible.

Billie then breaks through outward appearances once again, only to have them reimposed as the final arbiter. Admitting that she has adopted a stage name, she reveals her given name, Emma, and asks dismissively, "Do I look to you like an Emma?" Paul's reply affirms both their budding romance (legitimated by a virginal kiss) and Billie's pulchritudinous defiance: "You look like a lovely girl." Billie's innocence, signaled by Holliday's dimpled, impish face and the social effect of blondeness, is thus established as the base of her authority to critique corruption, even as her "stupidity" is linked to feminine materialism—the trope of woman-as-vacuous-mass-consumer.[17]

A pivotal dramatic exchange soon subverts this figuration, linking the assertion of women's economic prerogatives with symbolic vision. Following Paul's departure, Billie and Harry sit down to a game of gin rummy; in a rapid-fire routine, a dazzling display of physical comedy, Billie shuffles, deals, and wins hand after hand. Billie demands payment of precisely "fifty-five dollars and sixty cents," which Harry slams on the table. As he leaves the room, Billie deals a hand of solitaire. Harry turns and quietly beseeches her not to play all night, pleading, "It hurts your eyes." Temporarily humbled by Billie's superior skills, all within the rules of fair play, Harry displays one fleeting moment of nobility, accepting defeat and defending *her* ability *to see*. This theme develops in a quick succession of scenes depicting Billie's liberal education. As Billie wrestles with a reading list ranging from Tom Paine to the *Washington Post*, Paul notices her squint—another emblem of her sociopolitical myopia. He suggests wearing glasses and Billie laughs dismissively. Catching the embarrassed look on Paul's own bespectacled face, she says, tellingly, "Of course they're not so bad on men." Eyeglasses are thereby marked as a crucial (if obvious) symbol of intellect, firmly planted in the masculine domain, but attainable by any woman willing to trade vanity for vision.

Born Yesterday furthered this visual emphasis with shifting perspectives. In a sequence of scenes, Paul takes Billie sightseeing around the capital. Shot on location, wide framing establishes Billie's *visibility*, her presence in the public sphere legitimated by the authenticity of the mise-en-scène. This sequence revolves around Billie, as she wanders away from a congressional tour, captivated by the sight of a schoolgirl in blond pigtails gazing up at the painted ceiling of the Capitol dome. They stand as a pair, peering upward. The shot cuts to the dome's interior, establishing their point of view. These two diegetic looks, Billie seeing the girl who sees the dome, establish a third subjectivity as the audience sees through their eyes. The "girls'" subjectivity, and by extension, the audience's, is (re-)consecrated on the altar of democracy, a cinematic sacrifice of the innocents.

The sequence concludes as Paul guides Billie through Washington's public texts, from the Declaration of Independence at the Library of Congress to the Jefferson Memorial's rotunda inscription, with its avowal of "eternal hostility against every form of tyranny over the mind of man." Moved to clarify his point, Paul rants against "selfishness," which, he declares, leads inexorably to "fascism." Billie then cinches this vague popular frontism with a fistful of feminism. In response to Paul's assertion, quoting Alexander Pope, that the "proper study of mankind is Man," she adds, "Of course, that means women too. Yes, I know."

We next see Billie in her suite, wearing glasses, sitting on a pile of books and poring over one in her lap. Her spectacles are a reversal of the blonde-as-commodity spectacle, literally bringing her own vision into focus. Billie's public visibility while sightseeing meant, at least in part, that she remained an object of the gaze. Her glasses now symbolize her own newfound vision: Billie is the subject—and a monarch, enthroned on a pedestal of knowledge. But her reign is short-lived. Paul enters the suite and delivers a quip that reframes Billie's position as matronly, asking, "What are you trying to do with those books, hatch them?"

While this line certainly lends itself to a Freudian interpretation, Paul's joke relieving the tension wrought by Billie's patriarchal reversal, the scene's staging quickly undercuts this view. Billie, in soft focus, looks up, admitting that she had thought "the way to you was through your head." But now she is focused on learning, not romance. Paul joins her, sitting, the camera moving into a two-shot of the couple, their eyes at the same level. This image of gender equality was reinforced extratextually by press coverage that unanimously hailed Holliday as the film's star, as the "rightful heir to the throne" of women's comedy, praising the "wit," individuality, and smart "personality" of her performance, as well as her physical humor.[18] Alongside Holliday's self-effacing rejection of Hollywood "glamour," the result was a discourse that undermined the dumb blonde cinematic image, semiotically from within and explicitly from without.

The film also casts Billie in the role of democratic conscience, as she questions her own assumptions and others' motives. In a dialogue with Harry's corrupt congressman, she admits she has never voted. "It's easy," he insists, "you just push a button." She responds with deceptive naiveté: "Yeah, but which one?" Billie then quickly turns the tables. Com-

A Throne of Knowledge: In *Born Yesterday* (1950), Billie (Judy Holliday) and Paul (William Holden) replace spectacle with spectacles, showing the social power of intelligence and "vision."

Double Vision: Paul and Billie are framed as a figure of democracy and equality in *Born Yesterday* (1950), seeing eye to eye, as Harry (Broderick Crawford) hovers overhead, threatening violence and corruption.

bining her blooming sense of citizenship with Jeffersonian republicanism's notion of the woman's sphere as the source of public morality, she cuts to the heart of political corruption. No one voted for Harry, she insists, so why should he have a greater voice than anyone else? As Harry's lawyer enters, the congressman comments admiringly, "Quite a little girl." This figuration of feminine purity as the antidote for political poison is underscored as she aims directly at the lawyer's conscience. "I know what you feel bad about. You don't like to be doing all [of Harry's] dirty work because you know you're better than him," she pleads, pausing. "I'm not so sure, maybe you're worse." In an echo of Fritz Lang's *Metropolis*, Billie is the "heart" that mediates between the "head" and the "hands": Harry is an unsophisticated brute, so his blunt tactics are at least understandable; the lawyer, urbane and educated, should know better. Putting on her glasses, Billie turns to scrutinize the corporate contracts he brought her to sign, completing her threefold transition from spectacle to spectator and, finally, citizen-stockholder.

Born Yesterday's denouement is the triumph of Billie's brain over Harry's brawn. Threatened by her new knowledge, Harry descends into domestic violence, slapping Billie and demanding she leave the suite. She wanders Washington's streets, Paul's voice reverberating in her head, reciting Jefferson's disavowal of tyranny. (Still, authority is doubly gendered male, with Jefferson's authorial voice embodied in Paul's.) Returning to the hotel, wearing a spare black-and-white outfit reminiscent of a nun's habit, Billie declares Harry a "big fascist!" She and Paul hatch a plan to reveal his underhanded dealings. Secreting away incriminating documents into the safe hands of "the US mail," Billie demands that Harry "behave" himself, under pain of public disclosure.

Harry physically threatens Paul, but his lawyer intervenes, declaring that the days of strong-arm tactics have passed into a "new world" where force and reason have changed places and "knowledge is power." Billie again claims center stage, with a vocal assertion that "the people" *are* "the government," only slightly leavened with humor:

Billie: This country and its institutions belong to the people that inhibit it . . .

Paul: Inhabit it.

Billie: . . . inhabit it!

As Billie and Paul exit, the now-smart blonde cements this reversal of the old order, telling Harry, "When you steal from the government you steal from yourself, you dumb ox!" With Harry stunned silent, the lawyer concludes with a perfunctory soliloquy that nonetheless linguistically confirms this inversion of power: "To all the dumb chumps and all the crazy broads . . . who thirst for knowledge and search for truth . . . and make it so tough for crooks like you—and me." Holliday's outspoken blonde, *Born Yesterday* suggests, was perhaps out of the ordinary, even "crazy," but she was anything but dumb.

The film's final scene encapsulated its ambivalent representation of postwar gender norms. Fading into another exterior shot of Washington,

The Looming Fascist Threat: Billie's power of knowledge trumps Harry's domination by force in *Born Yesterday* (1950).

Paul and Billie are pulled over in their car by a motorcycle cop. Paul produces a marriage license, prompting the policeman to waive the speeding ticket—and affirming Hollywood's notion of a happy ending for Billie. Yet feminine intellect briefly triumphs with Billie's last line. As the cop encourages them to hurry along to their destination, she leans over Paul, placing herself physically and linguistically on top. "Oh, don't worry, we'll make it," she chirps. "It's a clear case of predestination." Smiling at the cop's confused countenance, she concludes, "Look it up." In a long shot of the car pulling away, presumably to some suburban idyll, the cop—that archetype of masculine authority—is left scratching his head in bewilderment, DC's monumental architecture as his backdrop.

Born Yesterday attempted to reconcile postwar demands for domesticity with democratic notions of feminine intellect, featuring wide-open shots of Washington sunlight and white marble, portraying feminine savvy not as a threat but as the epitome of integrity. The movie was also massively popular, with a box office of around $38 million in current dollars, despite scattered protests by conservative groups like the Catholic War Veterans, who objected to Kanin's and Holliday's politics. If anything, Holliday's offbeat image added to the movie's appeal, magnifying its sunny message that World War II had indeed safeguarded a pluralistic vision of democracy. Holliday's ties to the Left had led to her inclusion in the blacklisting bible *Red Channels*, but even that setback paled in comparison with her rave reviews and Academy Award.[19] In fact, as late as the film's release in November 1950, McCarthyism had not heated up to the point that such accusations imperiled her success. Within a year, that changed.

"MISS HOLLIDAY" GOES TO WASHINGTON

It is among the many ironies of Holliday's story that, having established her public visibility in *Born Yesterday* among the capital's sunlit monuments, when she was summoned to Washington to testify before Senator Pat McCarran's Judiciary Subcommittee on March 26, 1952, it was behind closed doors. The committee was known as the Senate's answer to HUAC (House Un-American Activities Committee), and the 1950 McCarran Act had strengthened federal powers to force communists to register with the government. In 1952, McCarran was pushing a bill that eased procedures for revoking citizenship and restricted immigration, particularly targeting East Europeans. While he left Holliday's interrogation in the hands of Senator Arthur Watkins and staff director Richard Arens, the hearing was clearly a form of political theater designed to support McCarran's bill by connecting Jewish entertainers with "subversive infiltration" of the industry. Of the four performers who testified that day, three were Jewish.[20]

By the committee's standards, Holliday was fair game. With her roots in the Cultural Front, close friends and family were among the communist associates Watkins and Arens pressed her to name. Through the 1940s, Holliday had supported left causes, including Pete Seeger's People's Songs, the Civil Rights Congress, and a Win the Peace Committee demonstration against fascist Spain. Yet she never joined the Communist Party and rejected any system that meant "being a slave to the state." Friends later remembered that, while she did not draw a distinct line between communists and socialists, she "knew about communism" enough to say that it "was not an answer. Socialism maybe, but not communism." Holliday's strategy to avoid naming names, therefore, was to downplay communist affiliations, emphasize her antifascist stance, and, most importantly, plead ignorance. As her publicity agent put it, Holliday would "play Billie Dawn" in front of the committee.[21]

Theater scholar Milly Barranger has offered a thorough examination of Holliday's McCarran Committee testimony, and correctly argues that she was "one of the first *Red Channels* performers to override the blacklist."[22] Yet Barranger's exclusive focus on Holliday's testimony leaves out the broader implications of her dumb blonde strategy. In particular, two aspects of Holliday's committee appearance were portentous for women's representations in Cold War America; neither can be understood except in relation to *Born Yesterday*'s themes of domesticity, intelligence, and national belonging. First was the issue of naming. In addition to suggesting connections between communism and ethnicity, Watkins and Arens impugned Holliday's marital status and her continued use of her "maiden" name—a Red Scare tactic commonly used against stalwart left-wing women to imply a lack of social propriety.[23] Second was Holliday's "stupidity" defense. By asserting that she had been "duped" by communist-front organizations, Holliday inadvertently reestablished the figure of the dumb blonde as an inadequate citizen, incapable of thinking for herself. Having once subverted it through *Born Yesterday*'s satire and her own iconoclastic publicity, she again became submerged within the dumb blonde image.

Holliday arrived in the hearing room dressed as Billie Dawn in a tight but tasteful black dress. Arens's questions immediately fixated on names, asking whether "Holliday" was her "stage name," what "other name" she had used, and whether she had a "married name." After she acknowledged these as "Tuvim" and "Mrs. David Oppenheim," Senator Watkins insisted that the official record list the latter as her "real name."[24] Having established her Jewish heritage, the committee had aimed squarely at her independence as a woman. Yet this tension threaded through the rest of her testimony, which the Senate's published report later highlighted by identifying her as "Miss Holliday"—a subtle reminder to the public that the actress had forgone the protections of traditional, male-breadwinner domesticity.

The bulk of the committee's interrogation targeted Holliday's politics, which she deftly sidestepped using Watkins's and Arens's own gendered assumptions against them. When Watkins asked about publicity photos taken of her at a Communist Party–backed waterfront strike in 1946, she spun him around with a dazzling display of double talk:

Senator Watkins: Do you know where it happened?

Miss Holiday: No.

Senator Watkins: The one you are talking about?

Miss Holliday: No.

Senator Watkins: It would be in New York; would it not?

Miss Holliday: Yes; it would have to be.

Senator Watkins: That is what I am trying to find out.

Miss Holliday: Yes.

Senator Watkins: You do have a recollection of being in a picket line?

Miss Holliday: Yes. Not in a picket line; but I had a publicity picture taken. . . . What was it for, strikers?

Exasperated, Watkins retorted, "I do not want to be in the position of testifying, I want to be in the position of interrogating you." At that point Arens, hoping to get to the heart of the matter, interjected, "With whom did you have your photograph taken." Holliday replied with impressively succinct wordplay, "With striking people."[25]

For another two hours, Holliday avoided implicating her mother, her "best friend" Yetta Cohn, and her fellow Revuers, each of whom had left ties. She kept her cool, putting her acting skills to work, as the committee outrageously pressed for her views on the McCarran Act and implied communist links to everyone from Eleanor Roosevelt to Albert Einstein. Holliday admitted that her uncle, Joe Gollomb, who had died two years earlier, was a "radical," but denied that he was her "intellectual mentor." Again raising the shield of gender norms, the most she divulged about the people who had asked her to support leftist causes was that they were usually someone's "secretary." In a prepared statement, she made a compelling case against the Red Scare, while also declaring herself "opposed to communism," asserting her devotion to "democracy" and her opposition "to any force which would deprive us of our freedom." "I believe in truth," she proclaimed, "and I believe in justice administered in the American tradition." Ironically, the most damaging testimony turned out to be self-inflicted. Ducking beneath her Billie Dawn persona, Holliday attributed her activism to "shallow thinking." "I have been awakened to a realization that I have been irresponsible," she reiterated, "and slightly—more than slightly—stupid."[26]

When the committee, falsely, assured Holliday that her testimony was confidential, her relief was audible. If the hearing had been televised, she said, "that would have been my last appearance." Yet the most ruinous revelation accompanying the release of Holliday's testimony in September was not that she was a "Red"—the conservative press and her Senate subpoena had already made that clear—but that she was "stupid." Reporters pounced, painting Holliday as an "innocent dupe." Most referred to her specifically as a "dumb blonde." Despite a brief dustup, and some disturbingly vitriolic public reactions—including an anonymous phone call from a woman telling the pregnant Holliday that "I hope you die in childbirth"—Holliday's tactic to save her career and compatriots worked. But the damage to her image as an intelligent woman was severe. After the fervor died down, only a single journalist made a serious attempt to revive Holliday's high-IQ image.[27] Other press coverage flattered her as a blonde beauty and gifted comic, but never again during her lifetime would the word *genius* be paired with the name Judy Holliday.

A WOMAN SUBMERGED

It is tempting to conclude Holliday's story as a simple tragedy, her life, public image, and career tattered by McCarthyism. The reality was more complex and subtle, but also more revealing. Holliday's strategy was fairly unique among women swept up in the Red Scare. For instance, as historian Landon Storrs has argued, left-liberal women in the federal government disproportionately suffered disloyalty charges, at around five times the rate for men. This was partially because the protections of "proper femininity" seemed incompatible with their positions of authority, making them threats to American social norms in the eyes of conservatives. Although no women were jailed for contempt during the McCarthy era, outspoken women in the culture industry who testified before Congress, such as Lillian Hellman, were almost always blacklisted.[28] The McCarran Committee was satisfied by Holliday's testimony because she relinquished her visible persona as Jewish, intelligent, and autonomous for the appearance of a dumb blonde who, by virtue of her feminine blankness, could be safely returned to the national fold. What they missed, however, was the central lesson of *Born Yesterday*, that appearances can deceive, which allowed her to run double-talking circles around them. Yet Holliday also fell into the 1950s trap of being publicly defined by surfaces—a return to the blonde-as-commodity spectacle without the escape of Billie Dawn's intellectual ignitions. Anxiety about appearances explains the committee's attraction to Holliday's dumb blonde display, which left no room for subversion to lurk underneath. There was safety in "shallow" waters. Of course, this was its own sort of self-deception. Holliday's intelligence may have been submerged, but it survived and occasionally broke the surface. Torpedoing, after all, is simply undermining in another medium.

Holliday's post-testimony film roles showed the complexities of women's containment in 1950s Hollywood. She continued to make successful films, although never on the scale of *Born Yesterday* and always playing parts determined by the studio. McCarthyism reduced her leverage, leaving Holliday, as her biographer plainly put it, "mired in typecasting." Holliday counted herself lucky that producer Harry Cohn took the risk of hiring her at all, unsure through 1953 whether audiences would pay to see a tarnished star.[29] They did, but mostly to be entertained by comfortingly familiar comedies. Each film, from *It Should Happen to You* (1954) to *Bells Are Ringing* (1960), featured the kind of romance that had suffused *Born Yesterday*, but without its smart satire and progressive politics.

Holliday's pre- and post-testimony public image is best illustrated by that ultimate symbol of 1950s rebellion and freedom: the car. Four of Holliday's seven pictures for Columbia ended with a shot of the film's happy couple in an automobile, always with her beau at the proverbial wheel, thereby confirming her successful romance. Only in *Born Yesterday* does Holliday disrupt this male-"driven" space, leaning over Holden to dazzle the traffic cop with her verbal virtuosity. A momentary victory? Of course. But also significant, as she cracked the dumb blonde facade with a burst of intellect that was mostly absent afterward. Holliday maintained a subversive streak, however, portraying independent women who often got the better of their male counterparts, even as they remained within the boundaries of domesticity. That contradiction was at the center of the dumb blonde image. It concealed as much as it revealed, making it an important symbol of the subterranean fifties, where feminism simmered beneath the surface, building up the pressure and heat that erupted with the 1960s Second Wave.

NOTES

1. Will Holtzman, *Judy Holliday* (New York: G.P. Putnam's Sons, 1982), 147; "Oscar Winners Get News of Victory in Small New York Night Club," *Los Angeles Times*, 30 March 1951, 2(N).

2. Milly S. Barranger, *Unfriendly Witnesses: Gender, Theater, and Film in the McCarthy Era* (Carbondale: Southern Illinois University Press, 2008), 9–33; "Obituaries Judy Holliday Dies; Played Dumb; IQ 172," *Boston Globe*, 8 June 1965, 35(N); Holtzman, *Judy Holliday*, 9–24, 298.

3. Natalia Ilyin, *Blonde like Me: The Roots of the Blonde Myth in Our Culture* (New York: Simon & Schuster, 2000), 30–50, 87–98, 141–56; Ellen Tremper, *I'm No Angel: The Blonde in Film and Fiction* (Charlottesville: University of Virginia Press, 2006), 10–13, 116–36, 147–82, 218–19; Joanna Pitman, *On Blondes* (New York: Bloomsbury, 2003).

4. Laurie J. C. Cella, "Narrative 'Confidence Games': Framing the Blonde Spectacle in 'Gentlemen Prefer Blondes'(1925) and 'Nights at the Circus' (1984)," *Frontiers: A Journal of Women Studies* 25, no. 3 (2004): 47–62; Maureen Turim, "Gentlemen Consume Blondes," and Lucie Arbuthnot and Gail Seneca, "Pre-text and Text in *Gentlemen Prefer Blondes*," in *Issues in Feminine Film Criticism*, ed. Patricia Erens (Bloomington and Indianapolis: Indiana University Press, 1990), 101–11, 112–25, respectively; A. H. Weiler, "By Way of Report: 'Affairs of State' Up for Filming—Anita Loos-Columbia Set Deals—Other Items," *New York Times*, 8 April 1951, 101; Lois W. Banner, "The Creature from the Black Lagoon: Marilyn Monroe and Whiteness," *Cinema Journal* 47, no. 4 (Summer, 2008): 4–29; James Harvey, "Marilyn Reconsidered," *Threepenny Review*, no. 58 (Summer, 1994): 35–37; Steven Shaviro, "The Life, after Death, of Postmodern Emotions," *Criticism* 46, no. 1, Special Issue: Material Media (Winter 2004): 125–41. See also Dennis Bingham, "'Before She Was a Virgin . . .': Doris Day and the Decline of Female Film Comedy in the 1950s and 1960s," *Cinema Journal* 45, no. 3 (Spring, 2006): 3–31.

5. Department of Commerce—Bureau of the Census, *Fourteenth Census of the United States: 1920—Population*, Supervisor's District No. 1, Enumeration District No. 1190, Ward of City: 17th, Sheet No. 11-B; Gary Carey, *Judy Holliday: An Intimate Life Story* (London: Robson Books, 1983), 4–5; Holtzman, *Judy Holliday*, 25–29; Winthrop Sargeant, "Judy Holliday," *Life*, April 2, 1951, 107–18; Mary Shank interview, Harry Shapiro interview, and clipping of Joseph Tuvim obituary, Box 28,644, Folder 4; Barney Josephson interview, Box 28,645, Folder 2; and Max Gordon interview, Folder 1a, Lee

Israel Research Notes, 8-MWEZ, Billy Rose Theatre Collection, New York Performing Arts Library.

6. Max Gordon, *Live at the Village Vanguard* (New York: St. Martin's Press, 1980), 33–36; Theodore Strauss, "Notes on Nightclubs," *New York Times*, 26 March 1939, 134(N).

7. Mary Shank interview and Max Gordon interview, Lee Israel Research, NYPL; Holtzman, *Judy Holliday*, 29–32, 49–53; Theodore Strauss, "Notes on Nightclubs," *New York Times*, 18 June 1939, 114(N); Michael Denning, *The Cultural Front: The Laboring of American Culture in the Twentieth Century* (London and New York: Verso, 1997), 77–83, 295.

8. Holtzman, *Judy Holliday*, 93–94. Holtzman insightfully notes that Holliday's translated name was its own form of resistance, rejecting the "stagy aliases" of the studio's publicity department.

9. John Chapman, "'Born Yesterday,' Witty Comedy, Invades Broadway: Paul Douglas, Judy Holliday Expertly Cast," *Chicago Daily Tribune*, 10 February 1946, E-6(N); Brooks Atkinson, "Good Acting Keeps Kanin Play at Top," *Los Angeles Times*, 18 May 1947, B-1(N); Lewis Nichols, "Broadway Comedy: 'Born Yesterday' Is a New Example of an Expert and Local Art," *New York Times*, 10 February 1946, 45(N).

10. Mark Barron, "Along Broadway: Judy's Older Though 'Born Yesterday'," *Los Angeles Times*, 30 January 1949, D-2(N); Tex McCray and Jinx Falkenburg, "With the IQ of a Genius, She Plays a Dumb Blonde," *Boston Globe*, 8 December 1949, 27(N); Frank Daugherty, "A Judy with Punch: Miss Holliday Proves a Vivid Personality On the Set of 'Born Yesterday,'" *New York Times*, 10 September 1950, 102(N); Sargeant, "Judy Holliday."

11. Leonard Lyons, "Manhattan Memos," *Washington Post*, 22 June 1946, 10(N).

12. "Katherine Hepburn Helped Judy Holliday in First Big Film Role," *Boston Globe*, 29 January 1950, 20-A(N); Holtzman, *Judy Holliday*, 132–39; Carey, *Judy Holliday*, 96–102; Orit Kamir, *Framed: Women in Law and Film* (Durham, NC, and London: Duke University Press, 2006), 135–59.

13. Laura Mulvey, *Visual and Other Pleasures* (Bloomington and Indianapolis: Indiana University Press, 1989), 14–26; E. Ann Kaplan, *Women and Film: Both Sides of the Camera* (New York : Methuen, 1983), 2, 23–35; Mark Garrett Cooper, *Universal Women: Filmmaking and Institutional Change in Early Hollywood* (Urbana, Chicago, and Springfield: University of Illinois Press, 2010), xxi–xxviii.

14. Janet Staiger, *Perverse Spectators: The Practices of Film Reception* (New York and London: New York University Press, 2000), 81; Kathy Lee Peiss, *Hope in a Jar: The Making of America's Beauty Culture* (Philadelphia: University of Pennsylvania Press, 2011, 1998), 6, 146–9.

15. Lary May, *The Big Tomorrow: Hollywood and the Politics of the American Way* (Chicago and London: University of Chicago Press, 2000), 180, 202–4; George Lipsitz, *Rainbow at Midnight: Labor and Culture in the 1940s* (Urbana and Chicago: University of Illinois Press, 1994), 51–65.

16. Wini Breines, *Young, White, and Miserable: Growing Up Female in the Fifties* (Boston: Beacon Press, 1992); Elaine Tyler May, *Homeward Bound: American Families in the Cold War Era* (New York: Basic Books, 1988).

17. Andreas Huyssen, *After the Great Divide: Modernism, Mass Culture, Postmodernism* (Bloomington and Indianapolis: Indiana University Press, 1986), 44–62; Tania Modleski, *Feminism without Women: Culture and Criticism in a "Postfeminist" Age* (New York and London: Routledge, 1991), 34.

18. E. S., "Holliday Screen Hit," *Los Angeles Times*, 15 November 1950, B-6(N); Daugherty, "A Judy with Punch"; Richard L. Coe, "'Born Yesterday' Is Chockful o' Laughs," *Washington Post*, 22 November 1950, B-8(N); "Earl Scheib Says," *Los Angeles Times*, 4 January 1951, C-2(N); Mae Tinee, "'Born Yesterday' Is a Hit: Judy Holliday Bows as Star in Beguiling Film," *Chicago Daily Tribune*, 20 January 1951, A-2(N); Richard L. Coe, "Kanin Play's Even Better on Screen," *Washington Post*, 2 February1951, C-7(N).

19. Holtzman, *Judy Holliday*, 146–47.
20. Barranger, *Unfriendly Witnesses*, 9, 17; "Testimony of Judy Holliday," March 26, 1952. *Hearings before the Subcommittee to Investigate the Administration of the Internal Security Act and Other Internal Security Laws of the Committee of the Judiciary.* US Senate. 82nd Congress. 2nd sess. *Subversive Infiltration of Radio, Television, and the Entertainment Industry.* Part 2. 1952 (Washington, DC: US Government Printing Office, 1952), 141–86.
21. *Daily Worker*, 30 November 1946, "Simon Rifkind," and "James Buffington," Box 28, 644, Folder 8, and "Screen, Stage, Radio & TV Archive," Folder 9, Lee Israel Research, NYPL; Holtzman, *Judy Holliday*, 162.
22. Barranger, *Unfriendly Witnesses*, 13–32, 16.
23. Landon R.Y. Storrs, *The Second Red Scare and the Unmaking of the New Deal Left* (Princeton, NJ: Princeton University Press, 2013), 86–106.
24. US Senate, "Testimony of Judy Holliday," 141–42, 147.
25. US Senate, "Testimony of Judy Holliday," 148–49.
26. US Senate, "Testimony of Judy Holliday," 161–63, 166–68, 175, 177, 181–83.
27. US Senate, "Testimony of Judy Holliday," 185; "Judy at Red Inquiry Told of Own Probe," *Washington Post*, 24 September 1952, 28(N); "Was Duped by Reds, Says Judy Holliday," *Los Angeles Times*, 25 September 1952, 32(N); "Innocent Dupe of Red Fronts, Actress Claims," *Chicago Daily Tribune*, 25 September 1952, B-4(N); R. H. Gardner, "But Not A Right Arm," *Baltimore Sun*, 14 March 1954, A-9(N); "Yetta Cohn," Lee Israel Research, NYPL.
28. Storrs, *Second Red Scare*, 89, 105, 326; Barranger, *Unfriendly Witnesses*, 7–8, 48, 60–64, 74–85, 124–25.
29. Holtzman, *Judy Holliday*, 182, 195.

BIBLIOGRAPHY

Banner, Lois W. "The Creature from the Black Lagoon: Marilyn Monroe and Whiteness." *Cinema Journal* 47, no. 4 (Summer, 2008): 4–29.
Barranger, Milly S. *Unfriendly Witnesses: Gender, Theater, and Film in the McCarthy Era.* Carbondale: Southern Illinois University Press, 2008.
Bingham, Dennis. "'Before She Was a Virgin . . .': Doris Day and the Decline of Female Film Comedy in the 1950s and 1960." *Cinema Journal* 45, no. 3 (Spring, 2006): 3–31.
Breines, Wini. *Young, White, and Miserable: Growing Up Female in the Fifties.* Boston: Beacon Press, 1992.
Carey, Gary. *Judy Holliday: An Intimate Life Story.* London: Robson Books, 1983.
Cella, Laurie J. C. "Narrative 'Confidence Games': Framing the Blonde Spectacle in 'Gentlemen Prefer Blondes' (1925) and 'Nights at the Circus' (1984)." *Frontiers: A Journal of Women Studies* 25, no. 3 (2004): 47–62.
Cooper, Mark Garrett. *Universal Women: Filmmaking and Institutional Change in Early Hollywood.* Urbana, Chicago, and Springfield: University of Illinois Press, 2010.
Denning, Michael. *The Cultural Front: The Laboring of American Culture in the Twentieth Century.* London and New York: Verso, 1997.
Department of Commerce—Bureau of the Census. *Fourteenth Census of the United States: 1920—Population.* Supervisor's District No. 1, Enumeration District No. 1190, Ward of City: 17th, Sheet No. 11-B.
Erens, Patricia, ed. *Issues in Feminine Film Criticism.* Bloomington and Indianapolis: Indiana University Press, 1990.
Gordon, Max. *Live at the Village Vanguard.* New York: St. Martin's Press, 1980.
Harvey, James. "Marilyn Reconsidered." *Threepenny Review*, no. 58 (Summer, 1994): 35–37.
Holtzman, Will. *Judy Holliday.* New York: G.P. Putnam's Sons, 1982.
Huyssen, Andreas. *After the Great Divide: Modernism, Mass Culture, Postmodernism.* Bloomington and Indianapolis: Indiana University Press, 1986.

Ilyin, Natalia. *Blonde like Me: The Roots of the Blonde Myth in Our Culture.* New York: Simon & Schuster, 2000.

Kamir, Orit. *Framed: Women in Law and Film.* Durham, NC, and London: Duke University Press, 2006.

Kaplan, E. Ann. *Women and Film: Both Sides of the Camera.* New York: Methuen, 1983.

Lee Israel Research Notes, 8-MWEZ. Billy Rose Theatre Collection, New York Performing Arts Library.

Lipsitz, George. *Rainbow at Midnight: Labor and Culture in the 1940s.* Urbana and Chicago: University of Illinois Press, 1994.

May, Elaine Tyler. *Homeward Bound: American Families in the Cold War Era.* New York: Basic Books, 1988.

May, Lary. *The Big Tomorrow: Hollywood and the Politics of the American Way.* Chicago and London: University of Chicago Press, 2000.

Modleski, Tania. *Feminism without Women: Culture and Criticism in a "Postfeminist" Age.* New York and London: Routledge, 1991.

Mulvey, Laura. *Visual and Other Pleasures.* Bloomington and Indianapolis: Indiana University Press, 1989.

Peiss, Kathy Lee. *Hope in a Jar: The Making of America's Beauty Culture.* Philadelphia: University of Pennsylvania Press, 2011.

Pitman, Joanna. *On Blondes.* New York: Bloomsbury, 2003.

Shaviro, Steven. "The Life, after Death, of Postmodern Emotions." *Criticism* 46, no. 1. Special Issue: Material Media (Winter 2004): 125–41.

Staiger, Janet. *Perverse Spectators: The Practices of Film Reception.* New York and London: New York University Press, 2000.

Storrs, Landon R. Y. *The Second Red Scare and the Unmaking of the New Deal Left.* Princeton, NJ: Princeton University Press, 2013.

Tremper, Ellen. *I'm No Angel: The Blonde in Film and Fiction.* Charlottesville: University of Virginia Press, 2006.

US Senate. 82nd Congress. 2nd sess. *Hearings before the Subcommittee to Investigate the Administration of the Internal Security Act and Other Internal Security Laws of the Committee of the Judiciary. Subversive Infiltration of Radio, Television, and the Entertainment Industry.* Part 2. 1952. Washington DC: US Government Printing Office, 1952.

TWO

The Fuzzy End of the Lollypop

Protofeminism and Collective Subjectivity in Some Like
It Hot

Melissa Meade

In Billy Wilder's 1959 comedy *Some Like It Hot*, Marilyn Monroe laments
having procured the "fuzzy end of the lollypop" in life. She blames herself for her life's misfortunes, for falling for the wrong men and getting
burned, and has joined an all-girl jazz band as a way out. She is Sugar
Kane, ukulele player and singer for Sweet Sue and Her Society Syncopators. The film's male leads, played by Tony Curtis and Jack Lemmon and
around which the plot revolves, have also joined the all-girl band to
escape their life's troubles. These two are Joe (later Josephine) and Jerry
(later Daphne), a pair of working musicians who end up running from
the Mafia after being in the wrong place at the wrong time. The story
centers on Joe and Jerry's adventures in transvestism, or cross-dressing,
as they don women's clothing and join Sweet Sue and Her Society Syncopators to facilitate their escape.

    In this chapter I look at the women in *Some Like It Hot*, situating the
film as a protofeminist text, one that connects gender politics of the First
Wave of the US women's movement to the Second Wave. As an ideologi-
cal text, it is neither straightforwardly feminist nor antifeminist, but one
in which we can see an anticipation of a feminist cultural politics in the
late twentieth century. The complicated and contradictory depiction of
women in the film captures a cultural ambivalence toward women's intellect; the women are simultaneously cunning and duped, witty and
dim, smart and naïve. Further, I argue that a collective female subject

emerges among the women in the all-girl band context, and that this collective subject becomes important for a collective feminist politics.

The film is set in 1929, and Joe and Jerry are out-of-work jazz musicians, struggling to find a new gig. They accept an out-of-town job, and while trying to borrow a car to get there accidentally witness the infamous Valentine's Day Massacre. This so-called Valentine's Day Massacre was a real-life gangster shooting in Prohibition-era Chicago, between Al Capone and Bugs Moran, killing seven. In his films, Wilder often incorporated intertextual references, using cameos and nods to real people and events.[1] Joe and Jerry, fearing Mafia retaliation and unable to find paying work as men, take a job that had been jokingly offered to them earlier in the film: as saxophone and bass players in an all-women touring jazz band, Sweet Sue and Her Society Syncopators. They pose as women with the names Josephine and Daphne in order to do so.

Billy Wilder does not make much of an effort to have the actors pass seamlessly as women. The costumes, wigs, and makeup are clunky, and much of the humor in the film derives from Joe and Jerry's obvious male status. We laugh because the transformation is incomplete. Indeed, Anthony Lane of the *New Yorker* noted in 2001 that the film "has almost nothing to tell us about transvestism, and surprisingly few suggestions about the topic of homosexuality."[2] He continues, "It only becomes truly fraught with sexual confusion if you try to decide what will happen after the *end* of the picture." The film ends with an iconic scene in which Lemmon, as Daphne, tries to deter the attention of a man who has been pursuing her throughout the film. The man, Osgood Fielding III, played by comedian Joe E. Brown, is proposing marriage, and Daphne lists the many reasons why the marriage would not work. Finally, exhausted by the ruse, Daphne comes clean as a man, and Osgood enthusiastically (and infamously) replies, "Nobody's perfect!"

In this way the end denies a neatly heteronormative resolution. Chris Straayer refers to this kind of film as "temporary transvestism," one in which sexual disguise is used in order to achieve something else, and to move the plot along in other ways. The cross-dressing is not an expression of sexuality, but a guise in order to tell another story, in this case running from the Mafia. Straayer suggests that this comedy of transvestism "both creates and controls homosexual possibilities," while also challenging and stabilizing traditional gender roles.[3] In the case of *Some Like It Hot* there are parallel heterosexual and homosexual narratives, each both "implied and real."[4] Joe (as Joe) and Sugar get together in the end, while Osgood and Jerry/Daphne may also have a chance of a happy romantic ending.

If we cannot see the film as insight into transgendered subjectivity, however, we can see the costuming and cross-dressing as calling attention to constructed identities and the gender performance required of everyday life. Joe and Jerry struggle in their costumes, in their heels, wigs, and makeup. Karen McNally writes that the film's key theme of disguise "provides a means of realigning gender identity,"[5] but that the lack of closure and the imperfect characters "represent fluid ideas of cultural, political and individual identity."[6] Joe and Jerry confirm traditional gender roles in some ways, while also embodying shifting gender roles of the 1950s, with hints of fluid sexuality and alignments with female subjectivity. They become part of the collective female subjective, alongside Sweet Sue, the Syncopators, and Sugar.

At the beginning of the film when Joe and Jerry cannot find work as men, the female administrators of the talent agency jokingly suggest that the only jobs available were for female musicians, either with all-female bands or in mixed-sex acts. Joe and Jerry discuss their financial woes and how they have resorted to taking loans from the female musicians in their bands, who seem to be doing fine. While female musicians may have started as a novelty, there is an overarching sense that their inclusion in the workforce will ultimately displace the male musicians. And in the context of economic struggles of the era (the stock market would crash in October 1929), it would be the men who would be culturally framed as suffering most.[7]

This depiction captures an anxiety associated with the "new woman" of the early twentieth century. Ushered in by the First Wave of the women's movement, the new woman was an independent career woman, who was thought to sometimes succeed at the expense of men.[8] The First Wave of the women's movement is generally understood as the feminism of the late nineteenth to early twentieth centuries and encompasses the activists who fought for women's full participation in politics and public life and to end male domination and female oppression. This First Wave of feminism culminated with women's suffrage in 1920. *Some Like It Hot* in part relies on a trope of a battle of the sexes, represented in the backdrop of the all-girl jazz band, Sweet Sue and Her Society Syncopators. This battle, however, has a limited economy, in part rooted in its temporal positioning vis-à-vis the Second Wave women's movement in the United States.

While set in 1929, *Some Like It Hot* was made in 1959, directly preceding the emergence of a Second Wave women's movement in the United States. The Second Wave, drawing from the work of the first and expanding its critique and analysis, began in the early 1960s. Popular texts such as Betty Friedan's *The Feminine Mystique* were important catalysts and generated the rallying cries of "the personal is political" and "sisterhood is powerful."[9] Women worked together to raise consciousness about what it meant to be a woman, instigated research agendas around gender, and changed our political systems to be more inclusive. They developed a collective female subject in order to effect change. If *Some Like It Hot* was made in the supposedly dormant time between the women's movements, it certainly acts as a cultural antecedent for the Second Wave and a bridge between the two.

The "all-girl," as they were called, entertainment acts were popular in vaudeville, theater, dance, and musical troupes from the 1920s through the 1940s. As Sheri Tucker and Kristin McGee assert, there were hundreds of all-women bands in the early parts of the twentieth century, and by the 1940s they were well represented by such popular acts as the International Sweethearts of Rhythm, the Ingenues, and Phil Spitalny's Musical Sweethearts.[10] Tucker argues that these feminized spaces were not racially or gender neutral, instead capturing the ways in which gender and race intersected, contradicted, and ultimately inscribed power.

In the early twentieth century quite a few films featured all-female dance troupes and musical acts. There were a multitude of genre flapper films in the silent era, for example, many of which do not exist anymore, as well as Dorothy Arzner's acclaimed *Dance, Girl, Dance* in 1940. The women in these films were often at odds with each other, competing for top billing and fighting over limited space for women. By the 1950s, however, all-women bands were not featured in film; by setting *Some Like It Hot* in 1929, Wilder is able to revive this depiction.

Wilder wanted to set the film in the "gangster era," seeing it as aesthetically cinematic. He saw the era as particularly photogenic, creating good background images in which he could tell a farcical story.[11] He wanted to satirize gangster films, and got the plot idea for men joining an all-female band from a 1935 French musical, *Fanfare of Love*.[12] The use of the all-women band as backdrop for the plot was foremost an aesthetic decision. In his production notes, he had extensive ideas for using the all-girl band for publicity events. Wilder was masterful at publicity, having concocted the infamous Monroe photograph over the subway grate, in which her skirt flares up, for *The Seven Year Itch*, a few year earlier.[13]

In a letter dated March 17, 1958, Wilder wrote directly to Marilyn Monroe, already well established in Hollywood, yet on a two-year respite from filmmaking, asking if she would be interested in doing the film. He wrote, "The time is 1929—the Era of Wonderful Nonsense, the age of jazz and flappers, of hip-flasks and 'It,' of the Charleston and the one-way ride."[14]

But, of course, the flapper era, the jazz age, was not only one of wonderful nonsense. It was a time of significant change for women and men, for challenges to gender behaviors, and it was the culmination of the First Wave of the women's movement in 1920, with women's suffrage. On the one hand, the age had come to represent an easy freedom, and on the other hand, flappers and jazz represented transgression and aggressive appropriations of freedom. Flappers, originally a British term for debutantes, became associated with young women who exhibited nontraditional clothing and behavior during and after World War I. Flappers were bolstered by many cultural forms, including literature, advertising, fashion, retail, and magazines, as well as the flapper films of the late 1910s to the early 1920s.[15]

The "flapper film," as a subgenre of silent romantic and social comedy films, was characterized by modern heroines and featured such actresses as Colleen Moore, Clara Bow, Louise Brooks, Virginia Lee Corbin, Madge Bellamy, and Joan Crawford. These films featured the modern style of the flapper, in behavior and dress, and the jazz age, resplendent with parties, dancing, drinking, and smoking. The women may have been at odds, but they were also independent and assertive.[16]

Lori Landay, looking at 1928's *Our Dancing Daughters*, starring Joan Crawford, asserts that when "female subjectivity is created out of the discourses of the culture industries, it is inextricably intertwined with self-commodification and self-objectification, with the split in sense of self between, to use John Berger's terms, the surveyor and surveyed."[17] The filmic female subject, as long as it is coming out of the context of Hollywood, can never quite escape the patriarchal and hegemonic gender and race relationships.

Landay continues, "Like other Jazz Age discourses of the paradoxical new woman that juxtaposed feminist and consumerist ideals, the flapper film performed the cultural work of reflecting, shaping, and (as comedy is wont to do) mocking emerging definitions of a modern femininity."[18] We see these paradoxes and gender contradictions reappear in *Some Like It Hot*, in the characters of Sugar Kane, band leader Sweet Sue, the rest of the Syncopators band members, and even Joe as Josephine and Jerry as Daphne. They perform "girl" in the all-girl band, and these girls were sexy, fun, youthful, well groomed, and musically accomplished.

The musicians of Sweet Sue and Her Society Syncopators, meant to parody the earlier flapper films, capture the sentiments and paradoxes of early twentieth-century femininity. Sweet Sue herself, the band leader, is forceful and commanding, insisting on hotter jazz from Joe and Jerry when they join in, and bossing the male manager around. Yet she is seen taking medicine for her ulcers, is worried and unable to control the band, and is ultimately a laughable and fangless leader. The band members, played by both actresses and offscreen musicians, are serious musicians as well as playful girls on tour.

Monroe, giving another indelible screen performance in her short film career, is a lightning rod for cultural sensibilities about women's intellect and capabilities. Perhaps no other Hollywood figure has received as much ink written as Marilyn Monroe; these books include biographies, fictional accounts, and academic treatises. As Clara Juncker pointed out in 2010, "In 1995, S. Paige Baty counted seventy books exclusively on Marilyn, and the number keeps rising."[19] She has been deemed victim, instigator, childlike, childish, wise, feminist, aspiring intellectual, gullible, and representative of feminine contradictions.[20] Monroe's body is also the quintessential "commodity fetish," as Karina Eileraas puts it, a "repository for myriad cultural fears, fantasies and longings about masculinity, femininity, sexuality, war and domesticity."[21]

In *Some Like It Hot*, at first it is Joe and Jerry who are doing the manipulating and the posing, but it becomes clear that Sugar Kane is in on the game, as well. When she meets Joe on the beach posing yet again, but this time as a wealthy male yacht owner, she contrives her own story, imagining what it is that would make her his perfect mate. She tells him of an imagined education and society-going days. When in the film she sings the 1920s tune "I Wanna Be Loved by You," in a startlingly suggestive gown, she is both ingénue and well-tred professional; she is clever and smart, and we can't quite believe her when she claims she "couldn't aspire to anything higher."[22]

Although Sugar and the rest of the Syncopators conform to classical Hollywood's sensibilities of women, as love interests for men, and as women waiting to be rescued, they by no means represent a hegemonic patriarchy, one in which women are still supposed to prefer domestic lives over working outside the home.[23] They are indeed working outside the home, building careers, making their own living, enjoying themselves, each other, and their work. Perhaps most significantly, they are seen working together, not as rivals but as united in a shared female subject.

The mise-en-scène consistently positions the Syncopators as body parts to be admired. We see this in one of the first sequences in the film, just as we are to meet Joe and Jerry playing with a male band—we see dancing girls in a mirror. We also see this in the band parties on the touring bus, lots of legs, sometimes with music; and we see it in scenes of men watching the female musicians as they arrive in their hotel in Florida, and as they move through their work. The Syncopators are not only the surveyed, however. Collectively they become a female subject that cannot be quite so simple. This is in large part due to the fact of the male interlopers, who call our attention so explicitly to the construction of femininity and the arbitrary designations of intellect and talent. Everybody in the film is performing; everybody is on the mooch; everybody is clever.

There is one particular sequence that captures the irony of Jerry and Joe watching Sugar, not only as a sexualized object, as expected (and they do elsewhere in the film), but also as the embodiment of perfected constructed femininity. It is the sequence in which we first see them in drag, and they comment on the awkwardness of their costumes. Then we see Sugar for the first time in the film, striding by, complete with trombone accompaniment and bounce. We see them watch her intently, not with the expected lust but also with fascination and admiration. Jerry says, "Look how she moves, she looks just like Jello on springs."[24] He wants what she has.

The sequence between Joe and Sugar, in which Sugar bemoans her "fuzzy end of the lollypop," is particularly apt for illustrating disrupted expectations of gender performance. Joe has just joined the Syncopators, as Josephine, and has found the group preparing to have an after-hours party on the tour bus. The party is strictly prohibited by management, and Sugar has been warned that another infraction will force her to leave the tour. Nonetheless, Sugar has gone to fetch ice for drinks, where Joe follows her. From the screenplay:

Sugar comes in, followed by Josephine with the cake of ice.

Sugar: (pointing to sunken washbowl) Put it here.

Joe: (dropping the ice in the bowl) Sugar, you're going to get yourself into a lot of trouble.

Sugar: Better keep a lookout.

Joe: If Bienstock catches you again—What's the matter with you, anyway?

Sugar: I'm not very bright, I guess.

Joe: I wouldn't say that. Careless, maybe.

Sugar: No, just dumb. If I had any brains, I wouldn't be on this crummy train with this crummy girls' band.

Joe: Then why did you take this job?

Sugar: I used to sing with male bands. But I can't afford it any more.

Joe: Afford it?

Sugar: Have you ever been with a male band?

Joe: Me?

Sugar: That's what I'm running away from. I worked with six different ones in the last two years. Oh, brother!

Joe: Rough?

Sugar: I'll say.

Joe: You can't trust those guys.

Sugar: I can't trust myself. The moment I'd start with a new band— bingo!

Joe: Bingo?

Sugar: You see, I have this thing about saxophone players.

Joe: (abandoning his lookout post) Really?

Sugar: Especially tenor sax. I don't know what it is, but they just curdle me. All they have to do is play eight bars of "Come to Me My Melancholy Baby"—and my spine turns to custard, and I get goose-pimply all over—and I come to them.

Joe: That so?

Sugar: (hitting her head) Every time!

Joe: (nonchalantly) You know—I play tenor sax.

Sugar: But you're a girl, thank goodness.

Joe: (his throat drying up) Yeah.

Sugar: That's why I joined this band. Safety first. Anything to get away from those bums.

Joe: (drier yet) Yeah.

Sugar: (hacking the ice viciously) You don't know what they're like. You fall for them and you love 'em—you think it's going to be the biggest thing since the Graf Zeppelin—and the next thing you know they're borrowing money from you and spending it on other dames and betting on the horses—

Joe: You don't say?

Sugar: Then one morning you wake up and the saxophone is gone and the guy is gone, and all that's left behind is a pair of old socks and a tube of toothpaste, all squeezed out.

Joe: Men!

Sugar: So you pull yourself together and you go on to the next job, and the next saxophone player, and it's the same thing all over again. See what I mean?—not very bright.

Joe: (looking her over) Brains aren't everything.

Sugar: I can tell you one thing—it's not going to happen to me again. Ever. I'm tired of getting the fuzzy end of the lollipop. [25]

If the First Wave of the US feminist movement focused on women's political and economic inclusion, the Second Wave of the feminist movement continued these struggles but took up as well a critique of phallocentrism and male cultural dominance. Sugar's dissatisfaction with the fuzzy end of the lollypop, in addition to being a comedic innuendo, anticipates such dissatisfaction. Although she downplays the importance of the all-girl group, calling it "crummy," it nonetheless gives her an important alternative to working and living in a male-dominated field. Here she is able to cultivate female friendship without the threat of male attention, and build a collective subject in this friendship and work. Or, as Bernard Dick put it, "Sugar wants friendship, and men want Sugar."[26] Such a critique and embodied alternative are protofeminist: they anticipate both the arguments and the strategies of the Second Wave women's movement.

This scene also demonstrates ways that Marilyn Monroe's character can be understood as a protofeminist subject. In this scene we see the guises of both feminine vulnerability and ambition, as well as the guises of both masculine control and disorientation. She is at once self-effacing and confident. After such linguistic maneuvering, it is indeed hard to believe that she is not "bright," for she has taken control of her professional life, made decisions, and is both assertive and independent, despite what she says.

Lieberfeld and Sanders contend that Sugar, throughout the film, disrupts normative masculine discourse, and we can see it clearly in this scene.[27] Sugar consistently contradicts Joe as Josephine. When he tries to correct her self-castigation, saying she's merely "careless," rather than "not very bright," she says "No." When he plays along with the trope of the predatory male, saying "you can't trust those guys," as if they are the actors and she is the acted upon, she quips, "I can't trust myself!" She embodies a full subject with both fallibility and strength, and with sexual agency. Even though the contradictions are self-effacing, she is controlling the conversation and not deferring to Joe.[28]

Curtis's character is protofeminist in that his positioning underscores the relationship between gender and power. Curtis, as Joe, is a man, but because he is in disguise as a woman he is unable to act, unable to fully assert himself. This points to changes in postwar masculinity, the accompanying fears of eroded masculine vitality, and changing power relationships between women and men. He is able to relate to Sugar through his femininity, and the battle of the sexes is resolved through female friendship. The relationship between Joe and Sugar can also be understood as protofeminist, with its sexual innuendo (both heterosexual and homosexual), and shared agency. Rather than fitting into a redomestication narrative, common for women in film in the 1950s,[29] *Some Like It Hot* depicts Sugar as clever, capable, able to act, and able to act in conjunction with other women. Rather than solely turning to a man for support, she first turns to the company of women.

Monroe as Sugar is a thin leading character, compared to Joe and Jerry, and in another depiction we might imagine this film as belonging to the "career woman" genre of the 1930s or 1940s, Katherine Hepburn or Rosalind Russell at her side. Her intelligence is on display as much as her body and sexuality. But right beside Sugar Kane is a collective female subject, constructed in their work and relationships, and collective intelligence. Sweet Sue is both nurturer and disciplinarian. The Syncopators are both playful siblings and serious coworkers. Even Joe and Jerry, and Josephine and Daphne, are part of the emergent collective female subject, as they fight off unwanted male attention, fit in, and expand the performance of femininity. What is partially at stake in this emergent female collective female subject is the struggle for women's intellectual representation.

Susan Glenn, in her research on women in early theater, theorizes a protofeminist activity within seemingly innocuous stage performances: "Although the stage did not so much resolve as register debates about changing gender roles and modern anxieties, there was nonetheless clearly identifiable moments when women's voices were either amplified or suppressed by stage spectacle."[30] *Some Like It Hot*, which many say is Wilder's most funny film, is about identity construction, manipulation, and disguise. At the center of this is the disputed category of woman, in the form of an all-girl band that hosts two men in disguise.

The band serves to organize the plot for farcical purposes, and also projects a vision of a female subject that is complex. Being set in 1929 and emulating flapper films, *Some Like It Hot* also serves a bridge between the first and second waves of the women's movement. In setting and character development there is an emergent collective female subject, and this subject both recapitulates and challenges prevailing gender ideologies. As such, it can be read as a protofeminist film, anticipating and articulating issues of women's subjectivity that will emerge more explicitly in the political and cultural arenas of the Second Wave women's movement.

NOTES

For assistance with this project I wish to thank the reference staff at the Margaret Herrick Library at the Academy of Motion Picture Arts and Sciences, the Cultural Studies Working Group at Colby-Sawyer College, the Center for the Study of Film and History, the NSRBH, Cricket Keating, Michel Gregory, and Laura Mattoon D'Amore.

1. Robert Horton, ed., *Billy Wilder: Interviews* (Jackson: University Press of Mississippi, 2001). Billy Wilder papers, f. 79, *Some Like It Hot*, Margaret Herrick Library, the Academy of Motion Picture Arts and Sciences, Beverly Hills, CA.

2. Anthony Lane, "Boys Will Be Girls," *New Yorker*, 22 October 2001, 76.

3. Chris Straayer, *Deviant Eyes, Deviant Bodies: Sexual Re-orientations in Film and Video* (New York: Columbia University Press, 1996), 402.

4. Straayer, *Deviant Eyes*, 418.

5. Karen McNally, "Introduction," in *Billy Wilder, Movie Maker: Critical Essays on the Films*, ed. Karen McNally (Jefferson, NC, and London: McFarland, 2011), 5.

6. McNally, "Introduction," 3.

7. Sherrie Tucker, *Swing Shift: "All Girl" Bands of the 1940s* (Durham, NC, and London: Duke University Press, 2000).

8. Patricia Marks, *Bicycles, Bangs, and Bloomers: The New Woman in the Popular Press* (Lexington: University Press of Kentucky, 1990); Martha H. Patterson, *Beyond the Gibson Girl: Reimagining the American New Woman, 1895–1915* (Urbana: University of Illinois Press, 2005); the Modern Girl around the World Research Group, Alys Eve Weinbaum, Lynn M. Thomas, Priti Ramamurthy, Uta G. Poiger, and Madeleine Yue Dong, eds., *The Modern Girl around the World: Consumption, Modernity, and Globalization* (Durham, NC, and London: Duke University Press, 2008).

9. Betty Friedan, *The Feminine Mystique*, repr. ed. (New York: W. W. Norton, 2001); Robin Morgan, *Sisterhood Is Powerful* (New York: Vintage Books, 1970).

10. Tucker, *Swing Shift*; Kristin A. McGee, *Some Liked It Hot: Women in Film and Television, 1928–1959* (Middletown, CT: Wesleyan University Press, 2009); Judy Chaikin, dir., *The Girls in the Band* (Artist Tribe, One Step Productions, 2011), DVD.

11. Vanessa Brown, "Broadcast to Kuala Lumpur," *Action*, November/December 1970, 64–69.

12. This was in 1951 made into a German film, *Fan faren der Liebe*, which is what Wilder credits in the title sequence of *Some Like It Hot*. Paul Kerr, "A Small, Effective Organization: The Mirisch Company, the Package Unit System and the Production Code of *Some Like It Hot*," in *Billy Wilder, Movie Maker: Critical Essays on the Films*, ed. Karen McNally (Jefferson, NC, and London: McFarland, 2011), 125.

13. Billy Wilder papers, f. 79.

14. Billy Wilder papers, f. 79.

15. Catherine Gourley, *Flappers and the New American Woman: Perceptions of Women from 1918 through the 1920s* (Minneapolis, MN: Twenty-First Century Books, 2007); Carolyn Kitch, *The Girl on the Magazine Cover: The Origins of Visual Stereotypes in American Mass Media* (Chapel Hill: University of North Carolina Press, 2000).

16. Lori Landay, "The Flapper Film: Comedy, Dance, and Jazz Age Kinaesthetics," in *A Feminist Reader in Early Cinema*, ed. Jennifer Bean and Diane Negra (Durham, NC, and London: Duke University Press, 2000), 221.

17. Landay, "The Flapper Film," 221.

18. Landay, "The Flapper Film," 225.

19. S. Paige Baty, *American Monroe: The Making of a Body Politic* (Berkeley: University of California Press, 1995); Clara Juncker, *Circling Marilyn: Text, Body, Performance* (Odense: University Press of Southern Denmark, 2010), 13.

20. Baty, *American Monroe*; Juncker, *Circling Marilyn*. See, most recently, Lois Banner, *Marilyn: The Passion and the Paradox* (New York: Bloomsbury, 2012).

21. Karina Eileraas, "Hello, Norma Jeane," *Ms. Magazine Blog*, 3 August 2012, http://msmagazine.com/blog/blog/2012/08/03/hello-norma-jeane (accessed 1 September 2012)

22. Billy Wilder and I. A. L. Diamond, *Some Like It Hot*, screenplay, 12 November 1958.

23. Harry M. Benshoff and Sean Griffin, *America on Film: Representing Race, Class, Gender, and Sexuality at the Movies*, 2nd ed. (Malden, MA: Wiley-Blackwell, 1999).

24. Wilder and Diamond, *Some Like It Hot*.

25. Wilder and Diamond, *Some Like It Hot*.

26. Bernard F. Dick, *Billy Wilder*, updated ed. (New York: DaCapo Press, 1996), 90.

27. Daniel Lieberfeld and Judith Sanders. "Comedy and Identity in *Some Like It Hot*." *Journal of Popular Film & Television* 26, no. 3 (1998): 128–35.

28. Monroe and Wilder had infamous public spats during the shooting of this film. Monroe was on a reduced working schedule, on doctor's orders, because of a recent miscarriage; Wilder claimed that she was demanding, uncooperative, and disruptive on set. Monroe worried that Wilder made her appear dumb in the film; Wilder characterized Monroe as having "breasts like granite and a brain like swiss cheese" (Lane, "Boys Will Be Girls," 74); Billy Wilder papers, Marilyn Monroe and Billy Wilder clipping files, Margaret Herrick Library, the Academy of Motion Picture Arts and Sciences, Beverly Hills, CA.

29. James Harvey, *Movie Love in the Fifties* (New York: Knopf, 2001).

30. Susan A. Glenn, *Female Spectacle: The Theatrical Roots of Modern Feminism* (Cambridge, MA, and London: Harvard University Press, 2000), 8.

BIBLIOGRAPHY

Banner, Lois. *Marilyn: The Passion and the Paradox*. New York: Bloomsbury, 2012.

Baty, S. Paige. *American Monroe: The Making of a Body Politic*. Berkeley: University of California Press, 1995.

Benshoff, Harry M., and Sean Griffin. *America on Film: Representing Race, Class, Gender, and Sexuality at the Movies*. 2nd ed. Malden, MA: Wiley-Blackwell, 2009.

Brown, Vanessa. "Broadcast to Kuala Lumpur." *Action*, November/December 1970, 64–69.

Chaikin, Judy, dir. *The Girls in the Band*. Artist Tribe, One Step Productions, 2011. DVD.

Dick, Bernard F. *Billy Wilder*. Updated ed. New York: DaCapo Press, 1996.

Eileraas, Karina. "Hello, Norma Jeane," *Ms. Magazine Blog*, 3 August 2012, http://msmagazine.com/blog/blog/2012/08/03/hello-norma-jeane (accessed 1 September 2012).

Friedan, Betty. *The Feminine Mystique*. Reprint ed. New York: W. W. Norton, 2001.

Glenn, Susan A. *Female Spectacle: The Theatrical Roots of Modern Feminism*. Cambridge, MA, and London: Harvard University Press, 2000.

Gourley, Catherine. *Flappers and the New American Woman: Perceptions of Women from 1918 through the 1920s*. Minneapolis, MN: Twenty-First Century Books, 2007.

Harvey, James. *Movie Love in the Fifties*. New York: Knopf, 2001.

Horton, Robert, ed. *Billy Wilder: Interviews*. Jackson: University Press of Mississippi, 2001.

Juncker, Clara. *Circling Marilyn: Text, Body, Performance*. Odense: University Press of Southern Denmark, 2010.

Kerr, Paul. "A Small, Effective Organization: The Mirisch Company, the Package Unit System and the Production Code of *Some Like It Hot*," 117–31, in *Billy Wilder, Movie Maker: Critical Essays on the Films*, edited by Karen McNally. Jefferson, NC, and London: McFarland, 2011.

Kitch, Carolyn. *The Girl on the Magazine Cover: The Origins of Visual Stereotypes in American Mass Media*. Chapel Hill: University of North Carolina Press, 2000.

Landay, Lori. "The Flapper Film: Comedy, Dance, and Jazz Age Kinaesthetics." In *A Feminist Reader in Early Cinema*, edited by Jennifer Bean and Diane Negra. Durham, NC, and London: Duke University Press, 2000.

Lane, Anthony. "Boys Will Be Girls." *New Yorker*, 22 October 2001.

Lieberfeld, Daniel, and Judith Sanders. "Comedy and Identity in *Some Like It Hot*." *Journal of Popular Film & Television* 26, no. 3 (1998): 128–35.

Marks, Patricia. *Bicycles, Bangs, and Bloomers: The New Woman in the Popular Press*. Lexington: University Press of Kentucky, 1990.

McGee, Kristin A. *Some Liked It Hot: Women in Film and Television, 1928–1959*. Middletown, CT: Wesleyan University Press, 2009.

McNally, Karen. "Introduction," 1–10, in *Billy Wilder, Movie Maker: Critical Essays on the Films*, edited by Karen McNally. Jefferson, NC, and London: McFarland, 2011.

The Modern Girl around the World Research Group, Alys Eve Weinbaum, Lynn M. Thomas, Priti Ramamurthy, Uta G. Poiger, and Madeleine Yue Dong, eds. *The Modern Girl around the World: Consumption, Modernity, and Globalization.* Durham, NC, and London: Duke University Press, 2008.

Morgan, Robin. *Sisterhood Is Powerful.* New York: Vintage Books, 1970.

Patterson, Martha H. *Beyond the Gibson Girl: Reimagining the American New Woman, 1895–1915.* Urbana: University of Illinois Press, 2005.

Straayer, Chris. *Deviant Eyes, Deviant Bodies: Sexual Re-orientations in Film and Video.* New York: Columbia University Press, 1996.

Tucker, Sherrie. *Swing Shift: "All Girl" Bands of the 1940s.* Durham, NC, and London: Duke University Press, 2000.

Wilder, Billy. Papers, f. 79, *Some Like It Hot*, correspondence. Margaret Herrick Library, the Academy of Motion Picture Arts and Sciences, Beverly Hills, CA.

Wilder, Billy, and I. A. L. Diamond. *Some Like It Hot.* Screenplay. 12 November 1958.

THREE

Brainy Broads

Images of Women's Intellect in Film Noir

Sheri Chinen Biesen

In the "golden age" of classic Hollywood, by the 1940s, representations of strong, intelligent, independent women in film challenged stereotypes, yet faced scrutiny. Several actresses such as Katharine Hepburn and Marlene Dietrich were labeled "box office poison" and ridiculed for their bold, passionate personas, which hurt their careers. Many women on screen encountered a double standard; they were criticized for shrewd behavior and independent mindedness—as crazy, angry, aggressive, or unduly masculine—whereas men were praised for having these same qualities: being strong, brave, and powerful cinematic heroes, applauded for using their brains, being determined, and showing conviction. Images of women's intellect in motion pictures, such as heroines in film noir crime narratives, strained against negative typecasting. Rather than being presented as thoughtful, multifaceted, intelligent individuals, women were often reduced to simplistic stereotypes—either lethal sexual temptresses or naïve victims—thus undermining their intellect in screen portrayals that emphasized sex and/or erotic violence: the toxic blonde *femme fatale* or gullible innocent *redeemer*. I will investigate screen images of women's intellect in film noir after World War II, such as Alfred Hitchcock's female gothic noir thriller *Spellbound* (1945), to examine how intelligent women were channeled from professional careers back into the home from 1945 to 1950.

As the war ended, smart hard-boiled women and brainy broads in classic 1940s Hollywood film noir were frequently imprisoned, ostracized, or commodified as sexual objects. In fact, even when women were shown working in a career, they were nonetheless marginalized and faced oppressive circumstances. Intelligent heroines included female scientists in noir pictures such as *Spellbound* and *Strange Impersonation* (1946), a secret agent in *Notorious* (1946), a dancer in *Gilda* (1946), a detective in *Lured* (1947), an artist in *Body and Soul* (1947), a widow in *The Ghost and Mrs. Muir* (1948), and a housewife in *Whirlpool* (produced in 1949, released in 1950).

Film noir and romantic comedy are known for strong, intelligent women who use their intellect on city streets as femme fatales or spar in a battle of the sexes to entice a mate. Yet, female intelligence is often portrayed as an intrinsically masculine quality that is countered and overtaken by a woman discovering her "femininity" and pursuing romance. This co-opting of female intelligence is seen in both film noir and comedy where a woman's intellect is marginalized in favor of more "feminine" or submissive qualities. Women are thus constrained or entrapped. Even in the films *Spellbound* and *Strange Impersonation* in which a woman is an accomplished scientist, she is ridiculed in terms of gender and sexuality as "frigid," threatening, unfeminine, or sexually undesirable to men. Women also face the double bind of being dismissed as less intelligent solely on the basis of gender stereotyping that favors male intellect.

For example, actress Katharine Hepburn, like her comedic heroines, was smart and athletic, a feminist whose mother was active in the women's suffrage movement. Hepburn was chastised for wearing pants and for dressing like a boy in *Sylvia Scarlett*. In fact, despite her established career at RKO, she was labeled "box office poison" by independent theater owners and essentially blackballed in Hollywood until her remarkable comeback at MGM, where she negotiated a long-term contract after buying out her contract at RKO, acquiring the screen rights and starring in the romantic comedy *The Philadelphia Story* in which she chose director George Cukor to glamorize and humanize her feminine screen persona opposite Cary Grant and James Stewart. By the end of the war, Hepburn played a tamer naïve ingénue in Vincente Minnelli's noir melodrama *Undercurrent* (1946). In this female gothic thriller, Hepburn's character is the daughter of a scientist, who then becomes a housewife trapped in a dangerous marriage where she is betrayed and victimized by her psychotic, murderous spouse (Robert Taylor) and is drawn to his mysterious brother (Robert Mitchum) as she solves a crime.

Film scholar Kathleen Rowe considers how gender and intellect are "constructed" in cinematic genres portraying the "unruly woman." She asserts that, for instance, romantic comedy "tolerates, and even encourages, its heroine's short-lived rebellion because that rebellion ultimately serves the interest of the hero" by way of activating laughter to cover up the "costs of a woman's acceptance of her proper place in patriarchy." Rowe observes that both melodrama and romantic comedy "tie a woman's rebellion to her acceptance or refusal of the terms of heterosexuality, yet melodrama dooms her rebellion from the start, not only teaching that a woman's lot under patriarchy is to suffer but making that suffering pleasurable."[1] Such gender distress is certainly evident in female gothic melodramas, as in Alfred Hitchcock thrillers *Spellbound* and *Notorious*, and noir crime films that frame images of gender and a woman's intellect according to a male point of view. In fact, in film noir a woman's intelligence is often portrayed in terms of her sexuality and conflated or transmuted into violent eroticism.

As early as 1955, French critics Raymonde Borde and Etienne Chaumeton recognized that film noir featured a bold archetypal woman with masculine attributes tied to her sexuality, "masterminding crime, tough as the milieu surrounding her, as expert in blackmail and vice as in the use of firearms—and probably frigid—has left her mark on a noir eroticism that is at times an eroticization of violence." They describe the infamous noir femme fatale as a shrewd spider woman, "frustrated and guilty, half man-eater, half man-eaten, blasé and cornered, she falls victim to her own wiles."[2] The fact that a woman is intelligent is seen as a dangerous threat. Her intellect and mental prowess are thus sexualized and masculinized to suggest that mental ability is inherently male, while at the same time she is commodified as a sex object for male consumption with the added lure of using her mind for violence, as in noir *Double Indemnity* (1944), *The Postman Always Rings Twice* (1946), and *Gun Crazy* (1949), originally titled *Dangerous Is the Female*.

Film scholar Janey Place observes how noir women were typically codified as either a sexual, often lethal, seductress who is "comfortable in the world of cheap dives, shadowy doorways and mysterious settings," or a naïve "good girl" who falls victim to those who prey on her innocence.[3] The archetypal gender binary of the "virgin" redeemer versus the "whore" femme fatale stereotype for women on screen marginalizes female characters and their intellectual portrayals. A masculine point of view in many noir films also suggests Laura Mulvey's "male gaze" in classic Hollywood films, including images of women in noir and comedy, while roman noir female gothic melodramas featured a woman's point of view and psychological distress.[4]

These stereotypes undermined women's intellect, ironically, even as films projected greater female independence and autonomy in the wake of strong, assertive gender roles such as the iconic Rosie the Riveter, acclaimed in propaganda growing out of the war years. Hitchcock's noir-styled female gothic suspense thrillers *Spellbound* and *Notorious* portrayed women's psychology, voyeurism, dreams, and nightmares with moody psychological noir montages and, as World War II drew to a close in 1945–1946, dealt with heroines working in some capacity in traditionally male-dominated occupations (like Rosie the Riveter) such as psychologists, scientific researchers, undercover secret agents, or detectives, who are trapped, marginalized, and victimized. In his female gothic thrillers, Hitchcock designed storyboard images of cinematic shots to psychologically convey a heroine's intellect and reveal her subjective point of view, often incorporating misogynism in his artistic vision. For example, in *Spellbound* and *Notorious*, Hitchcock created depictions of female intellect that heightened psychological and mental/emotional disturbances while smart gothic heroines considered how to solve a mystery involving crime and murder. Moreover, such noir gothic thrillers reflected changing gender roles, cultural tensions, and transformation in American society after the war leading into the postwar years.[5]

By 1945, Hitchcock's female gothic noir film *Spellbound* conveyed a woman's psychology, her occupation as a psychologist in an inherently masculine world, struggles with mental illness, and an asylum in dark shrouded style. Hitchcock initially wanted to film *Spellbound* (originally titled, *The House of Dr. Edwardes*) with clinical documentary realism, but instead incorporated eerie dream sequences based on stylized designs created by Salvador Dali that showcased Freudian psychoanalysis with elaborate surrealistic montages of a nightmare as gigantic voyeuristic eyes watch and peer into the minds of the characters, the soul of the viewer, and the psychological subject. Producer David O. Selznick was undergoing psychoanalysis at the time.[6]

Hitchcock's film concerns the study and science of the human mind and an intelligent woman's mastery of understanding her own and others' intellect, psychology, and emotions. His script introduced psychoanalysis as a "new medical science" that requires "neither drugs nor surgery," thus presenting an exploration of mental ability centering on female intellect: where analyst Constance Petersen (Ingrid Bergman) tries to decipher, understand, and cure her patients' psychological ills and in the process uses her shrewd mind to solve a murder crime and reveal her patient's identity. In fact, it is a smart woman who unlocks the mystery of the human mind.

Spellbound opens with a quote from Shakespeare's *Julius Caesar*: "The fault . . . is not in our stars. But in ourselves." It then explains,

> Our story deals with psychoanalysis, the method by which modern science treats the emotional problems of the sane. The analyst seeks only to induce the patient to talk about his hidden problems, to open the locked doors of his mind. Once the complexes that have been disturbing the patient are uncovered and interpreted, the illness and confusion disappear . . . and the devils of unreason are driven from the human soul.

This rumination on psychoanalysis (by Selznick's psychologist May E. Romm) then fades into a sanitarium.

Noir films like *Spellbound*, *Strange Impersonation*, and *Whirlpool* indicate the recurrent conflict between having a professional career as a psychological or medical scientist and being a woman. For instance, *Spellbound* and *Strange Impersonation* capture an era of stronger Rosie the Riveter female roles as the war ended in 1945–1946, after wartime women worked in essential nontraditional male jobs amid a war-related manpower shortage in America's home front while men went off to serve in the conflict. *Spellbound* and *Strange Impersonation* portrayed intelligent women—psychoanalyst Constance Petersen (Ingrid Bergman) and scientist Nora Goodrich (Brenda Marshall)—as deglamorized and masculinized as more androgynous in prim glasses, with hair pulled back into a tight bun, and wearing a plain scientific lab coat. However, they are able to both be successful career women in the psychiatry/scientific profession and engage in romance with a fellow doctor, such as John Ballantyne (Gregory Peck) in *Spellbound*. Yet, reflecting an evolving American culture at the end of the war in 1945–1946, intelligent female scientists or psychologists, such as Constance in *Spellbound*, also function as nurturing redeemers who are eventually feminized and aid troubled, traumatized returning war veterans (like Peck's character) in readjusting to civilian society as in real-life women and returning veterans in America were returning back to domestic home life.

In *Spellbound*, Bergman's character is erudite and uses her shrewd wits to navigate a man's world. Yet, she is trapped and ridiculed for her intellect. She is the only woman psychoanalyst/scientific doctor at the male-dominated psychiatric hospital, where she is demeaned, ostracized, marginalized, and sexually harassed by her male peers as frigid and unfeminine because she is an intelligent professional woman. In this noir film—directed, produced, and scripted by men—outrageous sexist patriarchal framing suggests that she is in need of a man for her to be not only complete as a woman, but also more successful as a female doctor. None of her male colleagues are subjected to this sort of scrutiny or sexual harassment. It is based solely on gender. In fact, it is clear she is more capable in her intellect and profession than her male colleagues. Hitchcock's script for *Spellbound* (penned by Ben Hecht) originally introduces Bergman's psychoanalyst as "arrogant," implying that female intellect connotes negative character traits in a woman simply because she is not male. However, Bergman's wonderful nuanced performance presents an intelligent professional woman who is capable, humane, and self-assured rather than arrogant. She is warm, caring, and intuitive, as well as extremely smart.

Nonetheless, Bergman's woman scientist is still objectified as a sexual entity by male colleagues who make sexual advances at her and mock her disinterest in them romantically. Ironically, although she is a respected analyst, she is disparaged by amorous male colleagues as naïve and not taken seriously before and after she falls in love with John Ballantyne. Even Constance's female patient is entrapped and marginalized, portrayed as a devious volatile woman whose intellect is subsumed by her

psychotic violent behavior as a nymphomaniac who assaults and sexually flirts with male orderlies. Yet, she paradoxically claims to hate men,
and misogynistically maligns Constance as "cold" and "frozen," equating
her mental ability as an analyst with frigidity and a lack of sufficiently
female or sexual qualities, as if to infer that intellect is a decidedly masculine arena off limits to women.

Constance and her psychiatric mentor Dr. Alexander Brulov (Michael
Chekhov) engage in Freudian psychoanalysis to analyze dreams, unveil
the disturbed criminal unconscious, and solve a murder crime. Constance's teacher (and her psychoanalyst), Alexander is an older, re-
nowned expert in the field of psychology, but calls her a "school girl" and
a "child" and insists he is wiser. Constance and Alexander diagnose mental illness symptoms including amnesia, schizophrenia, and a guilt complex. Alexander dismisses her love for the patient as "baby talk" —
"Women's talk! Bah!" — and derides "the usual female contradictions," at
one point saying, "You're not his momma. You're an analyst." (He then
sends her to the kitchen to make coffee for him.) She's depicted as a
woman trapped and possibly victimized by her maternal impulses and
assumed to have lost her intellect once she falls in love and cares for John.
Alexander says Constance was his best student/assistant, then tells her
that women make great analysts until they fall in love, at which point
they make the best psychological patients. Constance's relationship with
Alexander highlights her dilemma as a smart professional career woman
working in the field of psychology to study and analyze the mind. When
she pleads with Alexander to help her cure John (saying he only knows
science, not the heart), he replies that she is "twenty times crazier" than
John and says, "We both know that the mind of a woman in love is
operating on the lowest level of the intellect."

However, Constance capably functions as a female detective solving
the crime while treating, curing, and falling in love with her patient who
is suspected of murder. Her professional transgression of a clinical doctor
of psychology engaging in private sexual/love relations with a patient is
portrayed as acceptable precisely because Constance is a woman and her
more "feminine" qualities of vulnerability and sexuality are emphasized
to "soften" and contain her more threatening "masculine" intellectual
mental prowess and make her appealing and desirable to men. When
John descends the stairs in a psychotic state with dilated pupils and a
switchblade, Hitchcock leads viewers to believe he will murder Constance as she sleeps in the middle of the night (suggesting she is an
unsuspecting gothic ingénue victim) or her older mentor Alexander.

While Constance believes her patient/lover is harmless, Alexander
recognizes John's dangerous symptoms and sedates him with bromide in
a glass of milk—shown to simulate John's subjective point of view looking through the glass as he drinks it. Determined to treat him, Constance
analyzes his dreams with Alexander, who explains the importance of

Freud and dreams to John (a medical doctor who dismisses Freud). Despite those doubting her intellect and ability, Constance solves the crime when the murderer is revealed to be a rival doctor (Leo Carroll), the psychiatric director of the hospital—evocative of the insane patient's nightmare flashback in *The Cabinet of Dr. Caligari*. *Spellbound* features the valuable contribution of European talent filling roles during America's wartime labor shortage as in the film's émigré director Hitchcock; actors Bergman, Chekhov, and Carroll; and psychology adviser May Romm.[7]

Bergman's intellectual "scientific" psychoanalyst is a refreshing multi-faceted contrast to more one-dimensional female characters in noir films and demonstrated the influential role of psychology in Hollywood and American culture during this late wartime 1940s period, when filmmakers' real-life psychoanalysts—such as producer Selznick's psychiatrist May Romm, as well as Karl Menninger, Transylvanian psychiatrist Fraime Sertoroclos, and psychoanalysis student Eileen Johnston—were hired as technical psychiatry advisers for the film. In real life Bergman was a pupil of Chekhov, who had worked in German films and taught a new method of performance developing a more psychological style of acting drawing on the teachings of Konstantin Stanislavski to students Bergman, Peck, Elia Kazan, and others.

Film critics Stephen Farber and Marc Green observe that psychiatrists were usually male father figures. They suggest *Spellbound*'s female analyst protagonist played by Bergman was a novelty that "revitalized" a "woman-in-jeopardy thriller" by "presenting Bergman's character as a brilliant sleuth who sorted through the psychological clues presented by her disturbed patient" and "interpreted his dreams—replete with phallic ski poles and Cyclopean eyes—and solved the mystery of his neurosis with the aplomb of Sherlock Holmes."[8]

Calling Bergman a "trailblazing heroine," Farber and Green explain that "centering the story on a female psychiatrist may have seemed like a clever gimmick," but "there were also powerful similarities between the Bergman character and [Selznick's] real-life psychiatrist who was serving as his consultant." Bergman reveals that "Peck is an impostor—a madman, suffering from amnesia, who may have murdered the real Dr. Edwardes and taken his place. Eventually, with the help of her avuncular Viennese training analyst (Michael Chekhov), Bergman penetrates Peck's tortured psyche, decodes the symbolism of his dreams, exonerates him of the murder of Dr. Edwardes and unmasks the true culprit," the "embodiment of megalomania and silky duplicity, driven to murder by secret envy and a lust for power." Farber and Green also note that May Romm earned $1,500 for her consulting services on the film. "One of her principal duties was to serve as an unofficial censor, making sure the script didn't contain any embarrassing Freudian slips. She warned Selznick that a dream involving Peck and Bergman dancing was 'a symbol of sexual intercourse,' and Selznick promptly ordered it eliminated."[9]

Bergman's female detective in *Spellbound* solves the crime and the mysterious murderer's identity by using her woman's intellect to analyze Hitchcock's stylized Dali-inspired surrealist dream montage sequence, which reveals how noir gothic thriller films revolved around a woman's intelligence and subjective psychological point of view where dreams and nightmares depict a heroine's or antihero's inner psyche (in this case, to convey mental illness). In terms of depicting women's intellect, as evident in noir films *Spellbound* and *Whirlpool*, the female (and criminal) mind is often analyzed via invoking an oversimplified pop explanation of Freudianism and the unconscious, as in earlier films such as *Blind Alley*, where a psychologist explains the inner workings of the brain, ego, superego, and dreams to a psychotic gangster. In noir gothic films such as *Spellbound* and *Whirlpool*, psychoanalysis is portrayed as scientific, true, and wise. Even the doubter (John Ballantyne) is shown to be wrong. In fine noir form, the analysis of dreams is able to solve murders, a key part of being a film noir detective. In fact, Constance's sexual love affair with John is literally depicted in a visual psychological montage (a series of doors opening down a long corridor) as unlocking the doors of her mind and soul. Publicity for *Spellbound* promoted misogynistic sexual violence and questioned Constance's sanity, showing her trapped in an obsessive, dangerous affair where love compromised her intelligence. Posters featured John holding a switchblade as he embraces Constance with provocative taglines such as "Will he kiss me or kill me?," "The maddest love that ever possessed a woman," and "This is love! Complete . . . Reckless . . . Violent!"

By 1945 in terms of gender and masculinity, women and screen images of female intellect were influenced by what cultural critics observed as a changing American society as a result of the violence of World War II, which affected audiences and film noir crime pictures of psychological murder in the wake of grisly atrocities seen in documentary combat newsreels. The *New York Times* noted, "Crime Certainly Pays on the Screen: The Growing Crop of Homicidal Films Poses Questions for Psychologists and Producers."[10] Realization of the full extent of the shock and horror of the Holocaust, as well as postwar atomic trauma, also informed American cultural perspective in the shift from wartime to Cold War. The depiction of women's intellect, mental and physical entrapment, psychoanalysis, and European émigrés in *Spellbound* provides a contrast to later portrayals of women in institutional sanitariums as in *The Snake Pit* (1948).

Moreover, by the end of the war, images of noir screen women were already being cinematically transformed from intelligent professionals in the workplace to love mates in the home. Like the iconic reunion of the heterosexual couple in romantic comedy, even Hitchcock's female gothic noir thriller *Spellbound* ends with Constance not resuming her psychology career, but rather reunited with her man John, married, and leaving town together on a train, suggesting that, despite her capable intellect and ability, she may leave her profession. Like *Spellbound*, other female gothic thrillers and noir films such as *Strange Impersonation, Notorious, Gilda, Body and Soul, Lured, The Ghost and Mrs. Muir,* and *Whirlpool* followed suit regarding women's intellect.

As in *Spellbound*, the intelligent working woman protagonist played by Brenda Marshall in Anthony Mann's 1946 low-budget B noir *Strange Impersonation* (produced for "Poverty Row" Republic studio) is a female scientist. Nora Goodrich is a smart, capable chemist developing a new form of anesthesia for medical research and confidently lecturing an auditorium full of male scientists. When she chooses her career over marriage to a fellow scientist, which would jeopardize her research, and arrogantly proclaims her experiment will work, she has a drug-induced nightmare. In a wild noir flashback dream sequence, Nora becomes a victim of a lab accident and is disfigured by an explosion intentionally caused by her female lab assistant (who sabotages her and marries her scientist fiancé), revealing her psychological paranoia about her female sexuality and competition with other women as romantic rivals. By the end of her dream, Nora has a plastic surgery makeover in Hollywood to become as beautiful as a starlet, is framed for murder, is betrayed by her coworker friend, and wakes up to ask her fiancé how she looks. She then decides to give up her career, marry her fiancé, and fly off to Paris with him as the film concludes.

Following *Spellbound*, Hitchcock again directed Ingrid Bergman in the 1946 espionage noir thriller *Notorious*, also scripted by Ben Hecht. Cast against her wholesome "type," Bergman plays Alicia Huberman—not a respected scientist, but rather an apparently self-destructive alcoholic party girl, the daughter of a convicted Nazi collaborator at the end of the war, in a love triangle with romantic rivals, government agent Devlin (Cary Grant) and suspected Nazi Alexander Sebastian (Claude Rains).[11]

As Rosie the Riveter was redirected into the home, instead of being an intellectual career woman as in *Spellbound*, in *Notorious* Bergman poses as a housewife. Although her character self-deprecatingly professes that she is "no mastermind," she is surprisingly smart and insightful. American spy Devlin reforms and sobers (and has a torrid secret love affair with) Alicia—recognizing her mental ability as an intelligent, loyal, and sexually desirable woman. Devlin convinces her to go undercover as a secret agent in South America to romance and catch Alexander. Alicia puts herself in danger, even marrying the Nazi (despite Devlin's repressed jealousy), to break up a spy ring and solve war crimes for the good of the country. Notably, in *Notorious* Bergman's character not only masquerades as a trophy wife in a more domestic sphere (hiding her secret agent career), but she must use her intellect and feminine wiles to manipulate men. However, she is still trapped in a toxic marriage to a murderer (and his mother) and is nearly killed as a gothic victim. Hitchcock simulates

Alicia's disoriented perspective with an upside-down shot of Devlin, which turns completely around. He pushed the envelope of Production Code censorship with an extended series of steamy kisses between Alicia and Devlin, prolonging their *amore*, after which Alicia tries to curb her rebellious independence, be more domestic, and cook dinner for Devlin, but burns everything, declaring that the chicken caught fire—commenting on the smoldering intensity of their sexual relationship. Bergman's clandestine spy posing as a wife in *Notorious* contrasts with her more intellectual scientific career woman analyst in *Spellbound*, who reads clinical studies, publishes psychoanalytic research books, and attends professional conferences.

Like *Notorious*, another 1946 noir, *Gilda*, featured a beautiful, bright American woman—sultry, shrewd "working girl" nightclub singer-dancer Gilda (Rita Hayworth)—who relies on her sexuality and becomes involved in a South American love triangle (and espionage subplot) with fellow American Johnny Farrell (Glenn Ford) and his Nazi spy nightclub boss Ballin Mundson (George MacReady). Highlighting noir gender distress, in *Notorious* and *Gilda*, strong independent intelligent women are manipulated, used, mistreated, psychologically abused, trapped, victimized, marginalized, and sexually objectified in destructive relationships because of their gender, beauty, and desirability, which overshadow their intellect. For instance, despite working undercover to mentally solve the crime, Alicia Huberman is exploited for her sexual allure. She and Gilda marry Nazis and are expected to sublimate their intellect in service of sex and femininity, and to be sexually desirable to men. They are roughed up and psychologically distressed in these toxic affairs, then trapped in a dangerous marriage. Rita's Gilda is treated as a trophy wife, imprisoned and slapped around by both her sadistic Nazi and American ex-flame husbands. Bergman's Alicia is poisoned and almost dies—her Nazi mother-in-law (Leopoldine Konstantin) is depicted as the ultimate female incarnation of evil and duplicity, manipulating her "momma's boy" son Alexander to commit murder. Further, as World War II ends and shifts to Cold War relations, these noir heroines aid the capture of spies through romance, then give up their careers to fly off with their men and return to their American homes.

As gender evolved in a postwar environment, Gilda describes herself as "a dancer," but she is not an intellectual career woman as Alicia was in *Spellbound*. Instead, in *Gilda*—despite being produced, written, and supervised by women (including executive Virginia Van Upp)—Hayworth's noir heroine exudes erotic libido, creating a female sex symbol that the star later admitted she could never live up to, saying men went to bed with "love goddess" Gilda and woke up with her.

By 1947, in noir *Body and Soul*, a smart, intellectual artist (Lili Palmer) is reduced to exploiting herself and her body as a sexual object: wearing a bikini, pretending to be a beauty queen, and dancing with a local boxing champ (John Garfield) for a room full of yelping tough guys to earn fifty bucks because she can't support herself using her mind. Even shrewd femme fatale Hazel Brooks (as Alice) must use her body rather than her mind for sex and money and to lure a rich man.

In Douglas Sirk's 1947 noir *Lured*, Lucille Ball plays a hard-boiled brainy broad, an intelligent dance hall girl who becomes an undercover female detective to catch a serial killer. However, she must rely on (and is exploited for) her feminine beauty, body, and sexual charms: answering personal ads from dodgy characters, posing as a model and a maid, acting as "bait," being assaulted and nearly killed by the misogynistic murderer to solve the crime before she leaves her career to marry caddish nightclub entrepreneur Robert Fleming (George Sanders).

As seen in *Spellbound, Strange Impersonation, Notorious, Gilda, Body and Soul*, and *Lured*, wartime and postwar film noir reflected changes in American cultural gender roles during and after World War II. Strong World War II era Rosie the Riveter–style working female gender roles shifted just a few years after the war as women were channeled from career back into the home and more domestic roles. This postwar gender shift manifested itself in screen depictions of women's intellect, as shown by actress Gene Tierney moving to domestic roles: not playing a working career woman as in Otto Preminger's wartime noir *Laura*, but rather by the postwar late 1940s, playing housewives. Tierney plays a widow who has a supernatural affair and literally ghostwrites the bawdy autobiography of a dead sea captain in *The Ghost and Mrs. Muir*, but she is imprisoned in her haunted house on the Cornwall coast and betrayed by sleazy, adulterous Miles Fairley (George Sanders), who pursues her but actually has a second life married with kids.

In terms of women's intellect, by the end of the decade, in Otto Preminger's 1949–1950 noir *Whirlpool*, Tierney plays a beautiful, neurotic kleptomaniac who is married to a prominent psychologist. *Whirlpool* centers not on a shrewd female psychotherapist as in *Spellbound*, but instead on the disturbed housewife of a male doctor of psychology. Tierney is Ann Sutton, a wealthy suburban spouse neglected by her hardworking psychologist husband, Bill (Richard Conte), who is busy treating traumatized war veterans and attending a psychology conference in San Francisco, discarding her on the sidelines like an attractive prize trophy wife. Ann is depicted not as a smart professional career woman, but as a repressed, doll-like stay-at-home beauty who is treated as a sexual object by more aggressive men (including her husband) in the film. Ann is trapped, unhappy in her marriage, and ultimately exploited as her intellect is sabotaged by her own mental demons and by the psychotic, lustful greed of male predators. She is more gullible and marginalized intellectually than Bergman's shrewd analyst in *Spellbound*. Tierney's housewife is preyed upon by a psychic scam artist, and is victim of her circumstances as a married woman, and of her psychological affliction and kleptomania.

In *Whirlpool*, Ann is victimized, nearly killed, and framed by scam hypnotist David Korvo (Jose Ferrer) for a crime she did not commit: his murder of a former patient, who was a wealthy heiress he stole money from. Although set in Los Angeles, *Whirlpool* showcases not the iconic urban jungle of earlier gangster or noir films such as *The Big Sleep*, *Murder My Sweet*, *This Gun For Hire*, and *Double Indemnity*, but instead taps into the popularity of a growing, sprawling postwar suburban baby boom lifestyle in American culture after World War II in its well-to-do Southern California residential landscape.

Unlike earlier film noir such as Billy Wilder's *Double Indemnity*, Tierney's heroine in *Whirlpool*, like Bergman's working female psychologist in *Spellbound*, is not a lethal femme fatale, but more closely resembles a good girl gothic redeemer heroine who is falsely accused of murder and adultery. She interacts with the hypnotist to treat her mental illness, not because she pursues money or sex (as Barbara Stanwyck's nurse-turned-murderous-gold-digger-housewife does in *Double Indemnity*). In fact, she is well off and seems to have it all, which is precisely the reason Ferrer's criminal hypnotist takes advantage of her mental illness and exploits her for his own material gain. Paralleling a Cold War climate of ethnic xenophobia, Ferrer plays an ethnic villain in postwar noir *Whirlpool*. He hypnotizes Ann, commits murder, then frames her by hypnotizing himself after surgery.

As *Spellbound* revealed World War II–era American culture's esteem for working women in intellectual scientific professions of research, psychoanalysis, and Freudian psychotherapy, *Whirlpool* presents intellect, psychology, and the treatment of mental illness as a highly regarded man's profession, distinguishing it from hypnosis, which is presented as dangerous, a dubious masculine activity subject to illegitimate criminal elements that oppress and victimize housewives. Tierney's character's intellect is sublimated (more than Bergman's analyst) in a patriarchal intellectual and professional social universe where men exploit female intelligence at women's expense.

In *Whirlpool*, while Ann is marginalized and portrayed as crazy and criminal, her husband is a respected psychologist in the community. He's wealthy, famous, an invited speaker at a psychiatric conference who reads a hospital medical chart. Male intellect is valued. He helps ordinary people, war-traumatized soldiers, and his wife. His patriarchal understanding of psychoanalysis explains her mental problems of kleptomania rooted in her childhood resentment of her father. *Whirlpool* inverts the gender analysis of *Spellbound*, where Constance keenly deciphers John's psychological affliction after he witnesses a murder that brings back traumatic childhood memories of his brother's accidental death for which he feels responsible—precipitating his amnesia, guilt complex, and assumed identity. Moreover, Constance is intelligent, actively and perceptively engaged in piecing together and insightfully understanding her patient and his ailment in *Spellbound*, unlike Bill, who is completely oblivious to his wife's manic illness in *Whirlpool*. Furthermore, because Bill is so blind to his wife's psychological trauma, the criminally insane hypnotist (rather than a credentialed psychologist) scams, abuses, and victimizes her and other women—including Bill's female patient—by preying on wealthy housewives, widows, and heiresses who are vulnerable, sexually harassing and manipulating them, taking all their money, then blackmailing and murdering them.

Publicity for *Whirlpool* promoted Tierney's character's mental illness, hypnosis, and highlighted a distressing postwar marginalization of women's intellect and loss of sanity. The film's preview trailer begins with hypnosis and ends with *"Spellbound!"* Posters showed Tierney as Ann, hypnotized looking trance-like into a mirror with the tagline: "Tomorrow she will know what she did tonight!" and "Can a man make a woman do things she doesn't want to?"

By 1950, Gloria Swanson's aging femme fatale Hollywood star Norma Desmond in Wilder's *Sunset Boulevard* becomes a tragic figure suffering from mental illness and insane delusions that obsessively lead her to gun down William Holden's tormented screenwriter antihero Joe Gillis, whose dead subjective psychological point of view tells the story as he lays face down lifeless in her swimming pool. In fact, on the heels of psychological films noir such as Hitchcock's *Spellbound*, Preminger's *Whirlpool*, and Wilder's *Sunset Boulevard*, so many noir villains were depicted as psychotics that motion picture industry executives such as Twentieth Century-Fox's Darryl Zanuck actually complained about the overabundance of psychopathic criminal film antagonists in American noir cinema and sought to avoid them in the future.

By 1955, Robert Aldrich's Cold War noir *Kiss Me Deadly* captured American cultural fears of nuclear war and atomic trauma as it ends with a radioactive apocalyptic explosion. It opens as a doomed, barefoot, near-naked Christina Bailey (Cloris Leachman) flees in the night after escaping an insane asylum. She is depicted as a trapped, tormented, intelligent woman who recites poetry and philosophy and wisely understands the psychology of misogynistic gender relations, but is mysteriously pursued, tortured, and pushed off a cliff, meeting a violent demise after being beaten by thugs. Her insightful woman's intellect is thus destroyed. Ironically, she seems to be the sanest person in the film, but is imprisoned (locked up as out of her mind to silence her) and immediately killed off, suggesting a world gone mad amid the anxiety and paranoia of a corrupt, lethal, sadistic Cold War. Ads for *Kiss Me Deadly* clamored about salacious sexual violence toward women rather than celebrating their intellect: "I don't care what you do to me, Mike—just do it fast!" with "Blood-Red Kisses!" and "White-Hot Thrills!" as Mickey Spillane "Strips Down to Naked Fury!" Such exploitation marginalized cerebral minds as the erotic female body and ample flesh were emphasized.

As American culture evolved after World War II, by the mid to late 1950s, just a decade after the conflict, the dark psychological film noir crime trend and its depiction of women's intellect in bold femme fatales and working women ebbed in screen popularity with American motion picture audiences. However, the uniquely psychological predilection and female gender distress of noir crime films spawned an enduring legacy in subsequent pictures, including the psychological narratives of Alfred Hitchcock such as the voyeuristic *Rear Window* (1954) and mentally afflicted *Vertigo* (1958) and *Psycho* (1960), which were more male centered than his earlier 1940s female gothic thrillers with Selznick such as *Spellbound* with Bergman.

As evident in noir gender representation in films from *Spellbound* to *Whirlpool*, screen images of women's intellect in film noir evolved from working heroines to more submissive housewives in the postwar era. Later postwar films noir reimagined earlier images of independent female intelligence and reflected cultural changes in gender roles as strong Rosie the Riveter working women were channeled back into the domestic sphere after World War II. Notably, for example, as the war ended, even Bergman's independent professional "scientific" psychoanalyst career woman is married off at the conclusion of *Spellbound*, signifying a cinematic "taming" of noir gender and a sublimation of women's intellect to reinforce the status quo and, as Rowe suggests, her "proper place in patriarchy" by reuniting the classic Hollywood heterosexual couple.[12]

The legacy of these earlier World War II–era depictions of women's intellect in film noir lived on and influenced subsequent noir gender images. Wartime film noir like Hitchcock's *Spellbound* inspired later postwar noir productions, such as *Whirlpool* and *Kiss Me Deadly*, featuring intelligent women embroiled in—or being "framed" (by men) for committing—crime while battling their own psychological demons, domestic or societal misogynism, and physical, psychological, or institutional entrapment. The sublimation of women's intellect after the war is certainly evident in noir *Whirlpool* and its tormented housewife battling her psychological affliction and societal gender constraints as noir films reflected these broader changes in American society and intelligent wartime women shifted to postwar home life. Yet despite the shift from career-oriented to domestic-centered film noir and female gothic noir thriller narratives by the end of the decade, these postwar features nonetheless often directly mentioned earlier recognizable noir films and their familiar gender motifs, as in *Whirlpool*'s publicity actually citing *Spellbound* and drawing the comparison between Tierney's and Bergman's heroines. In the wake of *Spellbound*, as seen in Tierney's psychologically distressed housewife in *Whirlpool* and in Leachman's insane runaway in

Kiss Me Deadly, the postwar years seemed to destabilize noir women's intellect.

In a more domestic postwar cultural terrain that reversed and abandoned the working, capable Rosie the Riveter images of women's intellect such as *Spellbound* and *Strange Impersonation* in the war years, by 1950 Gloria Swanson's iconic film noir femme Norma Desmond in *Sunset Boulevard* is not only an eccentric homebody without a Hollywood career, but has actually gone crazy and lost her woman's intellect as she inhabits her morbid baroque mansion pining for her earlier fame and glory in delusional, egomaniacal splendor. Her murderous, suicidal inclinations were a far cry from Bergman's calm, intellectual clinical scientist rationally treating psychology patients in *Spellbound*. Ultimately, the portrayal of women's intellect in film noir at the conclusion of World War II, such as *Spellbound*, *Strange Impersonation*, *Notorious*, and *Gilda*, eventually transformed—as seen in the "tamed" intellect and curtailed independence of women in *Undercurrent*, *Lured*, *Body and Soul*, and *The Ghost and Mrs. Muir*, and the traumatized, psychologically unstable noir heroines in *Whirlpool*, *Sunset Boulevard*, and *Kiss Me Deadly*, as well as their legacy in Hitchcock's *Vertigo* and *Psycho*.

NOTES

1. Kathleen Rowe, *The Unruly Woman: Gender and the Genres of Laughter* (Austin: University of Texas Press, 1995), 112.

2. Raymonde Borde and Etienne Chaumeton, *Panorama Du Film Noir Americain (1941–1953)*, trans. from French by Paul Hammond (San Francisco: City Lights, 2002; first published 1955 by Editions du Minuit, Paris), 9 . Hitchcock's female gothic noir *Spellbound* featured a professional woman's intellect and psychological perspective solving crime. Many female gothic noir thrillers, including *Spellbound*, *Strange Impersonation*, *Notorious*, *Gilda*, *Lured*, and *Whirlpool*, fused a woman's subjective intellectual and psychological point of view with gender distress and artistic experimentation influenced by expressionism, surrealism, and documentary realism. *Spellbound*, *Strange Impersonation*, and *Whirlpool* are particularly noteworthy in terms of gender and the depiction of women's intellect because they deal with psychoanalysts, women scientists, and/or female protagonists battling psychological instability who are engaged in criminal activity and inhabit clinical psychiatric wards or insane asylums. Film noir was known for its gender distress, psychological points of view, and elaborate montages revealing the central character's conflicted, subjective inner psyche. Flawed, tormented gothic heroines and noir antiheroes grappled with volatile moods, psychological demons, and mental illness, trapped by traumatic fears and violent obsessions, constrained or imprisoned in claustrophobic environments or sanitariums.

3. Janey Place, "Women in Film Noir," in *Women in Film Noir*, ed. E. Ann Kaplan (London: British Film Institute, 1980), 35, 41–42.

4. Laura Mulvey, "Visual Pleasure and Narrative Cinema," *Screen* 16, no. 3 (1975): 6–18. Moreover, as in film noir, Hitchcock's roman noir female gothic cycle included psychic trauma; insanity; a tormented heroine's quest for psychological identity; elaborate flashbacks of haunting, surreal nightmare memories; and stylized subjective point of view—as seen in *Rebecca*, *Suspicion*, and *Shadow of a Doubt*, which influenced the noir style of *Spellbound* and *Notorious*.

5. As film noir became popular during World War II, European émigrés—such as Hitchcock; surrealist Salvador Dali; psychologist May E. Romm; writer-producer Joan Harrison; actress Ingrid Bergman; directors Billy Wilder, Fritz Lang, Robert Siodmak, Otto Preminger, and Douglas Sirk; and actor Michael Chekhov—cultivated a distinctly dark psychological breed of American crime films with fascinating images of women's intellect and subjective point of view. Noir gothic thriller films employed psychology and a female point of view to evade screen censorship and enable endorsement from American film industry Production Code censors. Émigré directors in Hollywood like Hitchcock were aware that depictions of insanity had been censored in British films, and thus ingeniously invoked psychological narrative techniques in their American noir films, tapping the interest in psychology in American culture at the time. In these American noir crime films, Hollywood and émigré filmmakers portrayed women's intellect and revealed American cultural views of changing gender roles, as well as representations of female intelligence and psychology during this 1940s period. (In fact, Hitchcock and Wilder served in psychological warfare units during World War II working on propaganda films, including documentaries depicting horrific atrocities of the Holocaust as Allies liberated Nazi concentration camps.)

6. *Spellbound*'s director Hitchcock and stars Ingrid Bergman and Gregory Peck were under contract to Selznick, who cut a good portion of Hitchcock's documentary opening and edited fourteen minutes out of Hitchcock's surreal Dali dream sequence.

7. Russian expatriate Chekhov, nephew of famed playwright Anton Chekhov, was nominated for a Best Supporting Actor Oscar as the accomplished psychoanalyst.

8. Stephen Farber and Marc Green, "Hollywood's Love Affair with Psychiatry," *New York Times*, 26 December 1993.

9. Farber and Green, "Hollywood's Love Affair with Psychiatry."

10. Lloyd Shearer, "Crime Certainly Pays on the Screen: The Growing Crop of Homicidal Films Poses Questions for Psychologists and Producers," *New York Times*, 8 August 1945; Sheri Chinen Biesen, *Blackout: World War II and the Origins of Film Noir* (Baltimore: Johns Hopkins University Press, 2005).

11. Hitchcock also cast former screwball romantic comedy star Grant against "type" to play a colder, more menacing noir antihero in female gothic thrillers *Suspicion* and *Notorious*.

12. Rowe, *The Unruly Woman*, 112.

BIBLIOGRAPHY

Behlmer, Rudy. *Memo from Darryl F. Zanuck*. New York: Grove, 1993.
Biesen, Sheri Chinen. *Blackout: World War II and the Origins of Film Noir*. Baltimore: Johns Hopkins University Press, 2005.
Borde, Raymonde, and Étienne Chaumeton. *Panorama Du Film Noir Americain (1941–1953)*. Translated by Paul Hammond. San Francisco: City Lights, 2002. First published 1955 by Editions du Minuit, Paris.
Farber, Stephen and Marc Green. "Hollywood's Love Affair with Psychiatry," *New York Times*, 26 December 1993.
Francke, Lizzie. *Script Girls: Women Screenwriters in Hollywood*. London: British Film Institute, 1994.
Leff, Leonard, and Jerold Simmons. *The Dame in the Kimono*. New York: Grove, 1990.
Mulvey, Laura. "Visual Pleasure and Narrative Cinema." *Screen* 16, no. 3 (1975): 6–18.
Place, Janey. "Women in Film Noir," 35–42, in *Women in Film Noir*, ed. E. Ann Kaplan. London: British Film Institute, 1980.
Rowe, Kathleen. *The Unruly Woman: Gender and the Genres of Laughter*. Austin: University of Texas Press, 1995.
Schrader, Paul. "Notes on Film Noir." *Film Comment* 8, no. 1 (1972): 8–10.
Shearer, Lloyd. "Crime Certainly Pays on the Screen: The growing crop of homicidal films poses questions for psychologists," *New York Times*. 8 August 1945.

FOUR

Troubling Binaries

Women Scientists in 1950s B-Movies

Linda Levitt

History is always an interpretation, as the past is understood through certain frames that shape perceptions. While there may be a strong sense that Second Wave feminism should be left in the past because of contemporary differences with some of its founding ideas, it remains a powerful lens for shaping perceptions of the past. This is particularly true with a view of the circumstances of middle class and affluent women working in the 1950s and 1960s, as these are the women and situations that motivated significant critique from the Second Wave. Of interest here is the way that Second Wave feminism, as a form of cultural critique, influences perceptions about midcentury media texts. The texts under discussion are science fiction B-movies from the 1950s. *B-movie* is a nebulous term, and much like Supreme Court Justice Potter Stewart's definition of pornography, "I know it when I see it." Film critic Chris Nashawaty, who wrote a book about legendary B-movie producer and director Roger Corman, says that in a double feature, the A-movie was the quality film with high production values and known stars, whereas "the B-movie was the shorter, cheaper, usually shoddier film tacked on to fill out the two-for-one bill. But hey, who cared? After all, at drive-ins, teenagers were usually too busy necking at that point to care about the second movie's plot—not that they'd be able to follow it anyhow."[1] Vince Rotolo, a lifelong film fan who runs the podcast BMovieCast, adds that for him "a good B-Movie needs to be filmed in black and white—with a few exceptions. It also needs to have a cool monster like giant bugs, gill men, 50 ft people, space ships, brains that jump on you and suck out your brains, pod people, etc."[2] These two definitions point to movies in which scientists take on some dangerous phenomenon, whether it be animal, man-made, or alien. A female scientist or traveling companion is typically among the ranks.

In 2012, the University of Denver published an extensive study of women in leadership positions in various industries. Of women completing degrees in STEM fields (science, technology, engineering, or math), fewer than one-third pursue careers in the fields they have studied. In fact, one in three women leaves the technology workforce within the first two years.[3] The reasons for these transitions are varied and complex, and are beyond the purview of this chapter. Of note, however, is that the number of women pursuing and succeeding in careers as scientists remains quite small.

Thus it is surprising to find a particular characterization of women as scientists in 1950s science fiction B-movies. The proliferation of female scientists in these films does not reflect the reality of women in the sciences at the time. Why, then, do they appear so frequently? One argument would be that including female scientists enhances the moviegoing experience: for male audience members, an attractive female character creates an aesthetic pleasure. If the moviegoer identifies with the heroic male lead, as Laura Mulvey[4] and others would posit, then the satisfying conclusion of the film includes winning the heart of the film's "leading lady" and enabling the "happily ever after" for the heroic male scientist who saves civilization from deadly creatures, nuclear meltdown, or another apocalyptic scenario.

Science fiction routinely posits an alternative present or a possible future: some of these realities are promising, and some are apocalyptic. The possibility of gender equality in the workplace is not far-fetched for an alternative reality, especially in light of a long history of women working quietly in the background in the sciences. Thus another perspective would be to argue that the inclusion of female scientists in B-movies allowed for the possibility of an intellectual career for young women in the audience. This is certainly the viewpoint of cultural critic Bonnie Noonan, who writes in her analysis *Women Scientists in Fifties Science Fiction Films* that the movies she watched as a teenager reflected her desire not so much to be a scientist, despite her affinity for the sciences, but her desire to have a career that could be taken seriously, like the women scientists she saw on film.[5]

In the decades since these films first played in theaters and drive-ins, it has become relatively commonplace for women to have fulfilling careers, although gender equality remains a daunting challenge across all professions. The recent proliferation of discussions about "work-life balance" indicates this inequality: the need to find a balance between professional and personal lives is addressed almost exclusively to women.

While men are beginning to join the conversation, gendered expectations that working women will take responsibility for childcare and other domestic issues before men make this a women's discourse. In a 2013 article, Kristin Rowe-Finkbeiner includes a lengthy quote from Joan Blades, cofounder of MoveOn.org, with whom she coauthored *The Motherhood Manifesto*. Blades notes that

> when mothers choose to "lean in" to high pressure jobs that entail working long hours, they often have guilt heaped upon them for supposedly neglecting their children. And when some choose to adjust their careers to have more family and personal time, they're often accused of betraying feminism. It's damned if you do, and damned if you don't.[6]

The discourse derived from Second Wave feminism would still have us believe that "you can't have it both ways": the happily ever after scenario in these films from the 1950s comes with an expectation that women give up their careers in science to become wives and mothers once the appropriate suitor is identified. Looking back at these portrayals occurs at an interesting moment in which the "she can have it all" superwoman debate is on the table once again. This chapter argues that there are women in B-movies who do have it all—they maintain the respect afforded to them as scientists and also win romantic partners, without having to sacrifice their professional interests to assume domestic roles instead.

Women scientists featured in 1950s B-movies include a broad variety of expertise: paleontologist Lee Hunter in *The Beast from 20,000 Fathoms* (1953); Dr. Patricia Medford, an entomologist in *Them!* (1954); biologist Stephanie Clayton in *Tarantula* (1955); and three scientists—Joanna Merritt, Marna Roberts, and Madame Elzevir, wife of the esteemed Dr. Pierre Elzevir—in *Gog* (1954). While these women often have the answers to save civilization, or willingly brave deadly encounters with the unknown, many of the depictions of female scientists also reify gender stereotypes about women, regardless of their intellectual prowess and independence. Whether a woman's expected destiny was a domestic life, the inclusion of female scientists in B-movies allowed for the possibility of an intellectual career for young women in the audience. Yet seeing these films and characters through a Second Wave feminist lens challenges the positive aspects of these portrayals.

BALANCING STEREOTYPES AND MAVERICKS

In her article "Feminist Film Theory," Anneke Smelik notes that early feminist film theory was focused on uncovering the stereotyping of women. She points out that feminist theorists believed that the "fixed and endlessly repeated images of women were considered to be objectionable distractions that would have a negative impact on the female spectator."[7] The 1954 Cold War sci-fi thriller *Gog* offers several good examples. A feminist critique would address some of the blatantly sexist events, such as the research assistant who weeps hysterically when the scientist she works with dies suddenly, only to be slapped across the face by another scientist who implores her to "get some men up here and restore order." Nonetheless, it is noteworthy that there are three women scientists at work in this underground laboratory where a space station is being built. Two of these scientists get little screen time, but it is worth taking a closer look at Joanna Merritt, an agent with the Office of Scientific Investigation (OSI). Joanna (although it is a gendered and antifeminist practice, this chapter follows the common habit of referring to male film characters by last name and female characters by first name, both in film dialogue and in critical reviews) is already acquainted with Dr. David Sheppard, who comes to the secret facility to investigate the mysterious death of a scientist, and more deaths follow. The nature of their acquaintance is made clear after Sheppard is introduced to various officials and scientists, when Sheppard and Joanna find themselves alone together. They embrace, and he asks about her time at the lab thus far, as the audience discovers that she too is an OSI agent. "So much has happened, so much has changed," she says. "You know what I keep thinking? It's silly. Mostly about slipping into a cocktail dress and waiting for you to ring the downstairs bell."

This is the only moment, until the end of the film, that Joanna reveals her feminine attributes. Like all of the other scientists at the lab, she wears standard coveralls that are the uniform for men and women alike and reveal little about one's body or sense of style. The intimate scene could be thought of as a gendered establishing shot: in this brief interlude, the audience is given access to the romantic side of both of the primary characters in the narrative. As such, viewers are able to frame their actions and interactions in the context of a romantic relationship. Joanna is consequently feminized, although her behavior and speech throughout the film tend to be firm, intellectual, and devoid of much emotion. She does, however, have a quick wit.

Joanna and Dr. Van Ness, the lab supervisor, take Sheppard on a tour of the facility. They observe an experiment in weightlessness, where a man and woman are training for a zero-gravity environment in space. After watching them for a while, Sheppard asks, "Why the girl?" Joanna replies, "We think women are better suited for space travel than men." Lest Joanna have the opportunity to make an argument favoring women over men, Van Ness quickly adds, "For one thing, they take up less space in a rocket."

As noted, this conversation can be considered from two different perspectives. A Second Wave feminist frame may have expressed dismay with both Sheppard and Van Ness for their blatant sexism. Sheppard objectifies the female astronaut in training, referring to her as "the girl" and questioning the appropriateness of her place in the space program. Then Van Ness adds that women are better because they are smaller, providing an idealized stereotype of the petite, fit woman. Nonetheless, there is still an opportunity for Joanna to offer what rhetorically sounds like a scientific truth: "We think women are better suited for space travel than men." Joanna has a strong and present personality, and the perspective she voices is not easily dismissed.

Because of the zero-gravity environment, the female astronaut is equally as strong as her male counterpart. She hoists him into the air easily, then pulls him back down. Her apparent strength leads Sheppard to comment, "I wouldn't like to be her boyfriend." Joanna delivers her witty retort "In space there's no such thing as a weaker sex," to which Sheppard replies, "That's why I like it here."

Finally, Joanna does prove women to be the weaker sex, but only physically. Joanna and Sheppard engage in a physical battle against the robots Gog and Magog, who are being controlled remotely by an aircraft flying over the laboratory. The robots are responsible for the deaths of the scientists, and finally try to initiate a nuclear reaction to bring the entire lab to its end. While their relationship has been somewhat balanced to this point, now Joanna cowers behind Sheppard, who protects her. They both get a dose of radiation. She loses consciousness, but he scoops her up and calls out, "Let's get her to the hospital, quick!" In the next scene she is safely in a hospital bed, he tells her she will be fine, and they kiss. The Americans launch their space station, when the air is fresh and crisp and clean, and the film ends.

Whether there is a happily ever after for David Sheppard and Joanna Merritt, her position does not seem to be diminished. The presence of women in positions of intellectual power seems tacitly accepted here, in a filmic world where imagination is boundless. Joanna has no internal conflict—she is not concerned about making choices about her life. Yet the taken-for-granted nature of female scientists in these films differs markedly from films that carry the ideology of post–World War II gender identity or of Second Wave feminism: for characters like Dr. Ellie Sattler in the *Jurassic Park* (1993, 2001) films or Dr. Eleanor Alloway in *Contact* (1997), their choice of careers leads others to question their scientific authority and personal motivation.

WHAT'S WRONG WITH PALEONTOLOGY?

Another set of binaries comes from women's studies scholar J. Kasi Jackson, who points out that "in addition to negotiating between detachment and empathy, the female scientist must balance professionalism with femininity."[8] The woman scientist is an outsider both in science, where her "feminine" empathy is not objective, and in society, where scientific rationality conflicts with assumed feminine traits. Jackson's observations relate well to Lee Hunter, a paleontologist in the 1953 giant creature movie *The Beast from 20,000 Fathoms*. Lee is a social outcast: as a woman, she doesn't comfortably fit in with her male colleagues, nor does she seem to connect with any other women. She is, in fact the only woman with any substance in the film, and no one doubts her place on the scene or the veracity of her research and observations. The other female characters are empty stereotypes: a nurse, a nun, a telephone operator, a screaming mother, and a bank of phone operators handling calls in the monster-created emergency. *The Beast from 20,000 Fathoms* fails the Bechdel Test,[9] which has three simple criteria for film: (1) it has to have at least two women in it, (2) who talk to each other, (3) about something besides a man.

Although it is unlikely that a 1950s science fiction B-movie would pass the Bechdel Test, it is employed here to draw attention to the strength of the female scientist in this film. Like Joanna Merritt, Lee Hunter is poised, confident, and smart. She is the assistant to Dr. Thurgood Elson, who is visited by a physicist named Thomas Nesbitt, who believes he has seen a dinosaur. No one takes Nesbitt very seriously, but Lee does. She establishes both her scientific prowess and her compassion after Nesbitt leaves Elson's laboratory. Of Nesbitt, she tells Elson, "When he first came to this country, I attended his lectures on the curative properties of radioactive isotopes. He's a brilliant man. Isn't his story in any way feasible?" Despite Elson's refusal, Lee decides to visit Nesbitt's office to offer her support.

Nesbitt's secretary informs him of Lee's arrival: "There's a Lee Hunter waiting for you. She's very pretty." In this moment, the narrative privileges Lee's femininity and sexuality over her intellect, framing Lee's invitation as both personal and professional. Sidney Perkowitz, a physicist and lay author, points out that female scientists are more likely to work on projects that are progressive and good for humanity rather than secretive and destructive. "But it's with looks that the discrepancy becomes really obvious. The female film scientist tends to be gorgeous,"[10] Perkowitz notes, and Lee Hunter matches his profile. Well-appointed and poised, Lee stretches the binary between smart and beautiful when Nesbitt asks why she would believe his claims. She says, "I have a deep abiding faith in the work of scientists. Otherwise I wouldn't be one myself." Here Lee ties her identity to science, a theme that is repeated throughout the film.

She invites Nesbitt to look at her collection of dinosaur drawings to see if he can identify the one he has seen. At her house, Lee is encouraging and nurturing. Before she takes out the drawings, she serves coffee and sandwiches. "You look tired. Why don't you just relax for a little.

Have a sandwich." Her care and concern inspire flirtation. Nesbitt sits on the floor, looking up at Lee perched on the sofa.

Nesbitt: Well it's funny. A girl like you, a paleontologist.

Lee: What's wrong with paleontology!

Nesbitt: Classifying old bones.

Lee: Old bones! If we didn't study the past, you wouldn't know anything about the atom. Dr. Elson says the future is a reflection of the past.

Nesbitt: You're fond of Dr. Elson, aren't you? How did you become his assistant?

Lee: I suppose by continually antagonizing him. I was one of his students, and to hear him tell it, all I ever did was challenge him or argue with him. I was afraid he was going to expel me. But instead he asked me to be his assistant after I graduated. So I graduated, and here I am.

In recent films, the origin story is often fraught with vulnerability. Like Lee, many women scientists from more recent films have a male mentor, often a father, uncle, or teacher. But where Lee is matter-of-fact about her relationship with Elson, contemporary stories tend to be emotionally weighted. Sharing the narrative of how she ended up in science is an opportunity for a female scientist to reveal a more emotional, tender side of her personality. Another perspective on the character is opened for the audience: in expressing doubts about her professional life, the female scientist diminishes her intellectual and professional strength. She does not get to have it all; rather, she sacrifices science for domestic life or chooses the inverse. The female scientist's origin story may also be woven into the narrative. In *Contact* (1997), for example, the audience learns early in the film that Dr. Eleanor "Ellie" Arroway's search for signals of extraterrestrial life is a metaphor for her search for signals from her father, whose death left her an orphan at age nine. As such, Ellie's work as a scientist is fundamentally personal and deeply tied to her emotional and familial life. She is confronted repeatedly by her choice of the rationality of science over an emotionally rich domestic life. Her dissertation director, who ends up being Ellie's nemesis, asks in an argument over her thesis topic, "What is it that makes you so lonely, Miss Arroway? What is it that compels you to search the heavens for life when there's so much of it being neglected right here at home?" In the original screenplay for the film, the next scene advances forward in time when Peter Valerian, Ellie's fellow scientist and sweetheart, comes to visit her while she is doing fieldwork in Puerto Rico. Rather than resuming their relationship, Valerian tells her he plans to marry another woman. The two begin a heated discussion about the improbability of Ellie getting funding to continue her research, let alone find signs of extraterrestrial life.

Ellie: Please, you're just as ambitious as I am, more—

Valerian: Maybe that's the problem. I want . . . a family, Ellie. I want kids. A townhouse on L Street instead of still living like a college kid. A real life. Maybe that makes me a sellout but I don't care anymore. It's what I want.

Ellie: And you think I don't want those things? You think I don't stay up half the night wondering if I've made the right choice living half a world away from you, wondering if any of this is worth what I'm giving up for it every day?

Even in her isolation, Ellie grapples constantly with an inner struggle to validate her choices. The decision, it appears, is made for her, as she loses her mate as a consequence of her dedication to science. In the end, however, Ellie does get to have it all, when she unexpectedly finds both scientific success and love. Unlike Ellie, Lee Hunter appears to have made her decision, as is understood by those around her. As previously noted, there is no evidence that Lee has any existing friendships or romantic relationships, making her dedication to science complete.

Toward the end of the film, the beast is located underwater, and Dr. Elson chooses to go down in a diving bell to investigate. Before the hatch is closed, he tells Lee exuberantly, "We're scientists! This is a great moment for me." She kisses the old doctor on the lips. When the doctor sees the monster under the water, he only wants to talk to Lee: she is the person to whom he reports his discovery, despite the presence of a core group of male scientists surrounding her. The beast kills Dr. Elson, and Lee and Nesbitt have their first embrace when he consoles her in Elson's office. The beast then appears at Coney Island, and Lee gives Nesbitt a long kiss on the cheek when he heads off with a soldier to shoot the monster with a radioactive isotope—the climax of the film. They hug at the end, when the monster is defeated, but this embrace is no more sexual than their first hug. Nesbitt gets his happily ever after at the end, and Lee appears to have it all too. As Nesbitt sees Lee as an ally and collaborator in the world of science, it is difficult to imagine that he would expect her to sacrifice her career, especially as she has likely inherited Elson's papers and projects.

PERHAPS NOT TYPICAL

Science fiction B-movies from the 1950s are rife with female characters who do not have the independence or determination of Joanna Merritt and Lee Hunter. Some female characters are primarily sexualized and seductive, where others are hyperemotional and present themselves as weak and needy. Despite the depiction of some women scientists, these films still reflect the gendered reality of their time: the cultural framework in which these films are set is undeniably sexist. Feminist film scholar Teresa De Lauretis argued that female characters are made to conform to the ideal image that the male protagonist has for them.[11] Regardless of their intellect or achievements, these characters are the object of the male gaze.

Ann Cragis, the only female character in *The Killer Shrews* (1959), offers a curious example of the science fiction woman of science: although she is the adult daughter of a scientist and is isolated on an island for a scientific mission—two typical circumstances for B-movie female scientists—she is not involved in any research. Ann appears to be there at her father's behest, and has been, until the night before the story begins, engaged to one of the scientists, Jerry Ferrell. Ann has broken her engagement due to Ferrell's failure to protect her from the killer shrews invading the scientists' compound. When Capt. Thorne Sherman arrives to deliver supplies and take her back to the mainland, Ann immediately begins flirting with him. Although she is a strong character, Ann is not a scientist. The inclusion of a female character who is present to be attractive, to function as the "damsel in distress," and to otherwise drive the plot forward is typical of science fiction B-movies.

Another film, *Attack of the Crab Monsters* (1957), similarly features an attractive female character who functions as a damsel in distress but is also, in fact, a scientist. Dr. Martha Hunter, a marine biologist, prefers to be called Marty by the other members of the expedition crew. Along with her fiancé, Dale Drewer, and several other male scientists, Marty travels to a remote island where another crew has disappeared without a trace. As the scientists set up camp and begin exploring, Marty remains in close physical contact with Drewer. He touches her on the shoulder when they stand together, puts his hand on the small of her back when they begin walking, and holds her hand when they walk or run across the island together. This degree of physical closeness is uncharacteristic of science fiction B-movies, yet it does not seem possessive or sexual. Marty is feminized not by her sexuality but by her domesticity: after one of the scientists is injured by a giant crab monster, she puts him to bed and takes care of him with maternal concern. Later in the film, when the male scientists leave to confront the giant crab, Marty stays behind, saying it's time that she should go fix dinner. She may be one of the scientists who can have it all, as she is engaged to her long-time partner, another scientist who, while physically demonstrative, also appears to accept her scientific mind.

Media theorist Mary Ann Doane has written extensively about masquerade,[12] and the tendency for women with power and authority to perform hyperfemininity as a means of concealing their power. Marty makes this choice, and her participation in the scientific discourse indicates she is capable of far more than cooking dinner. Filmic conventions help objectify Marty as well. Careful attention to framing places the one woman in a prominent position in virtually every scene, in ways that the viewer's eye, and the male gaze, fall naturally upon her. Similar framing techniques occur in *Creature from the Black Lagoon* (1954), one of the best-known science fiction B-movies. The female protagonist, a scientist named Kay Lawrence, is in a committed relationship with ichthyologist David Reed. Like Marty, Kay is the sole woman in the film. What sets apart *Creature from the Black Lagoon* is the creature's infatuation with Kay. Regardless of her scientific accomplishments, which are the topic of a discussion between Kay and another scientist who believes she has let her boyfriend take credit for her work, Kay is objectified not by the men but by the monster. It is a curious twist on the theme of examining the gendered nature of B-movies.

SECOND WAVE, SCIENCE, AND IDENTITY WORK

To consider Second Wave feminism as a lens for analyzing texts from the past requires an acknowledgment that no doors are closed on the Second Wave: the ideologies that shaped the women's liberation movement are still present, along with Third Wave feminism and postfeminist perspectives. Significant in this analysis is not necessarily moving beyond a Second Wave perspective but expanding the critical view to embrace other viewpoints simultaneously. Writing in 1971, political scientist Jo Freeman argued that one of the core concepts of sexism is that "women are here for the pleasure and assistance of men."[13] Freeman goes on to say,

> It is this attitude which stigmatizes those women who do not marry or who do not devote their primary energies to the care of men and their children. Association with a man is the basic criterion for participation by women in this society and one who does not seek her identity through a man is a threat to the social values.[14]

Scholarship in the decades since Freeman's assertions has argued that identity formation is a complex process, and every person forms and performs her or his identity in the context of interpersonal relationships. Women and men alike form their identities through others, and this does not diminish one's participation in society provided the self is at the center of self-identity. In other words, self-identity reflects, but is not dependent upon, the presence of others. Freeman's claim, then, has validity, especially when viewed with contingency. For women scientists in the 1950s, "association with a man" was "the basic criterion for participation by women" in society: science has been and remains patriarchal. As previously noted, women tend to abandon or simply not pursue professional life in the sciences; the lack of a welcoming, balanced space for women is one reason. With this in mind, it is noteworthy that B-movie women scientists seem undaunted by the patriarchal cultures in which they choose to work. Perhaps it is the influence of Second Wave feminism that makes more contemporary female scientists self-conscious about their sexism, gender, and self-identity.

Whether at the matinee or the drive-in, movie audiences in the 1950s were introduced to a new kind of B-movie character, the female scientist. Although men significantly outnumber women in these films, women were frequently featured in significant scientific roles, battling aliens, mutant forces, or giant bugs. A survey of these films indicates a spectrum of reception in which female scientists may be welcome or othered, depending on their circumstances and relationships to men within the patriarchal culture of a scientific organization. By looking at alternate and often opposing analyses of science fiction B-movies, it is clear that the self-consciousness of Second Wave feminism draws attention to the gendered nature of the female scientists, problematizing the issue for both film characters and their audiences.

NOTES

1. Chris Nashawaty, "NSFW: The 12 Best B-Movies Ever Made," *Huffington Post: The Blog*, 13 September 2013, http://www.huffingtonpost.com/chris-nashawaty/b-movies-you-need-to-see-_b_3921858.html (accessed 28 November 2013).

2. "Waffling with . . . Vince Rotolo of the BMovieCast," The Movie Waffler, July 2009, http://www.themoviewaffler.com/2009/07/podcast-profile-bmoviecast.html#.UpvqhN_I1UQ (accessed 22 November 2013).

3. Tiffani Lennon, *Benchmarking Women's Leadership in the United States*. University of Denver, 2012, http://www.womenscollege.du.edu (accessed 8 October 2013).

4. Laura Mulvey, "Visual Pleasure and Narrative Cinema," in *Film Theory and Criticism: Introductory Readings*, ed. Leo Braudy and Marshall Cohen (New York: Oxford University Press, 1999), 833–44.

5. Bonnie Noonan, *Women Scientists in Fifties Science Fiction Films* (Jefferson, NC: McFarland, 2005).

6. Kristin Rowe-Finkbeiner, "The Real Feminist Nightmare: It's Definitely Not Michelle Obama," *Politico Magazine*, 25 November 2013, http://www.politico.com/magazine/story/2013/11/the-real-feminist-nightmare-not-michelle-obama-100339.html (accessed 26 November 2013).

7. Anneke Smelik, "Feminist Film Theory," in *The Cinema Book*, ed. Pam Cook (London: British Film Institute Press, 2008), 491.

8. J. Kasi Jackson, "Doomsday Ecology and Empathy for Nature: Women Scientists in 'B' Horror Movies," *Science Communication* 33 (2011): 538.

9. "The Bechdel Test for Women in Movies," Feminist Frequency: Conversations with Pop Culture, 7 December 2009, http://www.feministfrequency.com/2009/12/the-bechdel-test-for-women-in-movies (accessed 24 October 2013).

10. Sidney Perkowitz, "Female Scientists on the Big Screen," *The Scientist*, 21 July 2006,   http://www.the-scientist.com/?articles.view/articleNo/24170/title/Female-scientists-on-the-big-screen (accessed 2 September 2012).

11. Smelik, "Feminist Film Theory."

12. Mary Ann Doane, "Film and the Masquerade: Theorising the Female Spectator." *Screen* 23, nos. 3–4 (1982): 74–88.

13. Jo Freeman, "The Women's Liberation Movement: Its Origin, Structures and Ideals," http://library.duke.edu/rubenstein/scriptorium/wlm/womlib (accessed 2 September 2012).

14. Freeman, "The Women's Liberation Movement."

BIBLIOGRAPHY

Attack of the Crab Monsters. Directed by Roger Corman. 1957. Netflix, 2013.

The Beast from 20,000 Fathoms. Directed by Eugène Lourié. 1953. Burbank, CA: Warner Home Video, 2003.

"The Bechdel Test for Women in Movies." Feminist Frequency: Conversations with Pop Culture, 7 December 2009. http://www.feministfrequency.com/2009/12/the-bechdel-test-for-women-in-movies (accessed 24 October 2013).

Contact. Directed by Robert Zemeckis. 1997.

Creature from the Black Lagoon. Directed by Jack Arnold. 1954.

Doane, Mary Ann. "Film and the Masquerade: Theorising the Female Spectator." *Screen* 23, nos. 3–4 (1982): 74–88.

Freeman, Jo, "The Women's Liberation Movement: Its Origin, Structures and Ideals," Duke University Library, http://library.duke.edu/rubenstein/scriptorium/wlm/womlib (accessed 2 September 2012).

Gog. Directed by Herbert L. Strock. 1954. Los Angeles: MGM, 2011. DVD.

Jackson, J. Kasi. "Doomsday Ecology and Empathy for Nature: Women Scientists in 'B' Horror Movies." *Science Communication* 33 (2011): 533–555.

The Killer Shrews. Directed by Ray Kellogg. 1959.

Lennon, Tiffani. *Benchmarking Women's Leadership in the United States.* University of Denver, 2012. htt://www.womenscollege.du.edu (accessed 8 October 2013).

Meyjes, Menno, Ann Druyan, Carl Sagan, Michael Goldenberg, and Jim V. Hart. "Contact (1997) Movie Script." Screenplays for You, n.d. http://sfy.ru/sfy.html?script=contact (accessed 20 November 2013).

Mulvey, Laura. "Visual Pleasure and Narrative Cinema." In *Film Theory and Criticism: Introductory Readings*, edited by Leo Braudy and Marshall Cohen, 833–44. New York: Oxford University Press, 1999.

Nashawaty, Chris. "NSFW: The 12 Best B-Movies Ever Made." *Huffington Post: The Blog*, 13 September 2013. http://www.huffingtonpost.com/chris-nashawaty/b-movies-you-need-to-see-_b_3921858.html (accessed 28 November 2013).

Noonan, Bonnie. *Women Scientists in Fifties Science Fiction Films.* Jefferson, NC: McFarland, 2005.

Perkowitz, Sidney. "Female Scientists on the Big Screen." *The Scientist*, 21 July 2006. http://www.the-scientist.com/?articles.view/articleNo/24170/title/Female-scientists-on-the-big-screen (accessed 2 September 2012).

Rowe-Finkbeiner, Kristin. "The Real Feminist Nightmare: It's Definitely Not Michelle Obama." *Politico Magazine*, 25 November 2013. http://www.politico.com/magazine/story/2013/11/the-real-feminist-nightmare-not-michelle-obama-100339.html (accessed 26 November 2013).

Smelik, Anneke. "Feminist Film Theory." In *The Cinema Book*, 3rd ed., edited by Pam Cook, 491–504. London: British Film Institute Press, 2008.

"Waffling with . . . Vince Rotolo of the BMovieCast." The Movie Waffler, July 2009. http://www.huffingtonpost.com/chris-nashawaty/b-movies-you-need-to-see-_b_3921858.html (accessed 28 November 2013)

FIVE

"The High Priestess of the Desert"

Female Intellect and Subjectivity in Contact

Allison Whitney

Science fiction narratives, given their explorations of technological and scientific innovation, frequently include intellectually remarkable characters. At the same time, the speculative nature of the genre treats the interior of the mind as a creative and dynamic space, such that science fiction spaces are often manifestations of thought—either transformed through new concepts and technologies or, in the case of some simulation scenarios, projected directly from the psyche. In most cases, the intellects that imagine these futures are gendered male, but in this chapter, I will discuss the figure of the brilliant female scientist in Robert Zemeckis's 1997 release, *Contact*, where Jodie Foster portrays Ellie Arroway, an astronomer who discovers evidence of an extraterrestrial civilization. I will discuss three elements of the film and its reception: the use of formal strategies and visual effects to align Ellie's cognitive and sensory powers with scientific technology; the way Ellie challenges patriarchal traditions in media representations of women, religious discourse, and government structures; and critics' conflicted responses to the film, particularly regarding Foster's performance and the intersections of intellect and sexuality in her star persona.

While *Contact's* story and characters had a mixed critical reception, its visual effects and sound design were almost universally lauded. Robert Zemeckis had solidified his reputation as a technical innovator with *Forrest Gump* (1994), which capitalized on new digital effects to, for example, place its protagonist in archival footage of historic events, or seamlessly "erase" an actor's legs when he plays an amputee. *Contact*'s visual effects are no less remarkable, in that they provide the high-concept spectacle that is expected of the science fiction genre to represent not only the cosmos in beautiful and moving ways, but also a mind, Ellie's mind, that is capable of understanding that cosmos. *Contact*'s opening sequence takes the form of a cosmic zoom, a technique that has been used for decades as a way of representing scale in the universe. Kees Boeke's 1957 book *Cosmic View* inspired several film adaptations, including Eva Szasz's *Cosmic Zoom* (1968), Charles and Ray Eames's *Powers of Ten* (1977), and the IMAX film *Cosmic Voyage* (Bayley Silleck, 1996), and in each case, the cosmic zoom represents the universe through a series of scale shifts, increasing exponentially by powers of ten. Cosmic zooms generally begin with a human body, then proceed to a vast cosmic scale in a matter of minutes, and in some cases, return to the human only to plunge inward to the subatomic level. *Contact* uses the cosmic zoom structure, beginning with a shot of Earth as seen from orbit, but here, the image is accompanied by a cacophony of broadcasts from the surface. As the sequence zooms out past neighboring planets, the broadcasts become progressively older, the premise being that it has taken them a longer time to reach further points in space.

As the zoom moves beyond the limits of the Milky Way, we hear the oldest of the transmissions, a faint snippet of Morse code, and then si-lence—a silence that persists for twenty-seven seconds—an eternity in mainstream cinema. The sequence reaches the furthest edges of the uni-verse, but then undergoes a radical reversal of scale, the zoom concluding with an extreme close-up of an eye. The eye belongs to the film's protago-nist, Ellie, in this scene portrayed as a child (Jena Malone), as she experi-ments with her radio set. This sequence's combination of sublime space imagery, true silence, and the close-up of the eye directly cite *2001: A Space Odyssey* (Stanley Kubrick, 1968), a film whose influence in science fiction is ubiquitous, including the now-common convention of close-ups of the eye representing a cognitive and spiritual transformation of the subject. However, the *Contact* cosmic zoom situates this transformative process in the eye of a female character, one whose intellectual and psychological experience will become the central focus of the film.

The decision to structure the cosmic zoom within a character's eye not only recalls science fiction traditions, but also conforms to the technical nature of a zoom, achieved through a change in focal length within the camera. In a zoom, cosmic or otherwise, the observer does not travel, but rather narrows or broadens the field of view through an internal process. Similarly, the sequence in *Contact* quite literally locates an ordered con-templation of the universe within the visual apparatus of the protagonist, anchoring the sequence in her eye. Meanwhile, as Stan Link argues in "Nor the Eye Filled with Seeing: The Sound of Vision in Film," *Contact*'s sound design maps outer space in terms of a historical synopsis, where sound becomes "ordered and 'uniformed' in a way imitating the ordered visual journey."[1] The sequence emphasizes the relativity of space and time, in large part because the sounds are easily recognizable, representing distinct styles of music, television theme songs, and notable moments in broadcast history, including the Space Shuttle Challenger disaster and John F. Kennedy's assassination.

Of course, the cosmic zoom, and particularly its unusual sound elements, serve a narrative purpose, as the premise of *Contact* is that a 1930s television signal reaches an alien civilization twenty-six light years away, and they see fit to send a response. Ellie, now a scientist who employs radio telescopes to search for extraterrestrial civilization, receives the signal, but the opening of *Contact* demonstrates that our imagining of the cosmos is as much an interior and subjective process as it is a collation of scientific data. *Contact* imagines the universe within Ellie's eye, an eye whose retina is an outcropping of her brain, a brain that contemplates the magnitude of outer space, and with its broadcast-centered soundscape, narrates it with cultural memory—all within a sequence that capitalizes on, and calls attention to, new technologies in filmmaking.

The film consistently aligns Ellie's persona as a scientist, her process as a thinker, and her sensory experiences with scientific instruments and technologies. In our first encounter with Ellie, she is using her radio set under her father's guidance, speaking with people around the country, and documenting her transmissions on a map. After speculating with her father about whether there are people on other planets, the sequence ends with Ellie musing, "I'm going to need a bigger antenna." In the next shot, we see the adult Ellie at the Arecibo Observatory in Puerto Rico, where she will be conducting her research. This sequence begins with a close-up of her face, and as she steps forward, the camera turns and moves upward to show the enormous radio telescope, with her standing in the foreground. Moments later, we see Ellie at work in the computer lab, a scene that begins with the camera looking out the window at the telescope, then turning to focus on Ellie, who sits in front of a bank of computers while wearing her headphones. Ellie's physical and cognitive connection to the radio telescope becomes more explicit when she unplugs the headphones, allowing the viewer to listen to the rhythmic sounds of the pulsar she has detected. A fellow scientist, Kent (William Fichtner) enters the lab and commends Ellie on actually listening to the radio signals rather than relying on computers to analyze them for patterns. Kent's own relationship to sound is especially marked since he is blind, and like Ellie, he will later use his acute hearing to discern levels of complexity in the extraterrestrial transmission. The film continually affirms that Ellie is a character whose senses, both visual and auditory, are both extended through and aligned with scientific instruments, from her childhood radio set to the most powerful telescopes, and who uses her senses as part of her scientific inquiry. Indeed, when Ellie detects the alien signal at the Very Large Array (VLA) in New Mexico, it arrives while she is again listening to her headphones. At the moment that it breaks through the static, the camera offers an extreme close-up of her closed eyes—eyes that open once she realizes that she is hearing something extraordinary. Meanwhile, her colleagues back at the station don't even notice that the computer has also detected the signal.[2]

The fact that Ellie makes her scientific discoveries in sensory, embodied terms is important in the way the film represents her cognitive processes. In the novel of *Contact* Ellie devotes considerable time to the painstaking process of decoding the signal through mathematical analysis.[3] In the film, however, the signal's arrival is rapid and sensational, expressed through a rhythmic pulse that exploits the visceral potential of contemporary sound systems. One might argue that this approach is more conducive to cinematic representation, as a suspenseful sequence with rousing sound design is arguably more exciting to audiences than watching someone work on a math problem. More important, however, is the fact that the film prioritizes a female character's visual and auditory power to a degree that one rarely sees in mainstream cinema. Ellie's eyes and ears, and the way her brain processes their inputs, align her body and mind not only with the advanced technology within the diegesis, but also the technology of filmmaking and theatrical exhibition, all of which invite the viewer to see, hear, and think along with her. When Ellie and her fellow scientists decode the alien signal, they discover that it includes instructions for a device that will allow a human to experience interstellar travel and communicate directly with the alien civilization. Ellie eventually makes this journey, encountering astonishing sights and sensations that are shared with the viewer. Meanwhile, the use of digital effects in this sequence also allows the film to visualize and dramatize Ellie's intellectual and emotional interior. As Stacey Abbott explains in "Final Frontiers: Computer-Generated Imagery and the Science Fiction Film,"

> As the journey accelerates, the dislocation of time and space caused by such speeds is shown through the appearance of a ghostly echo of her face that emerges and stretches beyond the boundaries of her body. Later, as she looks out at a celestial event, her image is digitally altered to create a surreal ripple effect, as if her countenance were being sculpted and reformed before the camera. The audience is looking at an image of the actress reinterpreted through computer technology.[4]

This reinterpretation of Foster's face, which allows the audience to not only hear but also see multiple simultaneous thought processes, combines both empirical observation and extreme emotional states to create a surprisingly nuanced representation of Ellie as a thinking subject.

While the film valorizes Ellie's visual and auditory sensitivities, it also employs retrograde gender dynamics in media representation to mark moments of disempowerment, moments that often coincide with Ellie's image appearing on television screens. For example, when Ellie's colleagues are watching the televised press conference where President Clinton addresses the alien discovery, one of them asks, "I thought Ellie was supposed to be on?" Moments later, we see Ellie reading her cue cards in preparation to face the press. However, when presidential aide Rachel Constantine (Angela Bassett) takes the microphone, she introduces David Drumlin (Tom Skerritt), Ellie's professional rival, as the leader of the scientific team that made the discovery. Not only does this moment resonate with the systematic erasure of women from scientific history, but it also demonstrates how women are excluded from media representations that honor their achievements. As David walks to the podium, the film's camera remains on Ellie, who sits down in shock next to a monitor showing David's face as he takes credit for her work. Later, when the billionaire industrialist S. R. Hadden (John Hurt), who has been funding Ellie's research, invites her to meet him on his aircraft, he demonstrates that he has been watching her career for some time by showing her a montage of images from her childhood to the present, concluding with an enlargement of her shocked face at the press conference. For the rest of their meeting, Ellie sits directly in front of that image, until Hadden offers to help restore her authority by offering her the primer that will allow her to decode the message embedded within the alien transmission. At this moment, Hadden turns to the monitor, and Ellie's image disappears to reveal the alien code.

Not only does television assist in Ellie's erasure from the narrative of scientific discovery, but it also serves to diminish her public image and to cast doubt on the veracity of her experience. For example, when Ellie is interviewed on television, she stammers and fidgets nervously, hardly portraying her high levels of competence. Meanwhile, when Ellie sets out to make her space journey, she wears a video headset to record her experience, but the device fails to corroborate her sensory experience, yielding nothing but static. Upon her return, mission control informs her that the system failed and that she did not in fact go anywhere. Ellie undergoes a hostile debriefing with Kitz (James Woods), the national security adviser, and this scene begins with a close-up of a television monitor showing Ellie's face. As the camera pulls back, we see that Ellie is sitting beside one of the monitors, and that there is another in the room beyond, each showing the same image. Kitz demands that she reconcile her story with "what we saw," showing her a series of videos from the various cameras trained on the machine, all of which seem to contradict her story. While it might make sense that Ellie's testimony would be videotaped, the multiplication of screens in this scene seems excessive, and also suggests that she, like the video footage of the machine, is being viewed not as a subject, but as an object to be scrutinized.

When Ellie is testifying before a congressional committee about her experience, she posits that the machine exploits the relativity of time and space, which is why her eighteen-hour journey appeared to take only a few seconds. Kitz offers the counter-argument that her journey never happened, but rather that she is suffering from a psychiatric "episode." The scene then cuts to an image of her colleagues at the VLA, who are watching the hearings on television. The camera moves around to look at the screen, revealing her image at the moment that she says, "Is that what you think? That I was delusional?" In a film like *Contact*, one that devotes substantial narrative import to a female character's perceptions and thought processes and that enthusiastically invites its viewers to experience awe, wonder, and visceral engagement with extended visual effects sequences built around that character's subjectivity, it is interesting that when Ellie is marginalized, doubted, and discredited, she is rendered not as an authoritative subject, but rather as a media image, and one that is clearly disempowered through the gendered imbalances that are ubiquitous in media culture. The film ultimately sides with Ellie, both in the ways it encourages the viewer to share her perceptions, but also in the revelation at the end of the film, when Rachel notes that though it is true that Ellie's video equipment recorded only static, and thus cannot corroborate her story, it did record eighteen hours' worth.

When it comes to the representation of female characters in mainstream cinema, a film centered on the exploits of a female scientist appears to be an improvement on Hollywood convention. However, some critics have argued that the film fails to address gender bias in the scientific community, something that Sagan's novel addressed quite consistently. In Carol Colatrella's essay "From *Desk Set* to *The Net*: Women and Computing Technology in Hollywood Films," she says that while the novel explicates how institutionalized sexism exacerbates Ellie's struggle to gain respect for her research, "the film takes an easier way out by imaging Ellie as the sole female member of a rather flaky team of scientists marginalized for their interest in 'little green men.'"[5] In some respects Colatrella is correct, as the film only hints at the sexism that the novel explicitly condemns, but I would argue that *Contact* challenges other forms of sexism, specifically the representation of women in the media, calling attention to both the novelty of prioritizing women's perceptions, while also addressing the ways women's images are used to nullify their power, and also the challenges women face as they negotiate the performance of femininity in other male-dominated realms, including government and religion.

In Peter Travers's review of the film in *Rolling Stone*, he compares the film to the novel, noting how the adaptation process forces *Contact* to acquire Hollywood traits that diminish the film's feminist messages. He writes,

> The book had a woman president; the film substitutes Bill Clinton in trick photography that allows the prez and Ellie to rub elbows like

Gump did with JFK and LBJ. The only other notable female is Rachel (Angela Bassett), a presidential aide who advises Ellie on where to buy a hot dress for a reception. No joke, though it should be.[6]

Regarding Angela Bassett's character, Jonathan Rosenbaum agrees in his *Chicago Reader* review that her presence in the film seems trite, that she is "less a character here than a form of demographic appeasement."[7] Ellie and Rachel have one private conversation in the film, when Ellie approaches Rachel after a White House meeting to ask where she can find "a really great dress" for a reception later that night. While this interaction appears to affirm sexist stereotypes, I would suggest a different reading. Both Ellie and Rachel are high-achieving women who work in conspicuously masculine and white power structures, where they are required to project an image of femininity that is necessarily bifurcated and contradictory. Ellie is aware that the reception, like any event in Washington, will be an important opportunity for her to advocate for herself, but that in order to do that effectively, she must strike a balance between glamour and professionalism. She assumes, correctly, that Rachel, an African American woman working in the White House, will be well versed in the intricacies of such a performance.

Indeed, in Karen Hollinger's study of female stardom, she notes how Angela Bassett's star persona is "composed of two major image clusters: (1) beauty, glamour, sexuality, and physicality; and (2) iconic status as a role model and a figure of strong black womanhood."[8] While the burdens of "role model" and "strong black woman" status often prove problematic for African American artists, the combination of glamour and competence that is so invested in Bassett's image suggests that her interaction with Ellie, and with Foster's star persona, is more complex than it appears.

Jodie Foster is an actor who both resists and inhabits conventional beauty standards and notions of femininity. In Christina Lane's "The Liminal Iconography of Jodie Foster," she explains how Foster's persona "encompasses such oppositions as masculine/feminine, public/private, gay/straight, in/out rather than submitting to their binary structure."[9] Lane describes further how Foster has cultivated a public image that is glamorous, citing her appearance in the 1989 edition of *Harper's Bazaar* as one of "America's Ten Most Beautiful Women," while also embodying "self-ownership, self-authorship, and, not least, heroic self-confidence."[10] In *Contact*, her character dresses in a manner that suits her profession and environment, so when she asks Rachel for shopping advice, it proves to be an act of "self-authorship." When Ellie arrives at the party, her dress is indeed "great," but Ellie's behavior makes clear that her appearance is part of an active strategy. Palmer Joss (Matthew McConaughey), with whom she has had a romantic relationship, approaches her and remarks that she looks beautiful, and she replies, "So do you." This remark is consistent with their ongoing flirtation, but it also suggests that Ellie is aware of her appearance in a way that men in Washington, or indeed anywhere, rarely have to be.

Meanwhile, Rachel consistently works to maintain Ellie's position of power, and advises her about how to manage White House politics. For example, she blocks David and Kitz's attempts to remove Ellie from the project, she reminds Ellie of the importance of diplomacy in political negotiations, and she remarks to Kitz that Ellie makes a good case for herself as an astronaut. At the end of the film, she also informs Kitz that Ellie will be receiving a substantial grant, and then confronts him with the information in the confidential report on Ellie's journey that supports her version of events. Rachel knows very well how and why women are silenced, discredited, and marginalized in the political system, and she uses her authority to advocate for Ellie. While it is true that by using Bill Clinton, Zemeckis would forgo the opportunity to cast Bassett as the president, it remains that the interaction between Ellie and Rachel, both as characters and in terms of the actors' respective star personae, allows for a level of commentary on how women of ambition and intelligence have to negotiate a delicate balance of gender codes to retain their power.

One of the central themes in *Contact* is the relationship between scientific thought and religious discourse, a relationship presented primarily through Ellie's friendship and romance with Palmer, a public intellectual and Christian thinker. Meanwhile, Ellie presents herself as an atheist, arguing that she believes in scientific method, and that a belief in God resting on faith alone is incompatible with her worldview. As Marie Lathers explains in *Space Oddities: Women and Outer Space in Popular Film and Culture, 1960-2000*, the film's ongoing debates about faith and science set up a narrative arc wherein Ellie ends up admitting that, upon returning from her voyage, she has no tangible evidence of her observations apart from her memory, which she recounts in testimony that parallels with Palmer's description of the mystical revelation that formed the foundation of his faith.[11] While Sagan's atheism clearly informs this dynamic in *Contact*, the film also takes on a political angle, where the implications of extraterrestrial contact are met with objection from the religious right, represented, ironically, by the character Richard Rank, portrayed by Rob Lowe.[12]

While *Contact* uses the relationship between religion and science to generate dramatic tension on a number of fronts, the film also draws upon a long tradition in science fiction where spiritual and scientific revelation go hand in hand. For example, *Contact* bears an uncanny resemblance to *Message from Space* (Lee Sholem, 1966), a film that takes place at a remote radio observatory in New Mexico, where a female scientist, Maria Herrera Flores Delgado (Gigi Perreau) is conducting research in exobiology. As is typical of science fiction films of that era, the male scientists at the station are surprised that the visiting researcher is a woman, and immediately try to take her on a date.[13] Their initial sexism, however, gives way to a rather nuanced series of debates on both faith and science. Maria explains that not only is she searching for extraterrestrial life, but she also has hypotheses that life on Earth may have been "seeded" by an alien civilization, and that humans have the potential to create artificial life. Meanwhile, one of the male scientists receives a visit from his father, a minister, who engages in extended discussions with all of the scientists about the complexities of reconciling religious faith with scientific practice. The minister, perhaps not unlike Palmer Joss, explains that he thinks scientific discovery, rather than countering religion, only compounds our wonder at God's creation. Even amid the occasional sexist comment, such as the men's opining that the coffee at the station will get better now that Maria is here, the minister still makes a point of valorizing Maria's research. *Message from Space*, curiously, does not include any actual messages from space, but it does make the unusual move of presenting a female presence as not only beneficial to, but perhaps even essential for, scientific discovery, which is itself conducive to greater religious experience.

In many respects, *Contact*'s take on the relationship between religion and science is more strained, and that tension takes on an especially gendered tone. When Ellie offers autobiographical accounts of how and why she became a scientist, or when she explains her relationship to organized religion, she uses examples that speak to the misrepresentation or invisibility of women from both traditions. For example, when she is telling Palmer about her early fascination with the solar system, she notes the paradox of the planet Venus being named after a goddess who embodies an ideal of female beauty, even though that planet is actually poisonous and volatile. Of all the things that could have intrigued her about the cosmos, it was this contradiction, based in a misreading of a feminine figure, that inspired her interest in astronomy. Later, she tells Palmer about her childhood experiences in Sunday school, when she would ask difficult questions like "Where did Mrs. Cain come from?" Her questions, rather than inspiring productive debate, resulted in their asking her father not to bring Ellie back to church. Ellie's questions about "Mrs. Cain" not only sought to reconcile biblical narratives with scientific logic, but they also speak to the ways religious institutions marginalize female figures. Ellie not only points out the logical fallacy of women's exclusion from scripture, but she also finds herself excluded from the community for raising the question at all.

Once she is shut out from institutionalized religion, Ellie embraces a scientific worldview, but even then, she continues to struggle to be taken seriously as a thinker and a scientist. After Ellie loses her position at the Arecibo Observatory, she relocates her research to the VLA. That is, until her colleague Kent notifies her that the government support for her project has been terminated, and that she is the laughing stock of the scientific community, who refer to Ellie as "the high priestess of the desert." This nickname is hardly a compliment, but rather a dismissal of her scientific inquiry as cultish and irrational. The name is also an indictment of her leadership and, by extension, the male scientists who work under her. For Ellie, religion is a clear source of alienation, as its traditions, narratives, and archetypes leave women belittled, mocked, or invisible.

Ellie responds to these traditions by distancing herself from religion, but even that decision leaves her vulnerable to criticism. While Ellie is in competition to be the first human to visit the extraterrestrial civilization, it is her atheism that bars her selection. Palmer, who is a committee member, asks if she believes in God. When she hesitates to answer, wondering aloud if it is a relevant question, another committee member notes that since the vast majority of the world's population holds some kind of religious belief, her lack thereof might make her an unsuitable representative of humanity. Meanwhile, David, who continually steals Ellie's thunder and takes credit for her work, lies to the committee about his religious faith in order to appeal to public opinion. To make matters worse, Palmer admits that because of his own love for Ellie, he did not want her to go for fear of losing her, which suggests that his question, one she could not answer in a politically auspicious way, was a form of sabotage. It is clear that the men in the film are free to employ religious discourse to their advantage, while for Ellie, it presents only impediments. Again, while the film may not thoroughly explore the barriers to women's advancement in scientific institutions, it does demonstrate how the combination of religious, political, and media discourses serve to marginalize and misrepresent women and their experience.

While *Contact* was popular with audiences, critics' reactions varied from enthusiasm to condemnation. The film was widely praised for its visual effects, and while some critics were excited by the progressive representation of a female scientist, others were highly critical of both Ellie's character and Foster's performance. Some critics complained that Ellie was not sufficiently glamorized, and that the emphasis placed on her intellect made her an unsympathetic or boring character. At the same time, many lamented that the romance between Ellie and Palmer lacked "chemistry." I would argue that these assertions rest on a discomfort with the role of high intelligence in Foster's star persona, a misreading of the intellectual component of erotic relationships, and critics' difficulty in identifying sexual attraction when it is represented from a female character's point of view.

When *Contact* was released in 1997, Foster had established a reputation as a woman of exceptional intellectual gifts, as both a child acting prodigy and a Yale graduate. Further, in her acting roles, she often played independent and intelligent characters, most notably in her performance as Clarice Starling in *The Silence of the Lambs* (Jonathan Demme, 1991), a character Foster described as a "feminist hero" in her Oscar acceptance speech for Best Actress. With this tradition in mind, Lisa Schwarzbaum's review of *Contact* in *Entertainment Weekly* praises the decision to cast Foster, saying there were "few actresses better suited to the lead role than Jodie Foster, whose rigorous intelligence radiates not only from her cool eyes but practically from her capable fingertips themselves." [14] Other reviewers cited Foster's capacity to exude intelligence, but for many of them, praise for her intellect came at the expense of sympathetic character traits. For example, Todd McCarthy's review in *Variety* praises Foster's performance as "very credible in her projection of innate intelligence, dedication to career and banishment of any personal life." [15] Meanwhile, William Holden in the *New York Times* writes,

> Although Ms. Foster gives a strong, fiercely intelligent portrayal of a driven scientist, her character exhibits little vulnerability. Even when shedding tears, Ellie is shown fighting them back, clenching her jaw, determined to solve the next problem. She never really lets go. [16]

These descriptions of Ellie link her intelligence to a lack of emotional depth, but they disregard the fact that for a woman in Ellie's position, working within predominantly male environments and high-pressure situations, "letting go" or displaying emotional vulnerability could have disastrous results, both practically and professionally—astronauts are not supposed to cry. At the same time, critics' descriptions of Ellie's emotional deficiencies ignore her close friendships, her ongoing love affair, her vivid memories of her father, and her powerful emotional responses throughout the film. Perhaps Ellie's relationships and feelings remain invisible to many critics because they do not conform to the narrow roles and rules for women in mainstream cinema, for unlike most female characters, Ellie's relationships are "about" Ellie, and their purpose in the narrative is to support her subjectivity, rather than to bolster the exploits of male characters.

Many critics had particular difficulty with the film's romantic subplot, and the representation of Ellie's body and sexuality. Rita Kempley's *Washington Post* review slams Foster's performance, and in describing Ellie's relationship with the religious Palmer, she says,

> Foster, who's as tense as Joan of Arc at a weenie roast, comes off as the more devout of the pair. Unconcerned about her appearance, obsessed with Vega, her character is an astro-nun. A lot of work goes into her performance, but the role is not an especially sympathetic or believably human one. [17]

Kempley's choice of Joan of Arc—a military leader and mystic who defied gender expectations in her dress and behavior—to describe Foster's performance, is quite telling of the ways her persona challenges Hollywood norms. First, it connotes Foster's then-closeted, yet widely suspected queer identity, which is an important factor in her resistance to strict gender binaries. Second, the comment about Ellie's lack of concern for her appearance is not only a tired stereotype of women in positions of power, but it also evokes the catch-22 for women in nontraditional fields, who find that expressions of femininity are at once compulsory for, and incompatible with, the job at hand. Indeed, one might wonder what kind of clothing, hair, or makeup choices Kempley would deem appropriate for a scientist who works in the jungle and the desert, or who wishes to be taken seriously at the White House. Finally, to describe Ellie as an "astro-nun" dismisses her sexual appetite and assertiveness, ignoring the fact that she sleeps with Palmer within a few days of meeting him.

While not all critics condemned the romance plot, Roger Ebert described it as a "brief but tender and important love affair," [18] most were resistant to this element of the film, claiming that the actors "fail to generate a single romantic spark." [19] One might argue that part of the appeal of mainstream cinema is its representation of romance, so it behooves critics to comment on its effectiveness in a given film. However, the level of attention devoted to "chemistry" in reviews of *Contact* seems disproportionate, especially in the context of a science fiction film whose primary attraction is arguably its elaborate digital effects sequences. The discernment of chemistry among film characters is, of course, highly subjective, but much of it relies on a set of long-established conventional scenarios, roles, and character interactions. I would argue that critics' difficulty in understanding Ellie and Palmer's relationship stems more from the film's refusal to objectify Ellie's sexuality, and to portray the film's erotic dynamics from her point of view, than any deficiency on the part of the actors' performances.

Contact defies romantic convention from the moment that Ellie and Palmer meet. Palmer approaches Ellie in a cantina near the Arecibo Observatory, and they begin an intense and flirtatious conversation about their respective research projects. In her audio commentary on the DVD of *Contact*, Foster offers an anecdote about the difficulties of shooting this scene, as they had trouble positioning the camera so it did not reflect in her glasses. [20] While Foster shares this detail to illustrate the intricacies of the filming process and Zemeckis's attention to technical detail, it also affirms the importance of this particular wardrobe choice: Ellie does not wear glasses all the time, so an easy fix would be for her to simply take them off. Instead, Ellie's glasses evoke two important traditions, where glasses represent high intellect, and where women's glasses, and their removal, are a means of concealing and revealing female beauty. As Cindy Conaway explains in her essay "'You Can See Things That Other People Can't': Changing Images of the Girl with Glasses, from *Gidget* to *Daria*,"

> More than most other aspects of costume design, they carry a freight that functions as a symbolic shorthand for the entire character. In his-

toric and contemporary mass media, glasses, especially on women, are an indicator of intelligence and the social limits that go with brilliance, and a barrier to sexual availability.[21]

Indeed, in most films, when female characters with glasses manage to enter romantic relationships, they often "surprise" the audience, their partner, and even themselves when they take off their glasses, revealing that they are in fact beautiful, and therefore worthy of sexual attention. *Contact* refuses this dynamic, and instead uses Ellie's glasses to mark her intelligence as anything but a sexual barrier. Palmer's opening line, "Arecibo, right?" makes it clear that he knows she is a scientist, and the more he learns about her scientific work, the more he is attracted to her. While she does take off her glasses as she leaves, it quickly becomes clear that contrary to the tradition of the woman with glasses lacking confidence, Ellie exercises considerable agency in her sexual life. While Palmer makes the first advance, she decides to return his attentions a few days later at a party, where, impressed by his intellect and moral courage in a debate with David, she asks Palmer "You wanna get out of here?" Once they are alone, he states his respect for her wonder at the universe as a foundation of scientific inquiry, and even her suspicions about religion. She sleeps with him in short order.

While both of them are physically beautiful—they are movie stars, after all—their mutual attraction rests largely on their intellectual connection. While such a dynamic is atypical of Hollywood romance, it is quite consistent with characters who are, in fact, intellectuals. Throughout the film, *Contact* continually defies audience expectations about romantic narratives and character motivation. For example, as Ellie prepares to leave Arecibo, she has a final moment in her room, where she looks at the note Palmer has left for her, containing his phone number and a request to "Please call." She then picks up the phone, causing the viewer to assume that she will call him, but instead she calls a colleague to strategize about her research. While the film connects her reluctance to enter a traditional romance with Palmer with her remaining grief over her father's death, it does not pathologize Ellie's personal life. If anything, traditional family bonds prove to be an impediment to space exploration, as one of the American astronauts who is considered for the voyage drops out because he wishes to stay with his family. This sense of family responsibility is more conventionally assigned to women, and often cited as a reason that women are less suitable to adventurous, high-risk careers, but *Contact* presents its female protagonist as willing to embrace a potentially fatal adventure for the sake of intellectual experience.

Rather than presenting Ellie's intellect and sexuality as being at odds with one another, the film allows Ellie to experience and act on her desires for both scientific inquiry and sexual expression, to conduct her relationships on her own terms, and to retain her own subjectivity. Ellie's character is therefore quite consistent with Foster's stated objective to redefine representations of female desire in cinema from a woman's perspective.[22] As Christina Lane explains, "Foster redefines sexuality as a fluid category—not merely as a rigid and confining projection of what men want, but instead as an orchestration of female fantasy and desire."[23] Further, in B. Ruby Rich's essay on Foster, she asserts, "It may be that Jodie Foster, whose position in the world owes so much to her perpetual willingness to take big risks, is preparing for the biggest risk of all: the gamble to fuse an active female sexuality with an equally active female authority."[24] I would argue that the negative critical responses to *Contact*, with their focus on the film's refusal to present a traditional romance, speaks to the effectiveness of Foster's risk taking and her efforts to confound sexist traditions in representing female desire.

In *Contact*, we have a film that proposes crucial revisions to both the science fiction genre and the cinema more broadly by offering a creative space built around the thoughts, feelings, and senses of a female protagonist. While demonstrating an awareness of women's negotiations of traditionally masculine structures of governance, belief, and representation, the film manages to propose new ways of rendering female subjectivity. The film not only valorizes Ellie's intellectual credentials, but it does so in a way that points to new film technologies and their capacity to offer artists new ways of sharing cognitive and emotional experience.

NOTES

1. Stan Link, "Nor the Eye Filled with Seeing: The Sound of Vision in Film," *American Music* 22, no. 1 (Spring 2004): 87.

2. It is interesting to note that when Ellie detects the alien signal, she is sitting on the hood of her car at the edge of a canyon, right next to the radio telescopes at the VLA. In reality, there is no such canyon in the vicinity of the VLA. While artificial landscapes such as these are ubiquitous in cinema, it is significant that the film positions Ellie in an archetypal landscape of the American frontier just as she makes her discovery. For an extended discussion of American frontier traditions in space imagery, see Elizabeth A. Kessler, *Picturing the Cosmos: Hubble Space Telescope Images and the Astronomical Sublime* (Minneapolis: Minnesota University Press, 2012).

3. Zemeckis's film is the product of an unusual adaptation process, as Carl Sagan initially wrote *Contact* as a screenplay, which he then published as a novel. The film that was ultimately produced is really an adaptation of both texts. Many thanks to Renée Lane for sharing her invaluable insights on the novel version of *Contact*.

4. Stacey Abbott, "Final Frontiers: Computer-Generated Imagery and the Science Fiction Film," *Science Fiction Studies* 33, no. 1 (March 2006): 101.

5. Carol Colatrella, "From *Desk Set* to *The Net*: Women and Computing Technology in Hollywood Films," *Canadian Review of American Studies* 31 (2001): 2.

6. Peter Travers, "Contact," *Rolling Stone*, 11 July 1997, http://www.rollingstone.com/movies/reviews/contact-19970711 (accessed 30 May 2013).

7. Jonathan Rosenbaum, "The Human Touch," *Chicago Reader*, 11 July 1997, http://www.jonathanrosenbaum.net/1997/07/the-human-touch (accessed 8 June 2013).

8. Karen Hollinger, *The Actress: Hollywood Acting and the Female Star* (New York: Routledge, 2006), 173.

9. Christina Lane, "The Liminal Iconography of Jodie Foster," *Journal of Popular Film & Television* 22, no. 4 (1995): 149.

10. Lane, "Liminal Iconography," 151.

11. Marie Lathers, *Space Oddities: Women and Outer Space in Popular Film and Culture, 1960-2000* (New York: Continuum, 2010), 196.

12. Lowe's performance is ironic in large part because of infamy stemming from a 1989 scandal where he appeared in a sex tape with an underage girl.

13. For a detailed discussion of the sexual personae of female scientists in cinema, see Bonnie Noonan, *Women Scientists in Fifties Science Fiction Films* (Jefferson, NC: McFarland, 2005).

14. Lisa Schwarzbaum, "Contact," *Entertainment Weekly*, 18 July 1997, http://www.ew.com/ew/article/0,,288679,00.html (accessed 12 November 2013)

15. Todd McCarthy, "Review: 'Contact,'" *Variety*, 7 July 1997, http://variety.com/1997/film/reviews/contact-2-1117341257 (accessed 30 May 2013).

16. Stephen Holden, "Contact," *New York Times*, 11 July 1997, http://www.nytimes.com/library/film/contact-film-review.html (accessed 5 June 2013).

17. Rita Kempley, "'Contact': Endless Orbit Follows Spectacular Launch," *Washington Post*, 11 July 1997, http://www.washingtonpost.com/wp-srv/style/longterm/movies/review97/contactkempley.htm (accessed 12 November 2013).

18. Roger Ebert, "Contact," *Chicago Sun-Times*, 11 July 1997, http://www.rogerebert.com/reviews/contact-1997 (accessed 5 June 2013).

19. Holden, "Contact."

20. Jodie Foster, audio commentary, *Contact: Special Edition*, directed by Robert Zemeckis (1997; Burbank, CA: Warner Home Video, 1997), DVD.

21. Cindy Conaway, "'You Can See Things That Other People Can't': Changing Images of the Girl with Glasses, from *Gidget* to *Daria*," in *Geek Chic: Smart Women in Popular Culture*, ed. Sherrie A. Inness (New York: Palgrave, 2007), 49.

22. Lane, "Liminal Iconography," 153.

23. Lane, "Liminal Iconography," 153.

24. B. Ruby Rich, "Never a Victim: Jodie Foster, and New Kind of Female Hero," in *Women and Film: A Sight and Sound Reader*, ed. Pam Cook and Philip Dodd (Philadelphia: Temple University Press, 1993), 61.

BIBLIOGRAPHY

Abbott, Stacey. "Final Frontiers: Computer-Generated Imagery and the Science Fiction Film." *Science Fiction Studies* 33, no. 1 (2006): 89-108.

Colatrella, Carol. "From *Desk Set* to *The Net*: Women and Computing Technology in Hollywood Films." *Canadian Review of American Studies* 31 (2001): 1-14.

Conaway, Cindy. "'You Can See Things That Other People Can't': Changing Images of the Girl with Glasses, from *Gidget* to *Daria*." In *Geek Chic: Smart Women in Popular Culture*, edited by Sherrie A. Inness, 49-63. New York: Palgrave, 2007.

Ebert, Roger. "Contact." *Chicago Sun-Times*. 11 July 1997. http://www.rogerebert.com/reviews/contact-1997 (accessed 5 June 2013).

Foster, Jodie. Audio commentary. *Contact: Special Edition*. Directed by Robert Zemeckis. 1997. Burbank, CA: Warner Home Video, 1997. DVD.

Holden, Stephen. "Contact." *New York Times*. 11 July 1997. http://www.nytimes.com/library/film/contact-film-review.html (accessed 5 June 2013).

Hollinger, Karen. *The Actress: Hollywood Acting and the Female Star*. New York: Routledge, 2006.

Kempley, Rita. "'Contact': Endless Orbit Follows Spectacular Launch." *Washington Post*. 11 July 1997. http://www.washingtonpost.com/wp-srv/style/longterm/movies/review97/contactkempley.htm (accessed 12 November 2013).

Kessler, Elizabeth A. *Picturing the Cosmos: Hubble Space Telescope Images and the Astronomical Sublime*. Minneapolis: Minnesota University Press, 2012.

Lane, Christina. "The Liminal Iconography of Jodie Foster." *Journal of Popular Film & Television* 22, no. 4 (1995): 149-53.

Lathers, Marie. *Space Oddities: Women and Outer Space in Popular Film and Culture, 1960-2000.* New York: Continuum, 2010.

Link, Stan. "Nor the Eye Filled with Seeing: The Sound of Vision in Film." *American Music* 22, no. 1 (2004): 76-90.

McCarthy, Todd. "Review: 'Contact.'" *Variety,* 7 July 1997. http://variety.com/1997/film/reviews/contact-2-1117341257 (accessed 30 May 2013).

Message from Space. Directed by Lee Sholem. Family Films Inc., 1966. 16mm.

Noonan, Bonnie. *Women Scientists in Fifties Science Fiction Films.* Jefferson, NC: McFarland, 2005.

Rich, B. Ruby. "Never a Victim: Jodie Foster, and New Kind of Female Hero." In *Women and Film: A Sight and Sound Reader,* edited by Pam Cook and Philip Dodd, 50-61. Philadelphia: Temple University Press, 1993.

Rosenbaum, Jonathan. "The Human Touch." *Chicago Reader,* 11 July 1997. http://www.jonathanrosenbaum.net/1997/07/the-human-touch (accessed 8 June 2013).

Schwarzbaum, Lisa. "Contact." *Entertainment Weekly,* 18 July 1997. http://www.ew.com/ew/article/0,,288679,00.html (accessed 12 November 2013).

Travers, Peter. "Contact." *Rolling Stone,* 11 July 1997. http://www.rollingstone.com/movies/reviews/contact-19970711 (accessed 30 May 2013).

SIX

Mad Men's Peggy Olson

A Prefeminist Champion in a Postfeminist TV Landscape

Stefania Marghitu

Mad Men (2007–present), an AMC original television series, depicts a sleek Manhattan agency during the 1960s golden age of advertising. Upon the show's premiere, audiences and critics initially praised the stunning re-creation of a bygone era dominated by the overtly sexist, racist, xenophobic, and anti-Semitic Madison Avenue executives. Beyond the men's philandering, chain-smoking, and bourbon-indulging proclivities, *Mad Men* is very much about its female characters. Although protagonist Don Draper (Jon Hamm) always resides at the forefront of the storyline, his former secretary turned copywriter Peggy Olson (Elisabeth Moss) is the series' true heroine, and likely one of the greatest feminist characters in television history. Peggy's narrative evokes Second Wave feminism and challenges what postfeminist television often fails to show: a woman actively participating in the workplace who is chiefly identified as a professional, and does not suffer from not pursuing traditional gender roles.

This chapter explores how *Mad Men* portrays Peggy in a prefeminist culture from the perspective of a present-day, postfeminist television landscape. I will first briefly chronicle feminism and postfeminism. For the purposes of this chapter, *prefeminism* will refer to the 1960s era on the verge of Second Wave feminism, as illustrated in *Mad Men*. Considered a precursor to this movement, Betty Friedan's 1963 book *The Feminine Mystique* stated that college-educated suburban housewives required more in their lives to achieve fulfillment than their roles as mothers and wives.[1]

Praising the working women of the 1930s and 1940s who thrived in male-dominated professions, she writes that upon the end of World War II, women retreated to the domestic sphere or to jobs based on gender expectations instead of their potential.[2]

Feminism, therefore, relates here to a set of goals laid out in 1966, when Friedan wrote the National Organization for Women's Statement of Purpose, summarizing the goals to "take action to bring women into full participation in the mainstream of American society now, exercising all the privileges and responsibilities thereof in truly equal partnership with men."[3] Workplace equality was a strong pillar of the movement, and, as Friedan stated, "we do not accept the traditional assumption that a woman has to choose between marriage and motherhood, on the one hand, and serious participation in industry or the professions on the other."[4] She also claimed that the importance of childbearing and rearing was still "used to justify barring women from equal professional and economic participation in advance."[5] In this Second Wave context, this chapter emphasizes the obstacles women must tackle when striving for workplace equality.

I regard postfeminism as an era beginning in the 1980s when cautionary tales of Second Wave feminism emerged in the mainstream media and press, as it is best chronicled in Susan Faludi's 1992 book *Backlash: The Undeclared War against American Women*.[6] One of the biggest critiques of Second Wave feminism was its alleged "overlooking and denigrating [of] the primacy of motherhood in women's lives."[7] Reactions against the movement led to "the disturbing postfeminist retreat from sexual politics to a more conservative pro-family vision."[8] Faludi declared that postfeminism was first used in the popular press of the 1920s, which declared First Wave feminism was no longer necessary when women were granted suffrage.[9] Friedan claimed that while women could vote, they hardly attempted to actively participate in politics.[10] Despite subsequent (if too meager) advances in this realm, the current postfeminist climate still faces the same problems, revealing a continuous pattern within feminist movements.

In *Mad Men*, Peggy proudly rises from the steno pool to become the first female copywriter for the company since World War II. She is constantly contrasted with head secretary/office manager Joan Holloway (Christina Hendricks), and to a lesser extent suburban housewife Betty Draper (January Jones). As articulated in Mimi White's essay "Mad Women," Peggy suffered in seasons 1–3 when the other women of the series were "more sophisticated and calculating, and more apt to use feminine wiles to get what they want."[11] White concluded that although Peggy did not make any gains from her passive sexuality, Joan did not necessarily benefit from her active sexuality, as she is not treated seriously as a professional. Much to the chagrin of both the female secretaries and male advertising executives, Peggy breaks expectations by excelling in advertising as a copywriter, eventually becoming a copy chief. When her professional success is on display, it often coincides with the disappointments of Betty, and particularly those of her co-worker Joan, due to their generation's reliance on traditional gender roles and dependency on men for fulfillment and purpose.

Seasons 4–6 of *Mad Men*, set in the mid to late 1960s right on the heels of Second Wave feminism, shifted from an emphasis on Betty to a detailed representation of the "mad women" within the workplace. Punctuated by the subsequent downfall of Don, these three seasons reflect a period in history that challenged the dominance of privileged white males. As a series in the "post-network era"[12] that heralded AMC's original programming success, *Mad Men* is also rare in the canon of feminist television criticism because it is not explicitly female centered or geared toward female audiences. *Mad Men* thus exposes feminist themes to an audience that may not be inherently interested in women's rights.

The now infamous pilot episode illustrates the sexual harassment and ingrained misogyny that Peggy encounters on her first day at Sterling Cooper. Freshly graduated from secretarial school, Peggy is initially seen in an elevator while a group of twenty-something ad executives provide less than subtle commentary on her looks. As senior secretary, or as she coins it later in season 1, "office manager," Joan gives her a welcoming tour, implying that the position functions as a step toward finding a husband, encouraging Peggy that "of course if you really make the right moves, you'll be out in the country, and you won't be going to work at all." The secretary job is described as "something between a mother and a waitress, and the rest of the time, well," and Joan gives a sly smile. She then unveils a typewriter, telling the new girl to not grow overwhelmed as the men who built it made it "simple enough for a woman to use." Sexism is thus embedded not only in the men of the office, but also in its women who believe they are not equally capable or intelligent because of their gender. The secretary position is not deemed worthy of a viable career or chance to progress as a professional, but as a stepping-stone to marriage and motherhood. By season 1, episode 2, "Ladies Room," Peggy renounces the junior ad men's relentless sexual advances and expresses her frustration to Joan, who responds, "You're the new girl, and you're not much, so you might as well enjoy it while it lasts." From the onset of the series, Joan takes advantage of her sexuality and femininity in a male-dominated workplace, while Peggy is reluctant to follow suit.

Despite its attention to period details, *Mad Men* serves as more of a critique on contemporary culture, suggesting that feminism is buried in a postfeminist society. Feminist TV scholars have already excelled in identifying the most important issues, themes, and representations in contemporary programming. In her 2006 book *Redesigning Women: Television after the Network Era*, Amanda Lotz describes the two dominant narratives about working women displayed in postfeminist TV. The first portrays

Joan (Christina Hendricks, left) and Peggy (Elisabeth Moss, right) clash over their views of a woman's role in the office in season 1, episode 2, "Ladies Room."

women pursuing "a liberal feminist agenda" by assimilating into male-dominated work environments, yet these shows suggest "women are ill-suited for professional roles or could not be both mothers and career women."[13] The second narrative represents women who could handle this balance effortlessly, yet these series "rarely [tell] stories about women doing work, despite attempting to associate themselves with the progressive trend of depicting women as qualified to work outside the home."[14] Further, Elana Levine's chapter in the 2013 edited collection *How to Watch Television*, "*Grey's Anatomy*: Feminism," argues how a standard of glorifying traditional gender roles becomes problematic:

> In this sort of "postfeminist" mindset, either feminism is identified as the cause of women's problems, in that the movement's embrace of women taking on greater professional roles purportedly failed to account for how to fit a personal life within such accomplishments, or feminism has succeeded so well that it no longer applied.[15]

The chapter goes on to describe how the hit medical series created by Shonda Rhimes, *Grey's Anatomy* (ABC, 2005–present), establishes a feminist fantasy of successful career women who often prioritize their professional goals over their romantic pursuits. This does not render them unfulfilled or undesirable by suitors. Within this fantasy, women and minorities hardly ever face prejudices or obstacles based on their societal limitations. Both Lotz and Levine cite *Ally McBeal* (Fox, 1997–2002) and

Sex and the City (HBO, 1998–2004) as popular series that depicted success-ful yet unfulfilled career women who were primarily concerned with their roles as girlfriends, potential wives, or consumers.

Peggy's narrative provides an unprecedented exploration of a career woman who rises through the ranks and achieves fulfillment through professional success. Although her love life is not as active the characters of *Grey's Anatomy*, *Ally McBeal*, or *Sex in the City*, she does not lament over her concerns as a girlfriend or potential wife and mother. In relation to negotiating work and traditional expectations, Joan's position is indic-ative of both prefeminist 1960s and early 2000s postfeminism. Historian Stephanie Coontz postulates that *Mad Men* is television's most feminist series because it reveals the abilities of its women characters, yet they never exceed beyond the parameters of the time.[16] She writes, "We should be glad that the writers are resisting the temptation to transform their female characters into contemporary heroines. They're not, and they cannot be."[17] *Mad Men* frequently exposes the state of modern-day wom-en who still face inequality in the workplace. In 1966, women's average national salaries quantified to 60 percent of men's. In 2010, women earned 81.2 percent of men's wages.[18] The series asserts the blurred lines between the past and present when dealing with discrimination in the workplace, revealing how complicated it is for a woman to advance in a male-dominated setting.

The series' predominantly female team of writers, which includes Lisa Albert, Marti Noxon, Katie Gordon, Cathryn Humphris, and Maria Jac-quemetton, aim to show the lack of progression in equality for working women, suggesting copywriters in the golden age of advertising are not far from TV writers in the new golden age of TV.[19] While TV auteurs in the form of show runners such as *Mad Men*'s Matthew Weiner often receive critical praise, the writers uncover the parallels between male-dominated creative workplaces in the prefeminist 1960s and postfeminist 2000s. As executive story editor Robin Veith informed, "It's less a prod-uct of the decade than viewers might think. The truth is that a lot of these moments that seem period and horrible for women come directly from experiences that I and the other women writers have had in our life-time."[20]

Peggy is first valued for her intellect and potential to serve as more than a secretary in season 1, episode 6, "Babylon." The women of the office participate in a focus group on lipsticks when the male creative team is at a loss for ideas. Middle-aged advertising executive Freddy Rumsen (Joel Murray) says he does not "speak moron" and suggests they "throw it to the chickens." Joan happily organizes the focus group as it reinforces her position as the alpha female amongst her inferiors. Peggy immediately stands out due to her lack of frivolity while the executives watch the women behind a one-way mirror. Joan, fully aware of her audience, flaunts her body for the men. When the group ends, Peggy brings the tissues full of lipstick imprints to Freddy, stating, "Here's your basket of kisses." He later acknowledges that Peggy created the ad campaign, exclaiming that "it was like watching a dog play the piano." When Joan informs Peggy that Freddy wants her to write copy for the cosmetic account, she is stunned. Joan mocks this pseudo-promotion, offered without a raise but entailing "more work and more responsibility," though she notes there may be entitlement to dinner money. Earnest Peggy replies unsurprisingly, "That's swell." Freddy, Joan, and Peggy are all seemingly shocked over Peggy's ability, yet treat it as an anomaly of little consequence or impact.

By season 2, episode 6, "Maidenform," Peggy is no longer a secretary, but a copywriter, yet she lacks the privileges that her male colleagues enjoy. Not privy to the out-of-office client meetings and internal memos, she asks Joan why she is not included in these communications:

Joan: I don't have your job. I never wanted it. You're in their country. Learn to speak the language.

Peggy: You don't talk that way.

Joan: I don't need to. And honestly, you've never listened to a word I've said. You want to be taken seriously? Stop dressing like a little girl.

Peggy stands out from her fellow secretaries during a focus group in season 1, episode 6, "Babylon," and is soon "discovered" based on her creative talents.

Joan yet again believes that success primarily equates to obtaining an external image. While she grows to resent Peggy for abandoning her secretarial position for a "man's job," as Joan clearly wishes to carry on creative work. In season 2, episode 8, "A Night to Remember," she handles a brief assignment to evaluate a series of television scripts. Joan brings them home and exuberantly details her new assignment to her fiancé, who replies that he assumed her job consisted of walking around while the office stares at her. He is visibly disgruntled as her task leads the couple to eat Chinese takeout rather than a usual home-cooked meal. He discourages Joan's recent development because it implies her subsequent disregard for her duties as a wife, which will soon become her only job when she is married. Later, her new role is assigned to a less-qualified male worker, and she rarely attempts to step outside of her margins again. These instances that show Joan's eagerness toward creative rather than clerical work are significant, suggesting that she is fully capable and desires to partake in it, despite the restrictions imposed on her at work and at home.

The contrasts between Joan and Peggy escalate as the series progresses, in which Joan's secretarial position remains largely the same and Peggy breaks new ground in the creative department. In season 2, episode 12, "The Mountain King," Peggy asks leading partner Roger (John Slattery) for Freddy's vacated office. He agrees, commenting, "You young women are very aggressive." When Peggy apologizes for her impoliteness, he jokes, "No, it's cute. There are thirty men out there who didn't have the balls to ask me." Immediately after, Joan arrives to introduce her successful and good-looking fiancé. In one of the most devastating scenes in the entire series, her future husband rapes her in Don's office. The following morning, Peggy moves in to her new office next door to Don's and behind Joan's desk. Joan offers cordial congratulations to Peggy, who thanks her and comments on how handsome her fiancé is, and Joan describes his many accomplishments. Peggy asks when the wedding will take place, but their small talk is cut off as a group of copywriters arrive and become befuddled and envious of their female cohort's new office. As soon as they disperse, Joan tells her the wedding will be during Christmas, but Peggy has already lost interest. Joan eventually goes through with the marriage despite his brutal treatment. In the 1960s, rape was not illegal if it occurred between a cohabitated or married couple. Even with the necessary advancements since then, it remains the most underreported crime in the United States today.[21]

For her work carried out in seasons 1 and 2, Peggy is enlisted to take on campaigns for women's products for her insight into feminine subjects, yet these accounts are never for the high-profile clients. In most cases, those clients only wish to deal with fellow men. As the series begins to highlight single working women in the city in season 4, the reformed agency of Sterling Cooper Draper Pryce (SCDP) also explores this demographic. Just as Betty's role diminishes after season 3, the agency deemphasizes the role of the housewife consumer who purchases cleaning products, groceries, and other basic family amenities. Therefore, a "new woman" figure emerges, yet she is not yet separated from traditional gender expectations. Season 4, episode 4, "The Rejected," represents the various workplace shifts since the first focus group in season 1, episode 6, "Babylon," as well as the differences in new career women and traditional secretaries.

In season 4, episode 2, "Christmas Comes but Once a Year," Peggy argues with Freddy, who returns to the company for the first time since season 2, over how to sell Pond's Cold Cream. She favors an approach that enhances "the experience of putting it on, looking in the mirror" and "indulging yourself." Freddy counters that "if young girls started using it, maybe they could find a husband and stop being so angry." An infuriated and offended Peggy calls the man who first discovered her talent "old-fashioned." The company continues with her indulgence proposal by conducting a new focus group. As a sharp contrast to the previous group held in season 1, Peggy is accepted as a leader of the creative team, and her ideas are valued and put forth over Freddy's seemingly antiquated suggestion.

New psychologist and marketing expert Faye Miller (Cara Buono) directs the group to study the eighteen- to twenty-five-year-old single women demographic of the cream, testing Peggy's hypothesis on the office secretaries. Faye is depicted as educated and successful as well as blonde and beautiful, as she is involved in a secret affair with the series' prime Lothario, Don. In "Babylon," a middle-aged German female psychologist served as a company consultant, and the male ad executives compared her to a man. This transition reveals that the revamped company, SCDP, is now confronted with attractive, feminine women who are also intelligent and can excel in male-dominated areas. Faye, who only appears in season 4, represents a career woman depicted in television whose struggles are rarely shown. However, her extreme professionalism suggests a lack of empathy that Peggy still values along with her ambitions. For example, when Peggy asks Faye about a secretary, Dottie, who sobs during the focus group, the psychologist is only concerned with the experiment's results, not the possible emotional repercussions it triggered. In season 4, episode 9, "Beautiful Girls," Faye shows a rare vulnerability when she reveals that her difficulty with children is rooted in her choice to have both a career and an advanced degree.

During the group, Faye attempts to decode the beauty rituals of the secretaries while Peggy, Freddy, and Don watch the experiment from another one-way mirror. She evokes a response from Dottie, the most susceptible focus group member, who laments over how she was never beautiful enough for her ex-boyfriend. Peggy's indulgence approach ultimately fails, as the secretaries are generally not concerned with how beauty products make them feel about their own self-worth, but how they can help them keep a man. As the focus group concludes, Freddy smirks, victoriously boasting, "My strategy was right. All they want to do is get married, and they'll buy anything to help." Dottie becomes the embodiment of the insecure female consumer unable to find fulfillment outside of male approval. Although a small percentage of women like Peggy and Faye stand outside the standard secretary/consumer, the majority's compliance with Freddy's hypothesis shows how progress can be limited by traditional expectations based on beauty and relationships. Furthermore, the advertising agency setting also reveals how little has changed in contemporary postfeminist marketing strategies, and how the pleasures of consumerism often denote women's self-fulfillment.

Despite the failure of Peggy's innovative strategy rooted in individual gratification, she is ahead of her time for suggesting this tactic. As a young professional with her own income and no marital ambitions, she suggests the company pitch a product in correlation to the immediate benefits for a woman. This refers to the concept of being satisfied as a woman without having to consider how a man could control her self-perception. By stressing women's own gratification with Pond's, Peggy's strategy prefigures Second Wave feminist ideology privileging a woman's independence; it implies a desire to disregard the reliance on a feminine identity defined by men.

With feminism slowly ascending to the mainstream by the 1970s, companies began to target a new demographic of single working women with disposable incomes, with an example being the viewers of *The Mary Tyler Moore Show* (1970–1977). Centered on one of the first career women on American television, the series' pilot sees its protagonist starting a promising job as a producer at a television news station after breaking off her engagement. It details the benefits of Mary's professional choices and her rewarding life in the city with her cantankerous new family at her workplace, yet she does not struggle with explicit sexism or inequalities. Mary is depicted as happily single, social, and professionally successful. She also uses birth control and enjoys the company of men. Peggy, the first female copywriter for SCDP since World War II, represents the working women of the 1930s and 1940s, who retreated to the home once their male counterparts returned from combat. These are the women that Friedan commends in *The Feminine Mystique* for their capabilities, and Peggy's professional trajectory also foreshadows the career woman model that Mary Tyler Moore first personified, and was later prevailed in series such as *Cagney and Lacey* (1981–1988), *Designing Women* (1986–1993), and *Murphy Brown* (1988–1998).

It is highly important that the series shows Peggy as attractive to many men around her, as she is a part of several romantic flirtations, flings, and partnerships. Although her workaholic nature can interfere with her relationships, her position does not prohibit her from intimacy.

In season 4, Peggy meets a potential love interest, Abe (Charlie Hofheimer), a handsome yet fumbling left-leaning journalist who refers to the African American civil rights movement as "an inequality the world has its eyes on." Peggy replies that she is not a political person. She insists that she is frequently denied the same rights as African Americans, citing that she cannot be a member of the private men's clubs where most advertising executives hold their meetings. Abe condescendingly replies, "All right Peggy, we'll have a civil rights march for women." She soon leaves their first date, realizing his ignorance to her situation. *Mad Men* has frequently revealed that even the most liberal individuals of the 1960s retained a sexist attitude, as Abe only mockingly predicts the imminent women's liberation movement. As the only female copywriter she knows of, Peggy remains unaware that her situation is not what Ellen Riordan describes as "the unique responsibility of each individual woman, rather than a basic social dilemma which society must solve." [22] In a prefeminist era, Peggy is oblivious to the larger political implications of her seemingly personal situation.

Season 5, episode 11, "The Other Woman," focuses on the options women have in advancing their careers. It also represents how "Woman" functions as "The Other." This episode demonstrates Peggy as the most triumphant of *Mad Men's* leading women for demanding to be taken seriously based on her mind rather than relying on using her body or men to advance. As it centers on the newly downsized ad firm striving to land a big client, the prospect of securing the lucrative car company Jaguar is much more about the women of SCDP than its men. "The Other Woman" begins while the entire creative team (without its second in command to Don, Peggy) continues to slack in their preparation for the Jaguar pitch, accomplishing no actual work. Don has placed Peggy in control of all the other accounts as he spearheads the sought-after campaign. Despite her consistent success with products geared toward both men and women, her superiors attest that clients such as Jaguar and Mohawk Airlines do not wish to hire a female copywriter, even if she is the most experienced of the group. We see over Peggy's shoulder as she gazes at the male copywriters through the clear glass surrounding of the conference room; they are provided a sumptuous lunch of lobsters and caviar for their mere participation in the high-profile car campaign. Then in an eye-line match, we see Peggy on the outside looking in, with Don's silhouette reflected on Peggy. She is now visibly "in his shadows," unable to step out on her own in this environment. She is also literally and figuratively unable to break down the "glass ceiling," a term coined in 1987 to describe the invisible barriers women in corporate America face in terms of advancement and equal pay. [23]

She later saves a campaign by proposing a new commercial idea on the spot. When Don suggests her male inferior fly to Paris for the filming instead of her, she exposes the injustice: "I guess I'm not in charge of everything." Her responsibilities are not high priority. She organizes various small-scale campaigns and is never rewarded financially or with respect commensurate to her male colleagues. When Peggy struggles to be assertive and ambitious, the office views her as "pushy," while her male colleagues' aggression is construed as ambition. In psychological studies of contemporary workplaces, women who step outside of typically female-oriented fields or positions encounter similar struggles when it comes to assertiveness and success.[24] This demeaning situation ultimately leads Peggy to pursue a new career outside of SCDP.

Throughout the professional developments of Peggy and Joan in season 4, Peggy succeeds due to her intellect while Joan advances due to her attractiveness. Peggy's romantic life evolves while Joan's marriage ends, as she finally rejects her husband's cruelty. When Peggy first meets with a rival agency in "The Other Woman," she curls her hair, wears bright pink lipstick, and pairs a blue and orange scarf with a matching, color-coordinated dress with a plunging V-neck. Yet her future boss is only interested in her talent, stating that other potential employers will first ask if she will soon become married or pregnant, knowing this will end a woman's career. At this point, she is living with her now boyfriend Abe, yet the episode does not include him, choosing to stress the importance of her professional advancement over her romantic progression. In season 5, episode 5, "Far Away Places," the introductory scene opens with Peggy and Abe's dispute over her workaholic tendencies; her boyfriend states most men would leave when they are placed second. In the following episode, "At the Codfish Ball," she fears he might end their relationship, but Joan suggests he will propose. He instead hopes they will move in together, to the disappointment of her conservative Catholic mother. When Peggy returns to tell Joan, she states that marriage is just a piece of paper, and Joan agrees to its banality when she remarks on her husband's newfound loyalty to the military above their marriage. Joan suffers as a divorced single mother. For Peggy, living with her mate is less of a sacrifice than the potential consequences of marriage, and further indicates how her modern take on work and relationships benefits both her personal and professional life. In *Mad Men*, Betty's and Joan's marriages are revealed as both personal and professional entrapments, as they must first adhere to their duties as wives. Betty quits her lucrative modeling career upon marrying Don, and Joan quits her job when she is first wed, but she eventually returns when her husband cannot fully provide for the both of them.

During the meeting, Peggy's future employer offers her a salary of $19,000 for her position as copy chief, approximately $133,000 by today's standard according to the United States Bureau of Labor Statistics Inflation Calculator.[25] With her new salary, she is not only a minority in the 1960s, but also in the twenty-first century. Peggy previously mentions the Equal Pay Act of 1963 (season 3, episode 5, "The Fog") when she asks for a raise to match the salary of her male peers. Don rejects the request, aware that he does not have to legally abide by the act, which is still the case today with the gender pay income gap.

In Jennifer Allyn's editorial for *Forbes Woman* online, the corporate managing director for PricewaterhouseCoopers LLP urges the next generation of women to view Peggy's success as an inspiration to "break new ground, only this time instead of leaping from the steno pool to junior copywriter as Peggy did, they need to ascend from middle management to the executive suite."[26] According to Allyn, the Second Wave goal of not accepting the "token appointment of a few women to high-level positions in government and industry as a substitute for serious continuing effort to recruit and advance women according to their individual abilities" has yet to be accomplished in American society.[27]

In her closing scenes at SCDP, Peggy reaches for a handshake after she gives Don her formal resignation. This leads to a close-up of Don's farewell through a prolonged, passionate kiss on her hand. This gesture represents that for Don, Peggy is first and foremost a woman who was initially his secretary, and only secondly a professional. With this departure, her success is no longer contingent upon her association with Don. In season 4, episode 7, "The Suitcase," she revealed to Don that her male peers accuse her of sleeping with him to advance her career. Peggy personifies the rise of both women and youth, and her absence will be a difficult loss for her former company, which previously devalued a woman's creative input. In this same episode, Joan also advances, becoming the only female partner at SCDP. However, she does not reach this position for her intellect or talent, but rather for agreeing to have sex with a Jaguar employee who told the company it was the only way they could do business together. Once again, the contrast between Joan advancing due to her sexuality and Peggy for her intellect is illuminated.

Peggy is also most emblematic of Second Wave feminist ideology through her drive for women's solidarity. In season 5, episode 4, "Mystery Date," she even attempts to transcend racial borders when she invites co-worker Dawn to stay with her upon discovering that the African American secretary has been sleeping in the office due to fear of race riots in the city. The two engage in an honest and friendly conversation:

Dawn: I was gonna say, I hope you won't tell Mr. Draper about me sleeping there. You two talk sometimes.

Peggy: Nah. We have to stick together. I know we're not really in the same situation, but I was the only one like me there for a long time. I know it's hard.

Dawn: I appreciate that.

Peggy: Do you want to be a copywriter?

Dawn: No, I like my job.

Peggy: Yep. You're right. Copywriter's tough. Especially for a woman. . . . Do you think I act like a man?

Dawn: I guess you have to, a little . . .

Peggy: I try, but . . . I don't know if I have it in me. I don't know if I want to.

Peggy is uncertain of how to succeed in her career without "acting like a man" because of the lack of precedent of successful career women she encounters in her profession. Her attempt at female unity is tainted by bad judgment on her part as she says good night. She pauses at the thought of leaving Dawn alone in her living room with her purse on the coffee table, after rejoicing earlier that she was recently given a large sum of cash. The only thing more casual than the sexism in *Mad Men* is racism, and Peggy's attempt at solidarity ultimately fails because of this unconscious attitude. Dawn becomes noticeably aware of her potential confidante's actions, and Peggy cannot hide it when she uses the excuse of throwing away empty bottles. In the morning, she discovers Dawn's note placed on top of her purse, in which she curtly thanks her for her hospitality and apologizes for the inconvenience. Peggy's undeniable guilt and regret still makes her an anomaly for her time, understanding the need to make connections between other women in her workplace, and not wishing to have made such a foolish prejudice based on race.

Peggy is able to succeed in a man's world when it comes to her career, but the pre–Second Wave era, along with contemporary postfeminism, proves to be a difficult environment for women to unite as minorities in a patriarchal society. Therefore the connection between Peggy and Joan not only shows the subtle differences in generations when it comes to career opportunities, but also a complicated relationship between them as the women negotiate their patriarchal surroundings. Peggy fails in one of her most feminist actions at the office in taking on sexual harassment and showing support for Joan. In season 4, episode 8, "The Summer Man," a freelance copywriter continually makes lewd jokes at Joan's expense, showing no remorse. Peggy is given permission by Don to fire him, and she is both surprised by her own authority and determined to reprimand the wrongdoer. Peggy hopes Joan will appreciate her efforts, but Joan tells Peggy, "No matter how powerful we get around here, it doesn't matter because they can still draw a cartoon. So you just proved I'm another meaningless secretary and you're a humorless bitch." Joan also suggests that a dinner date with a client could have produced the same results with less dramatics, showing once again how she handles situations through her own strengths. Joan's strategy shows how her individual charm can solve her own problems, while Peggy's stance hopes to make an example and set a precedent for unacceptable and inappropriate behavior. This represents a strong generational divide between Joan in her early thirties and the twenty-something Peggy, who will benefit from, and also perhaps contribute the most to, the forthcoming Second Wave feminist movement. She actively acknowledges the copywriter's act as a punishable offense in the workplace, preceding Second Wave feminism's attempt to define and convict sexual harassment.

By the latter part of season 4 and up to season 6, Joan and Peggy begin to form a friendship and a sense of mutual respect, exemplified in the season 4 finale, "Tomorrowland," as they discuss how Don's engagement overshadowed Joan's recent promotion that does not include any financial benefits, as well as Peggy's victory of landing the first new account for the agency in several months. By season 6, Joan attempts to spearhead an Avon campaign with Peggy as her creative partner, signaling a potential new era of women in command of their own careers as well as expressing the desires of women consumers. However, Joan suffers when she endeavors to bypass the systematic rules of business in order to gain control of the account. When Peggy saves her from a fatal error in the process, Joan's humble appreciation further ushers in a chance for cooperation between the former adversaries. Despite the abundance of obstacles she faces, Peggy never retreats and rarely compromises. With her new position as copy chief, she finally achieves the career advancement that her talents should have earned her long before.[28] The feminist goal of the series is further divulged when Joan is a cautionary tale in the narrative of social limitations that result in a reliance of traditional gender roles.

Season 5 ends with series protagonist Don Draper coming to terms with women on the verge of Second Wave feminism, although the movement has yet to be discussed in the series. We first see what SCDP is like without Peggy in the season 5 finale, "The Phantom." A group of pantyhose clients express dissatisfaction with a new pitch and protest that they initially signed on with the company for a woman's point of view, which is now clearly absent. The men of SCDP are now no longer able to articulate the needs of female consumers through campaigns based on traditional expectations. The next scene shows Peggy as the new copy chief of an agency, yelling at a young team of male copywriters. Throughout the series, Peggy aims to emulate Don and "act like a man" to survive in the workplace, as there is no precedent for being an assertive woman and leader without a "masculine mindset." She later runs into Don at a cinema and expresses her satisfaction of a future business trip to Virginia, even though it is not Paris. Although she earned a substantial promotion, Peggy's new position shows the everyday struggles that both career men and women encounter. She has also yet to develop her own identity as a new leader. Yet for the first time, Don and Peggy are equals, meeting as two creative directors from rivaling advertising agencies.

Season 6 begins with Peggy as the creative head with a new boss who values her talent. By episode 6, "For Immediate Release," her former and current superiors decide to merge agencies. Her new boss, Ted, proclaims, "You are the copy chief at one of the top twenty-five ad agencies in the country, and you're not even thirty. I'm jealous!" Don and Ted ask Peggy to write the press release announcing the new company, as she is the only nonpartner who is informed of the news. She returns to clerical tasks and the former work environment that limited her abilities, yet this time she is more equipped to negotiate her role as a valued employee. *Mad Men* illustrates the experiences of contemporary women who must make difficult choices in their personal and professional lives at the expense of understanding the struggles of Second Wave feminism in terms of workplace equality. In her 2012 cover story for the *Atlantic*, "Why Women Still Can't Have It All," Anne-Marie Slaughter's only television/ pop culture reference is as follows:

> I owe my own freedoms and opportunities to the pioneering genera-
> tion of women ahead of me—the women now in their 60s, 70s, and 80s
> who faced overt sexism of a kind I only see when watching *Mad Men*,
> and who knew that the only way to make it as a woman was to act
> exactly like a man.[29]

Slaughter writes that both women and men cannot "have it all" during this critical juncture in American history, and a close viewing of *Mad Men* makes clear how much of the past is present within the today's postfeminist society.

Throughout the series, Peggy has been compared to other women, but another strong contrast is between her and Don. When he is aloof and absent, Peggy often takes control of a campaign and shines. Season 6 ends with Don's professional and personal downfall, when his fellow partners ask that he take a leave of absence and his wife threatens to leave him. However, he begins to show honesty with his children, leading to a hopeful conclusion for the series' principal protagonist and antihero. Peggy is heartbroken by her former boss, who moves to California to repair his marriage, yet as a consequence, she is given Don's position. In essence, this demonstrates that during the 1960s, while women like Peggy achieved success against the odds, men like Don often crumbled amidst a tumultuous and altering era. We last see her sitting in Don's office chair, clearly foreshadowing her next step as a leader.

With *Mad Men*'s final season beginning in 2014 and concluding in 2015, the series finale will likely prove that both men and women cannot have it all by the end of the 1960s, just as Slaughter suggested they cannot in the 2000s. Yet the series also claims that for women, "having it all" can be more than marriage and motherhood, and retreating from university or workplace to the home should not be once again a glorified path. It decries that the Peggys, Joans, and Bettys of today all have the capability to thrive professionally. In the 2013 series finale of the NBC workplace sitcom *30 Rock*, show runner and star Tina Fey predicts that *Mad Men*'s grand conclusion will bring the show's long-term role reversal to fruition: a chastened Don begins to work for Peggy. Her humorous enthusiasm and prediction of simple gender reversal is of course not the solution to workplace equality, but it indicates that narrative closure and audience satisfaction would come from Peggy's career triumph.[30]

NOTES

1. Betty Friedan, *The Feminine Mystique* (London: Penguin Books, 1963), 5–20.
2. Friedan, *Feminine Mystique*, 21–29.
3. Betty Friedan, "The National Organization for Women's 1966 Statement of Purpose," National Organization for Women official website, 29 October 1966, http://www.now.org/history/purpos66.html (accessed 21 May 2012).
4. Friedan, "Statement of Purpose."
5. Friedan, "Statement of Purpose."
6. Susan Faludi, *Backlash: The Undeclared War against American Women* (New York: Crown Publishers, 1992).
7. Faludi, *Backlash*, 87.
8. Faludi, *Backlash*, 81.
9. Faludi, *Backlash*, 50.
10. Friedan, *Feminine Mystique*, 35.
11. Mimi White, "Mad Women," in Mad Men: *Dream Come True TV*, ed. Gary R. Edgerton (London and New York: I.B. Tauris, 2011), 152.
12. *Post-network era*, as defined by Amanda Lotz in her 2009 book *Beyond Prime Time: Television in the Post-network Era*, indicates a shift away from the dominance of US networks ABC, CBS, NBC, and Fox and onto newer programming from HBO, Showtime, AMC, FX, and online outlets.
13. Amanda Lotz, *Redesigning Women: Television after the Network Era* (Urbana and Chicago: University of Illinois Press, 2006), 145.
14. Lotz, *Redesigning Women*, 145.
15. Elana Levine, "*Grey's Anatomy*: Feminism," *How to Watch Television*, ed. Ethan Thompson and Jason Mittell (New York: New York University Press, 2013), 139.
16. Stephanie Coontz, "Why *Mad Men* Is TV's Most Feminist Show," *Washington Post*, 10 October 2010, http://www.washingtonpost.com/wp-dyn/content/article/2010/10/08/AR2010100802662.html (accessed 22 May 2013).
17. Coontz, "Feminist Show."
18. United States Department of Labor, "Women at Work: BLS Spotlight on Statistics," Bureau of Labor Statistics, February 2011, http://www.bls.gov/spotlight/2011/women/ (accessed 15 July 2013).
19. Amy Chozick, "The Women behind 'Mad Men,'" *Wall Street Journal*, 7 August 2009, http://online.wsj.com/news/articles/SB10001424052970204908604574332284143366134 (accessed 20 July 2013).
20. Rachel Bertsche, "*Mad Men* and the Real Women behind Them," *CNN Living*, 17 August 2009, http://articles.cnn.com/2009-08-17/living/o.women.and.mad.men_1_women-writers-robin-veith-young-women?_s=PM:LIVING (accessed 21 July 2013).

21. Dean G. Kilpatrick, "Rape and Sexual Assault," National Violence against Women Prevention Research Center, Medical University of South Carolina, 2000, http://www.musc.edu/vawprevention/research/sa.shtml (accessed 21 May 2013).

22. Ellen Riordan, "Commodified Agents and Empowered Girls: Consuming and Producing Feminism," *Journal of Communication Inquiry* 25, no. 3 (July 2001): 279–97.

23. Ann M. Morrison, Randall P. White, and Ellen Van Velsor, *Breaking the Glass Ceiling: Can Women Reach the Top of America's Largest Corporations?* (Saddle River, NJ: Pearson Education, 1987).

24. Madeline E. Heilman, Aaron S. Wallen, Daniella Fuchs, and Melinda M. Tamkins, "Penalties for Success: Reactions to Women Who Succeed at Male Gender-Typed Tasks," *Journal of Applied Psychology* 89, no. 3 (June 2004): 416–27.

25. United States Department of Labor, "CPI Inflation Calculator," Bureau of Labor Statistics, http://www.bls.gov/data/inflation_calculator.htm (accessed 21 June 2012).

26. Jennifer Allyn, "*Mad Men*—Why Gen Y Women Need to Tune In," *Forbes*, 14 August 2009, http://www.forbes.com/2009/08/14/mad-men-peggy-olson-forbes-woman-leadership-gen-y.html (accessed 16 May 2013).

27. Friedan, "Statement of Purpose."

28. "Establishing *Mad Men*," DVD special feature, *Mad Men: Season 1* DVD, Los Angeles: Lionsgate Home Entertainment, 2008.

29. Ann-Marie Slaughter, "Why Women Still Can't Have It All," *Atlantic*, July/August 2012, 89.

30. The author would like to thank Lee Grieveson, Melvyn Stokes, Leslie Streicher, and Lindsey Alexander for their input and encouragement on the earliest versions of this chapter. Further thanks to Harvey Cohen, Conrad Ng, Sigi Preissl, Ben Stevens, and Elisa Jochum for their editing expertise. To Daniela, Dan, Elena, Dumitru, Vali, and Emil. To Conor. And to every friend who has watched an episode of *Mad Men* with me, shared a link, or has listened to me discuss my work on the series. Finally, my humble gratitude is given to the editor of this collection, Laura D'Amore.

BIBLIOGRAPHY

Allyn, Jennifer. "*Mad Men*—Why Gen Y Women Need To Tune In." *Forbes*, 14 August 2009. http://www.forbes.com/2009/08/14/mad-men-peggy-olson-forbes-woman-leadership-gen-y.html (accessed 16 May 2013).

Arthurs, Jane. "*Sex and the City* and Consumer Culture: Remediating Postfeminist Drama." *Feminist Media Studies* 3, no.1 (2003): 83–98.

Bertsche, Rachel. "*Mad Men* and the Real Women behind Them." *CNN Living*, 17 August 2009. http://articles.cnn.com/2009-08-17/living/o.women.and.mad.men_1_women-writers-robin-veith-young-women?_s=PM:LIVING (accessed 21 July 2013).

Blaszcyk, Regina Lee. "*Mad Men* and the Odd Power of Focus Groups: Echoes." *Bloomberg*, 22 March 2012. http://www.bloomberg.com/news/2012-03-22/-mad-men-and-the-odd-power-of-focus-groups-echoes.html (accessed 21 May 2012).

Boggs, Glenney Colleen. "*Mad Men*'s Scarlet Women." *Huffington Post: The Blog*, 26 March 2012. http://www.huffingtonpost.com/colleen-glenney-boggs/mad-mens-scarlet-women_b_1380745.html (accessed 16 May 2013).

Brabon, Benjamin A., and Stephenie Genz. *Postfeminism: Cultural Texts and Theories.* Edinburgh: Edinburgh University Press, 2009.

Brown, Helen Gurley. *Sex and the Single Girl.* Fort Lee, NJ: Barricade Books, 1962.

Chozick, Amy. "The Women behind 'Mad Men.'" *Wall Street Journal*, 7 August 2009. http://online.wsj.com/news/articles/SB10001424052970204908604574332284143366134 (20 July 2013).

Coontz, Stephanie. "Why *Mad Men* Is TV's Most Feminist Show." *Washington Post*, 10 October 2010. http://www.washingtonpost.com/wp-dyn/content/article/2010/10/08/AR2010100802662.html (accessed 22 May 2013).

Doyle, Sady. "*Mad Men*'s Very Modern Sexism Problem." *Atlantic*, 2 August 2010. http://www.theatlantic.com/entertainment/archive/2010/08/mad-mens-very-modern-sexism-problem/60788/ (accessed 2 May 2013).

Edgerton, Gary R., ed. *Mad Men: Dream Come True TV*. London and New York: I.B. Tauris, 2011.

"Establishing *Mad Men*." DVD special feature. *Mad Men: Season 1* DVD. Los Angeles: Lionsgate Home Entertainment, 2008.

Faludi, Susan. *Backlash: The Undeclared War against American Women*. New York: Crown Publishers, 1992.

Friedan, Betty. *The Feminine Mystique*. London: Penguin Books, 1963.

———. "The National Organization for Women's 1966 Statement of Purpose." National Organization for Women official website. 29 October 1966, http://www.now.org/history/purpos66.html (accessed 21 May 2013).

Gill, Rosalind. "Empowerment/Sexism: Figuring Female Sexual Agency in Contemporary Advertising." *Feminism and Psychology* 18, no. 35 (2008): 36–60.

Hanisch, Carol. "The Personal Is Political." In *Notes from the Second Year: Women's Liberation*, edited by Shulamith Firestone and Anne Koedt (self-published, 1970). Available at http://www.carolhanisch.org/CHwritings/PIP.html (accessed 21 May 2012).

Heilman, Madeline E., Aaron S. Wallen, Daniella Fuchs, and Melinda M. Tamkins. "Penalties for Success: Reactions to Women Who Succeed at Male Gender-Typed Tasks." *Journal of Applied Psychology* 89, no. 3 (June 2004): 416–27.

Kilpatrick, Dean G. "Rape and Sexual Assault." National Violence against Women Prevention Research Center, Medical University of South Carolina, 2000. http://www.musc.edu/vawprevention/research/sa.shtml (accessed 21 May 2013).

Kim, L. S. "'Sex and the Single Girl' in Postfeminism: The F Word on Television.'" *Television & New Media*, 1 November 2001. http://tvn.sagepub.com/content/2/4/319.full.pdf+html (accessed 2 April 2013).

Levine, Elana. "*Grey's Anatomy*: Feminism," 138–47, in *How to Watch Television*, edited by Ethan Thompson and Jason Mittell. New York: New York University Press, 2013.

Lotz, Amanda D. *Redesigning Women: Television after the Network Era*. Urbana and Chicago: University of Illinois Press, 2006.

———. "Postfeminist Television Criticism: Rehabilitating Critical Terms and Identifying Postfeminist Attributes." *Feminist Media Studies*, 14 December 2010.

Lotz, Amanda D., and Sharon Marie Ross. "Bridging Media-Specific Approaches." *Feminist Media Studies* 4, no. 2 (2004): 185–202.

Martinson, Jane. "*Mad Men*: It's All about the Women Now." *Guardian: The Women's Blog*, 26 March 2012. http://www.guardian.co.uk/lifeandstyle/the-womens-blog-with-jane-martinson/2012/mar/26/mad-men-about-women-now (accessed 20 April 2013).

Matlack, Tom. "Is *Mad Men* a Feminist Show?" *Huffington Post*, 13 July 2009. http://www.huffingtonpost.com/tom-matlack/is-imad-meni-a-feminist-s_b_230097.html (accessed 9 March 2013).

McRobbie, Angela. "Postfeminism and Popular Culture." *Feminist Media Studies* 4, no. 3 (2004): 67–82.

———. *The Aftermath of Postfeminism: Gender, Culture and Social Change*. London: Sage, 2009.

Modleski, Tania. *Feminism without Women: Culture and Criticism in a 'Postfeminist' Age*. New York and London: Routledge, 1991.

Morrison, Ann M., Randall P. White, and Ellen Van Velsor. *Breaking the Glass Ceiling: Can Women Reach the Top of America's Largest Corporations?* Saddle River, NJ: Pearson Education, 1987.

Riordan, Ellen. "Commodified Agents and Empowered Girls: Consuming and Producing Feminism." *Journal of Communication Inquiry* 25, no. 3, (July 2001): 279–97.

Slaughter, Ann-Marie "Why Women Still Can't Have It All." *Atlantic*, July/August 2012, 89.

Stoddart, Scott F., ed. *Analyzing Mad Men: Critical Essays on the Television Series*. Jefferson, NC, and London: McFarland, 2011.

United States Department of Labor. "Women at Work: BLS Spotlight on Statistics." Bureau of Labor Statistics, February 2011, http://www.bls.gov/spotlight/2011/women/ (accessed 15 May 2012).

———. "CPI Inflation Calculator." Bureau of Labor Statistics. http://www.bls.gov/data/inflation_calculator.htm (accessed 21 June 2013).

White, Mimi. "Mad Women," 147–58, in *Mad Men: Dream Come True TV*, edited by Gary R. Edgerton. London and New York: I.B. Tauris, 2011.

Worthington, Nancy. "Progress and Persistent Problems." *Feminist Media Studies* 8, no. 1 (2008): 1–16.

SEVEN

A Deeper Cut

Enlightened Sexism and Grey's Anatomy

Mikaela Feroli

Throughout the 1960s and 1970s, feminism exploded because of the frustrating and degrading nature of blatant sexism, particularly regarding the work place. When Betty Friedan wrote *The Feminine Mystique* in 1963 and coined the "problem that has no name," women learned that their days were more valuable than baking cupcakes and making sure their husbands were satisfied. Similarly, girls on college campuses were no longer satisfied receiving their "Mrs." degrees and demanded change. Women began to recognize that femininity is a performance, consequently switching their focus to create beauty beyond the mirror. Through "consciousness raising," feminists created an awareness, insisting women had more potential than what society allowed them to express. Primarily, women constructed a sense of sisterhood that ideally rebuilt their confidence and self-image. This new image was their "push back" toward the absurd representations of women throughout the media. Their push back, however, disturbed the status quo. Much of the media twisted and fabricated the feminist message as anti-men and anti-fun.[1] This stigma, which survived, versus the true legacy of Second Wave feminism, led to the present-day media representation and impression that feminism is detrimental to the American society.

Some scholars speculate why feminism fell rapidly in the 1980s. Scholar Susan J. Douglas, author of *The Rise of Enlightened Sexism* and *The Mommy Myth* (with coauthor Meredith W. Michaels) argues that enlightened sexism is to blame. Douglas describes "enlightened sexism" as any rhetoric that suggests there has been "plenty of progress" due to feminism, "so now it's okay, even amusing to resurrect sexist stereotypes involving girls and women."[2] It is utilized mainly through various media that bombard the American public, often skewing the progression and representation of women and girls. Because of the chokehold media has on society, members are encouraged to mock femininity as long as society remembers "the progress we have made." In addition, "while enlightened sexism seems to support women's equality, it is dedicated to the undoing of feminism."[3]

Domesticity is deeply entrenched in the ideology of the American lifestyle. It coerces men and women to engage in gender performance. According to Joan Williams, "Men and women [serve] to justify and reproduce breadwinner/housewife roles by establishing norms that [identify] successful gender performance with character traits suitable for those roles."[4] Masculine norms are typically performed by men who are straightforward and hardworking, while feminine norms are typically performed by women who are delicate and emotional. In 1936, 82 percent of Americans (both male and female) told pollsters "that a married woman should not earn money if her husband was capable of supporting her."[5] At the time, social norms dictated that men worked in the market place and women stayed within the home to care for the family. This system created the notion of ideal worker and caregiver. By definition the ideal worker can "work full time and overtime and take little or no time off for childbearing or child rearing," and because of the structure of the American working system, "good jobs" such as "high-level executive and professional jobs [means] caregivers often cannot perform as ideal workers."[6] Due to their "inherently" caring, emotional, and soft nature, women are often considered caregivers, while men are judged ideal workers due to their "inherently" dedicated, competitive, and emotionally detached behavior.

Feminist struggles have explicitly addressed this work of inequality since Seneca Falls, and despite resistance, women have been clawing their way up the ladder of heteronormativity and misogyny. As a result many policy changes have transpired that provide women platforms to success. Statistically, the labor participation of women has grown 2.6 percent annually since 1950.[7] Despite this increase, women primarily still work in dead-end jobs.[8] Dead-end jobs include those where little to no advancement can be found and the "majority of these dead-end positions are in office and administration support."[9] In 2011, 73.4 percent of office and administration support occupations were women.[10] One would never know of this misrepresentation, though, if our popular media were to be believed. Various television shows, magazines, books, music, and commercials claim that women are disproportionately succeeding in high-demand professional jobs.

Media plays a major role in the perception women have of themselves as individuals, and how it forms deep impressions on American culture. Advertisements are a common place for such ideologies to play out. Marketing companies aim to target certain demographics for specific products in order for their products to profit. Therefore, when domestic products target women, specifically mothers, they create an archetype for "normal women." Companies create commercials that portray happy homemakers who have time, endless energy, and the desire to create a perfect lifestyle for their families. Through these commercials, companies preach that their products will better the lives of a mother's child, suggesting that if a woman does not purchase the products, her child's development and well-being may be in danger. Clothing advertisements often monitor how women should look by emphasizing impossibly stick thin women with enormous breasts, creating a body "norm." Whether these exaggerated features are maternal, feminine, or masculine and even "if you think they're preposterous, you assume you'll be judged harshly by not abiding them. In this way media portrayals can substitute for and override community norms."[11]

Enlightened sexism ensures that many women, especially young girls, see the "F-word" (feminism) as undesirable: a hairy, antifashion lesbian who hates men. What is all too often forgotten is that feminists also urge girls and women to be powerful, successful, and smart. From this urgency, young females today understand their history as the oppressed sex, and consequently choose not to act as a victim. Yet, this knowledge creates a divide especially for millennials; it forces girls and women to straddle the 1970s feminist pressure of being top of their class, while playing three sports and working, all while being fashionable and sexy. They are encouraged to laugh off sexism because "sexism is now 'cool.'" Enlightened sexism's pervasiveness in American culture made sexism funny. It seduced girls and women into a false sense of security and power. And though magazines, music, and television represent women in power positions, even these "successful" characters are actually finding themselves standing behind and serving men, often relinquishing their own dreams because of the expectations society enforces on girls and women.

Take, for example, the popular television show *Grey's Anatomy*. Produced by Shonda Rhimes, the series is a medical drama that premiered in 2005. Since then, Rhimes has become a model of female success. Her success is important to note due to the few women producers in Hollywood, let alone black women. Of producers and directors, 40.7 percent are women, and statistically Asian and white women are more likely to work in higher paying management, professional, and related occupations than black women. Yet, the fact that a black woman created a hit series in a difficult profession adds to misrepresentation of achievement.[12]

Since initial airing, there have been nine drama-filled seasons that involve sex, crying, death, and more sex. Unlike other shows at the time, *Grey's Anatomy* has several ground-breaking characters who, without careful examination, appear to have overcome sexism. The main character, Meredith Grey (Ellen Pompeo), is the centerpiece of the show. She fights to keep sanity and faith in a predominantly male work force. Her superior, Miranda Bailey (Chandra Wilson), is a strong, powerful black woman, who struggles with the difficulties of working motherhood. Lastly, Grey's best friend, Cristina Yang (Sandra Oh), is a die-hard Asian American surgeon, who only concerns herself with her identity as a surgeon. Watching the development of these characters who "kick ass" in the surgery room, mouth off to their male counterparts, and crave sex just as much as guys, might persuade viewers that these women have transcended sexism; such a perception might even suggest that real-life women have as well. However, this show is not much better at providing a compelling feminist role model than *Leave It to Beaver*. At least people of today can mock June Cleaver, but those watching the characters of *Grey's Anatomy* may miss the subtly rooted sexism. Through its characters and plot lines, *Grey's Anatomy* comments on slut shaming, the maternal pedestal, work-life conflict, working motherhood, feminine roles, and femininity, though not always for the better.

MEREDITH GREY

Meredith Grey appears to be a common twenty-first-century woman starting a new medical career in a dominantly male workforce. "As late as 1970, only 14 percent of all doctoral degrees were awarded to women, only 8 percent of all students enrolled in law schools were women, and only 8 percent of all medical school graduates were women," but by 1990 enrollment statistics rose to 40 percent.[13] In the pilot, "A Hard Day's Night," Grey's seemingly feminist attitude quickly manifests when she flies off the couch only to stumble over her one night stand, presumably after a fun-filled night of drinking. The banter that follows (between Derek Shepard [Patrick Dempsey] and Grey) provides viewers with the knowledge and perception that in this series women are sex objects, but they also objectify men.[14] Even Grey's casual attitude of bringing a man back to her place, but then promptly kicking him out in the morning by openly instructing him to leave seemingly replaces the notion that women cannot have carefree sexual encounters.

Shepard, Grey's one night stand, ironically turns out to be her boss. This turn of events leads to a long road of hurdles Grey must clear in order to prove her deserved spot as an intern at Seattle Grace Hospital. Unintentionally, having slept with her superior, Grey was vulnerable to her fellow interns' criticisms that she, as a woman, "needed" to sleep with her boss to get ahead. In "A Hard Day's Night," Shepard promised a chance to scrub in on a surgery to the intern who correctly solved a difficult case. Grey, and fellow intern Cristina Yang, worked diligently together to solve the patient's illness. After learning Shepard was her boss, in confidence, Grey told Yang of her encounter with Shepard and promised the surgery to Yang, if they were correct. Ultimately, Grey's prediction was right, and even though Yang explained their hypothesis to Shepard, he awarded the surgery to Grey. Rather than congratulating Grey on her successes, Yang claims that the only reason Grey was awarded the surgery instead of her was because she slept with Shepard, and furthermore only got into medical school because she had a "famous" mom.[15] This excerpt demonstrates how women are taught to blame and humiliate other women for being sexual and successful. Yang did not commend Grey for her knowledge; instead she reverted back to the slut shaming rooted into the psyches of many young women and girls. The media often reinforces the stereotype that her sexuality, not her intelligence, is the only reason why she got there. As a true working woman, especially in the medical field, she completed her tasks despite endless obstacles. Even though as of 1990 women earned 70 percent as much as men in the medical field and were being pressured to stay in female specialties like gynecology, Grey had pushed herself to the top.[16] Despite the odds, and despite her sexual encounters, Grey deserved her spot as an intern, but was shamed and belittled, creating self-doubt. This is a double bind for women as they are both shunned for and desired for their sexuality.

As time passes, Grey continues to sleep with her boss and deals with the repercussions of her decisions. To unsuspecting viewers, Grey is an ideal working feminist. She works as many hours as her counterparts and endures as many surgeries. Yet, for some reason her life is in shambles. More often than not, Grey finds herself in scenarios that utterly disrupt her life and sometimes almost end it. In episode 17 of season 2, "As We Know It," Grey thrusts her hand into a man's body cavity to support a grenade he accidentally shot himself with, though everyone else had the sense to protect themselves. Repeatedly, viewers see Grey struggling with the intensity of the situation, but she continues to put her life on the line. If Grey moves her hand even an inch the bomb could explode killing her and several other people. At one point, she begins to speak erratically as if she was going to die until the bomb squad captain calms her down, "I know that I'm this ass who has been yelling at you all day. So you pretend that I'm not; you pretend that I'm someone you like, whatever you need. But you need to listen to me," and in a mirage the captain's image shimmers into a calm-faced, reassuring Shepard, who insists, "I know [you're scared], it'll be over in a second. You can do this Meredith."[17] This reassurance by Shepard shows not only Grey but viewers that the strong feminist Grey depicts needs male support in order to complete the task. One can argue that Shepard's support is providing a plot line for the growth of their love; however, in an interview Rhimes stated, "For a long time the show has essentially been a love story [of friendship] between Meredith and Cristina more than anything else." [18] However, even with this proclamation Rhimes and writers demonstrate enlightened sexism through the devaluation of women's confidence by repeatedly placing Grey into situations where her insecurities (of worthlessness) and fear intensify.

After several seasons of pain and humor, Grey and Shepard finally end up happily married. Shepard worked his way up the surgical chain to become the new chief of surgery. With his position came new responsibilities that forced him to make the difficult decision to take a woman off of life support. Distraught by the pain of losing his wife, Gary Clark (Michael O'Neill), enters the hospital with a gun intending to kill the man who took her from him. Clark injures Shepard (by shooting him in the heart) and reemerges as Yang is surgically repairing Shepard's heart. Almost immediately Grey steps in and announces to Clark as he points the gun at her,

> You want justice right? Your wife died, I know what happened. Derek told me the story. Lexie Grey is the one that pulled the plug on your wife, she's my sister. Dr. Webber, he was your wife's doctor. I'm the closest thing he has to a daughter. And the man on the table, I'm his wife. If you wanna hurt them, the way that you hurt, shoot me. I'm your eye for an eye. Tell Derek that I love him and that I'm sorry. [19]

When analyzed, this wrenching moment suggests that Grey fears and believes her very existence causes injury to those around her; thus, if she were removed from the equation everyone's life would be better. At first glance, Grey is sacrificing her life for the people she loves, an outstanding virtue, but simultaneously she is taking blame for the pain that she is not responsible for and wishes death upon herself before her husband and others. In subsequent episodes throughout the series Grey's self-sacrificing actions are ridiculed in an irrational manner. Moreover, in the middle of her plea she miscarries. Not only does she almost fail as a wife, she fails as a mother because she could not protect her unborn child. Therefore, this occurrence in the show does not demonstrate a simple sacrifice for a loved one; instead, *Grey's Anatomy* enforces the idea that women are emotionally irrational and men are logically bold.

This observation of fear and worthlessness is further verified in future episodes where Grey has lost her will to survive. After growing to love Grey for her endless (bordering desperate) love for Shepard, the viewer learns that Grey comes from a complicated past that primarily involves the family she tries to ignore. At the beginning of the series, it is suggested that her abandonment issues stem from her father who was driven out by her mother at the early age of five. However, the relationship that plagues Grey is that of Ellis Grey (Kate Burton), her mother. Through flashbacks and comments by other colleagues, viewers learn Ellis was hard core and unsympathetic. Ironically, Ellis was diagnosed with early onset Alzheimer's. One miraculous day, Ellis wakes lucid, and when prompted by Grey about her life, Ellis is quickly disappointed to learn Grey has become "no more than ordinary." Dejected, Grey retorts, "You want to know why I'm so unfocused, so ordinary? You want to know what happened to me? You! You happened to me!"[20] Grey blames her mother for her fate, and Ellis is used as a textbook example of Second Wave feminism "gone wrong." Ellis was one of those women who valued her career more than her family. Consequently, she has a detrimental relationship with her daughter, which causes Grey agony for the rest of her life. Moreover, Ellis's husband wanted nothing to do with her. She failed as a wife and a mother in her quest for a career. In various moments throughout the series Ellis's "bad mothering" haunts Grey. In a confession to Dr. Owen Hunt (Kevin McKidd), as he is grappling with the impending abortion that his partner, Cristina Yang, wants to have, Grey explains to him about the difficulties of both the mother and unwanted child perspective:

> Do you know what it's like to be raised by someone who didn't want you? I do. To know you stood in the way of your mother's career? I do. I was raised by a Cristina. My mother was a Cristina. And as the child she didn't want, I am telling you, don't do this to her, because she's kind and she cares and she won't make it. The guilt of resenting her own kid will eat her alive.[21]

The pressures of American motherhood provide a complex plot line that helps drive home enlightened sexism. As mentioned before, enlightened sexism's primary goal is to break down feminism. And a crucial way feminism was targeted and deemed as negative transpired through the conflation of good and bad mothering. If Ellis was a "perfect mother—the woman for whom childbearing supersedes all other identities and satisfactions"—she would be proud of her daughter no matter what profession she chose or man she fell in love with.[22] Furthermore, it shows women they must obtain perfect work-life balance in order to produce healthy children so they are not riddled with issues like Grey.

Shortly after Grey and Ellis's damaging conversation in season 3, a traumatic ferry crash occurs in Seattle Harbor. Grey is sent to tend to the tragedy by helping patients. While trying to help an older man, Grey gets knocked into the icy waters of Seattle Harbor and begins to drown. Since Ellis's comments had inflicted such deep pain for Grey, it appeared that she gave up on life.[23] She is in the process of drowning when Shepard jumps in after her to carry her limp body out of the water. This literal act of Shepard saving Grey again positions Grey as a woman who needed to be saved by a man. The show "bombards [viewers] by overlapping and often colliding streams of progressive and regressive imagery, both of which offer . . . very different fantasies of female power."[24] The feminist power Grey tried to hold onto throughout the past seasons slipped through her hands, and those watching are encouraged to root for a heart-wrenching star-crossed love story. Furthermore, it reinforces the idea that what mothers do has dire consequences on the well-being of their children—so dire, in fact, their children will try to end their lives.

MIRANDA BAILEY

Miranda Bailey shamelessly uses her confident, sarcastic personality to drive home the point that even though she is a woman, she is the best surgeon around. She is a self-assured, dominant woman who tries to break down barriers involved with the work-life conflict. As a black working mother Bailey embodies the trappings of enlightened sexism. She was cast as a primary character, indicating to viewers to perceive her as more important than a mere "diversity" character. Although in reality, the working-poor rates for black and Hispanic women are significantly higher than for white and Asian women.[25] Having one of the most ad-mired characters be a black working mother insinuates that black women have "made it." Similar to Grey's character, no matter how hard Bailey tries to succeed, there are battles to spoil her riches.

To be taken seriously, women in power positions often need to be stricter than their male counterparts, leaving them vulnerable to being denounced as a "bitch" or "cold hearted." Accordingly, Bailey's sexist nickname is the Nazi. One Thanksgiving, due to the lack of staffing, a visiting resident was filling in for Bailey's boss. Unknowingly speaking to the person he was searching for, Dr. Kent explains,

> Dr. Kent: Look, I'm only here for one day and I don't need my ass kissed. All I need is to tell you what to do and you do it. And I don't like mistakes.

> Dr. Bailey: I don't make mistakes

> Dr. Kent: Whatever, there's only one resident I want in my OR; a guy they call the Nazi. Do you know him?

> Dr. Bailey: The Nazi?

> Dr. Kent: He gets a great word of mouth, stellar rep, balls the size of Texas?

> Dr. Bailey: That big? Sounds like an impressively talented man, this "Nazi."

Dr. Kent: Do you know him or not?

Dr. Bailey: Never heard of him but I'll be sure to keep an eye out.

Dr. Kent: For now you can work on smaller cases. A guy just came in to curtain three. Page me if you get confused.

Dr. Bailey: I'll be sure to do that.

Dr. Kent expected the Nazi to be a man because of the characteristics associated with the reputation.[26] He assumed that Dr. Bailey's abilities were less comparable to a man's and assigned the less difficult and confusing cases to her. When Dr. Kent finally realizes Dr. Bailey is the Nazi, his dumbfounded expression explains it all. Bailey defies gendered work traits, but is rarely rewarded for her accomplishments. Moreover, her success within the workplace often discredits her ability to mother.

She finds it difficult to juggle her spheres due to the challenges of the work-life balance. Bailey's struggles for work-life balance are evident in the ways her character strives for equality. "In the wake of the women's movement [women] were supposed to be autonomous, independent, accomplished, yet pore-less, slim, nurturing, and deferential to men."[27] This new belief designed a system where women who work are scrutinized, and women who are "less work-centered [are seen] as having 'dropped-out' or 'given up.'"[28] Therefore, no matter the decision, Bailey's efforts are negated on both sides. However, her work reputation suggests Bailey would be a poor mother because she lacks the development of her nurturing side, yet fostered those abilities "to succeed in the male-dominated public sphere."[29]

Bailey struggled with the decision to have a family knowing the difficulties of balancing the two. However, she believed she would be able to carry out her dreams as a surgeon while having a lovely, functional family without feeling guilty of her "choice." The idea of choice regarding working motherhood provides a platform that sets women up to fail. If it is a literal choice—meaning choosing to work, or have a family, or manage both—then women are overwhelmed with outside opinions and expectations. As Douglas and Michaels point out, women are persistently told they are choosing wrong no matter what decision they make.[30] Bailey chooses both. She does her best to keep up with the demands of surgery and motherhood, but often finds herself failing due to the impractical pedestal of motherhood. One-third of the American public believes that women with small children at home should not work at all, insinuating that those who work are wrongly organizing their lives.[31] The media perception that mothers are a main influence and provider for their children shames working women into feeling inadequate about their choices.

When Bailey tries to receive a promotion she needs to work twice as many hours. According to a study conducted at the University of Michigan Law School, "women are more willing than men to sacrifice wages and promotions for the joys of parenting."[32] Bailey contradicts this social norm and in turn is reprimanded. During opening scenes of "Lay Your Hands on Me," the camera cuts to Bailey's household where Bailey's husband, Tucker Jones (Cress Williams), is taking laundry out of the dryer, while Bailey is reminding him that she fed and changed their son and to call the building manager. He ignores her until she is about to walk out the door.

> Tucker: (still folding laundry with little Tuck crying in the background) Miranda.
>
> Bailey: Oh you're talking to me now, now that I'm on my way out the door?
>
> Tucker: You're always on your way out the door.
>
> Bailey: (exhaustedly) Tucker . . .
>
> Tucker: Look are you interested in being a part of this family or not?
>
> Bailey: (walking away and out the door) OK I can't do this now. I don't have time for this.
>
> Tucker: (slams down laundry he was folding)

Because Bailey is not around as much, and Tucker is left at home to tend to a majority of the household chores and child rearing, he becomes resentful and Bailey is belittled. As Williams argues, "'working-mothers' take on an impossible task, and ultimately fail to meet their children's needs."[33]

This notion is later reinforced when that same afternoon, Tucker brings their son into the hospital because he "found Tuck under the book shelf and under 'all those medical books.'"[34] He tells Bailey that "somebody left the baby gate open," and immediately Bailey knows he blames her for the accident. Tucker yells, "If you weren't in such a hurry to get out of the house this morning and get to work there wouldn't be this problem. Why do you think he even went into that room? You're the only one who goes in there. He went looking for his Momma and ended up in the hospital." Tucker blames Bailey for causing this accident through her focus on work, symbolically, through her medical books, and literally because she was not there to stop it. If she was not a working mother and spent more time at home watching Tuck he would not feel the need to go "looking for his Momma."[35] This situation depicted through *Grey's Anat-*

omy reinforces "those [women] who 'choose' to work full-time (and even overtime) because [they] have to, want to, or both, are . . . selfish mothers with absolutely wrong priorities."[36] Those women who want to have both identities in life are often forced to minimize the importance of one because of the way that the American system is built. Capitalism, autonomy, and success are three attributes that are admired in society and often "successful motherhood requires relinquishing one's autonomy to a sometimes dangerous, always preposterous view of women and children."[37] In the end, as Douglas and Michaels explain, it is nearly impossible for women who are good workers to be seen as good mothers because it is abnormal and strange to be both, ergo "working mother" or a woman without children both mean "deviant."

CRISTINA YANG

Cristina Yang, on the other hand, is deviant on all levels. She is a passionate surgeon whose sole desire is to cut. She snaps crude comments, does not take no for an answer, and strives for success. Viewers can interpret her as a strong female character who unabashedly owns her sense of accomplishment. When talking to a male coworker who is whining about a headache she retorts, "Look, I'd rip your face off if it meant I got to scrub in."[38] She completely disregards the gendered expectations of women because presumably she does not need a man to define herself, hates children, and throws domesticity out of the window. Asian Americans are often depicted as "well-educated, competent, highly competitive and ambitious," which Yang exhibits, but she also displays "negative characteristics such as being socially awkward, unsympathetic and lacking femininity."[39] Despite her lack of femininity, Yang's steadfast approach toward work never impedes her sexuality and sexual encounters. Therefore, Yang's character appears to provide an icon for a certain type of ruthless woman to look to and feel like the fight for equality is over.

After seeing Yang whip into work via motorcycle and watch her colleagues avoid her robot-like persona, Yang is a heroine for women who eschew the formal gender codes of their work environment, wishing instead for crass commentary and disgust for common "girlish" characteristics. After a long day of banter and pleading amongst colleagues, Yang and three other colleagues are shown in the pediatrics wing. With Yang's back to the babies and the others swooning, Grey finally concedes to allow her coworkers to move into her house. Turning to Yang, Grey exhales, "I can't believe I caved" and with a quick roll of the eyes, Yang bluntly comments, "I blame the babies, they make you toxic" and strides off.[40] For all of the women who think babies are repulsive and are assaulted by advertisements and beliefs that the one sole purpose of being a woman is to love children, here they have a character to identify with. Moreover, she once said to her now ex-fiancé, Preston Burke (Isaiah Washington) as she showed him her filth-ridden apartment for the first time, "I don't do laundry, I buy new underwear . . . I don't wash dishes, vacuum or put the toilet paper on the holder."[41]

Yang's thirst for power and surgeries evokes a desire for passion. As such, she develops a relationship with her superior Preston Burke because they are both attracted to that passion. Yang's attempts to keep a strictly physical relationship with him fails because she finds herself a "victim" of love. In passing comments between Grey and Yang, Yang's indifference to emotion is apparent by calling love a problem.[42]

Yang: Burke said he loved me . . .

Grey: Are you going to say it back?

Yang: Of course not, everybody has their problems.

Quickly viewers notice that Yang circumvents emotion, and because of this her strong persona is often challenged.

After Yang and Burke's rocky relationship begins to take hold, Burke is caught in the crossfire of a dramatic shooting scenario at the hospital.[43] After being shot, Burke suffers nerve damage and cannot perform surgeries properly because his hand occasionally tremors. Before her "victimization" Yang would have walked the other way in order to protect her career. However, Yang steps in to support Burke in order to keep his condition secret. She assists with complex surgeries beyond her level so no one knows of the severity of his condition. If the situation between Burke and Yang were to be discovered, irreparable damages from the hospital such as firing could occur. Even though Yang was previously depicted as coldhearted and selfish, Yang assists and risks her career to give Burke the necessary encouragement for his success. One day the truth escapes, and in the end it is Yang who is blamed for pushing Burke too hard and too fast.

Yang: (confused, but firm) We crossed the line. Together. I crossed the line with you.

Burke: (curtly) You dragged me across the line. You made us a team. You told Shepherd I was fine. You said nobody has to know. I was out there on my own. You made us a team.

Yang: (louder) I did what you needed me to do. You were standing there looking at me telling me your whole life was your hands, if you couldn't operate, if you couldn't be Preston Burke.

Burke: That was your concern, not mine! . . . Do you know how scared I am when we go into surgery? I don't have to just worry about my career now. I have to put yours on my back too.

Yang: We are a team!

Burke: There is no team. There is no team! There is only me, once again, making allowances for your emotional shortcomings!

Throughout this dialog Yang insists that they are a team and whatever happened occurred because they pursued it together, despite them both knowing Yang led Burke to the road of recovery. Yet, Burke spins the situation around and asserts his dominance and control by assuming the burden of the possibility of their defamed reputations, because he is making up for Yang's lack of emotions. Because Yang took the dominant position when Burke was vulnerable, the attitude and passion that Burke once admired in her backfired due to his insecurities and her lack of emotional appeal. Quite often a man is depicted to have emotional shortcomings, but their relationship problems are frequently placed upon the woman because she is too hysterical or emotional. Yang is still blamed for her relationship problems, and even more harshly because of her resigned emotional personality. [44]

Yang's lack of femininity is further criticized when she denies the "typical" fiancée role. Burke proposes to Yang unexpectedly after they settle their differences involving the tremor scandal. Because of her simple attitude toward relationships and indifference to conventional aspects of life, it takes her several days to accept his proposal and even longer to accept the idea of having a lavish, traditional wedding. During the middle of studying for their intern examination at Yang and Burke's apartment, Yang and the other interns are deeply invested in procuring and memorizing the correct answers. Although, in the middle of answering questions Burke steps in front of Yang and forces bites of cake into her mouth. Exasperated and annoyed, Yang obliges Burke by tasting a couple of the cakes in the middle of shouting out answers. After one taste test too many Yang shouts out an answer, but needs Burke to determine if her or another intern is correct.

Yang: (about the cake) Look baby, I don't care. Is Alex right or am I?

Burke: You don't care? Learn to care or I'll get another bride.

Yang: (exhausted) I love it. I love all cakes. Now break the tie.

This quick exchange presents several characteristics about Yang and Burke. [45] Firstly, Burke must force Yang to participate in the decisions involving their wedding. Secondly, Yang is forced to drop what is important to her in order to appease his desire for her femininity. After realizing this, Yang is forced to relinquish her wishes and succumb to the demands of femininity code. This compliance goes so far that on the day of her wedding Yang wanders into the hospital hours before the ceremony with her hair half done and dragging her dress. The quick camera shot of her face only allows the viewer to see her pained expression, but not what has happened to it.

Grey: (turns around) Woah!

Yang: (destitute) Mama took my eyebrows. She took my eyebrows and now I am a Burke.

Burke's mother has transformed Yang into someone unrecognizable not only physically, but mentally. To ease her pain and regain her identity, Yang and Grey find Dr. Bailey in order to let Yang scrub in on a surgery.

Grey: Dr. Bailey, Cristina needs to cut something. I can't explain it in a way that won't make you glare, but they took her eyebrows and they called her a Burke. She really needs to cut somebody open.

Bailey: (annoyed) Yang. Go do married things. Get out of this hospital.

Yang: (desperately) HEY! . . . hey . . . You have to let me cut because I am standing here eyebrow-less with no dignity left. I am a surgeon Dr. Bailey, but right now I don't feel like one . . . I feel like somebody else.

First and foremost, Yang considers herself a surgeon and not a bride. Because this identity fosters her dominant qualities instead of her feminine, Yang loses her sense of self in order to please those around her, and ultimately Burke leaves her on their wedding day after explaining he wishes to be with someone who complies more with the femininity code.

As of the most recent episode at the time of this chapter's completion (November 2013), Yang has been engaged twice and married once, and has had one abortion and one ectopic pregnancy. She repeatedly reminds not only her friends, but her husband, Owen Hunt, that she does not want children. Yang has chosen a path that involves herself, her career, and her husband versus having a "traditional" family because she lives for surgery. Despite that, Yang finds herself pregnant again. Racked with despair, Yang desperately wants an abortion despite her husband's wishes. On many levels this act of defiance conveys feminism through pro-choice and resistance to the desires of her husband. Grey tries to explain to Hunt, as a child of a mother who did not want her, "Trying to pretend that [Yang] loves a kid as much as she loves surgery will almost kill her, and it'll almost kill your kid."[46] Fundamentally, there is nothing wrong with the choice not to have children. However, gender expectations force women into motherhood when they have no inclination to bear children. When the media reinforces these stereotypes, they typically override what the public actually wants versus the wants of the media.[47] Adrienne Rich, author of *Of Woman Born: Motherhood as Experience and Institution*, sees "motherhood as a patriarchal institution imposed on women 'which aims at ensuring that . . . all women shall remain under male control.'"[48] Yang tried to resist that control.

However, Yang's husband, Hunt, wants nothing more than to have a child. He knew coming into the relationship that Yang never wanted children, but later revealed that he hoped he could change her. He tries to change her opinion on having children even though she has expressed a multitude of times she does not want children. Since Hunt is an ideal worker based on his sex, historically "under common law, a man was entitled to have his wife follow him wherever he wanted to live. Men no longer have that entitlement . . . but men as a group still enjoy it as a matter of social custom" and Hunt felt that his desire to have children overruled his wife's.[49] Troubled by her husband's misery, Yang could not initially follow through with the abortion she seriously wanted to have. Seeing the despair between both parties Grey tries to reconcile and talk sense into Hunt. Grey reveals, "She didn't have the abortion. She wants to but she can't do it because of you. Because she loves you and instead of loving her, you're punishing her. And for what? For being the woman that you fell in love with?"[50] When Yang finally made the decision to get the abortion, Hunt feigned support until the couple came head to head in the middle of a party:

Yang: (tears in eyes) It all comes back to this?

Hunt: (nodding) Crazy, right? That I would ever bring it up again.

Yang: Yes. Yes! Yes! Ok, it was a horrible situation, but it's over. Is it too much to ask to just try and forget it?

Hunt: (scoffing) YOU KILLED OUR BABY! YOU DON'T EVER FORGET THAT!

Hunt refuses to support Yang and love her for the person she is. And Yang's punishment for not following gender norms was that Hunt walked out on her and had an affair, ripping Yang apart. She may not want children, but she loves her husband. The emotional roller coaster that viewers see reminds women that if they do not want to have children, and choose to listen to their own aspirations rather than the demands of their husbands, their lives will be destroyed.

Since the surgical field is demanding, it is automatically deemed a male profession because "the ideology of domesticity held that men 'naturally' belong in the market because they are competitive and aggressive; [and] women belong in the home because of their 'natural' focus on relationships, children and an ethic of care."[51] This principle instantly marginalizes men as the potential caretaker, and places women at the center of their children's lives, necessarily keeping them out of the workplace. Therefore, any woman who chooses to work is abnormal. Yang is pressured to take a domestic role, forcing Yang into a situation where she feels helpless.

Grey: And maybe you wanna be a mom, too, and that's why you can't go through with [the abortion].

Yang: I wish I wanted a kid. I wish I wanted one so bad because then this would be easy. I would be happy. I'd have Owen and my life wouldn't be a mess, but I don't. I don't want a kid. I don't wanna make jam, I don't wanna carpool, and I really, really, don't wanna be a mother. I wanna be a surgeon. And please, get it. I need someone to get it. And I wish that person was Owen and that any minute he'd get it and show up for me. But that's not gonna happen. And you're my person, and I need you to be there at six o'clock tonight to hold my hand because I am scared, Mer, and sad because my husband doesn't get that. So, I need you to.

Yang does not want to have children and loses her husband because of it.

CONCLUSION

Grey, Yang, and Bailey often find themselves in emotionally demanding predicaments that embellish on the fact that they are women, but find themselves in these predicaments because they are women. Enlightened sexism has played an important part in the psychological development of the millennials' upbringing. Millennials were taught they can be whoever they want to be, and that the fight for women's equality is over. Be that as it may, the pervasiveness of enlightened sexism in everyday life has maintained the policing of gender roles. According to Girlguiding, 87 percent of girls aged eleven to twenty-one believe that women are judged more for their looks than their abilities.[52] This statistic and belief demonstrates even though society claims there is gender equity, it is far from reality. This reality is fortified through media in American culture and the acceptance of current ideologies. When individuals of past generations felt oppressed they formed coalitions in order to right the wrongs society was enforcing. However, certain people of today are turning a blind eye to the false consciousness of domesticity. It creates platforms for systems like enlightened sexism to rule the media and enforce gender roles that often impede the success and happiness of different types of women. Demonstrated through *Grey's Anatomy*, three women faced constant turmoil due to their aversion to gender codes. We need to make a deeper cut, to delve more deeply beneath the surface to see that in America's superficial society there is still a great divide between the sexes.

NOTES

1. Peter Braunstein and Michael William Doyle, *Imagine Nation: The American Counterculture of the 1960s and '70s* (New York: Routledge 2002), 44.

2. Susan J. Douglas, *The Rise of Enlightened Sexism: How Pop Culture Took Us from Girl Power to Girls Gone Wild* (New York: St. Martin's Griffin, 2011), 9.

3. Douglas, *The Rise of Enlightened Sexism*, 10.

4. Joan Williams, *Unbending Gender: Why Family and Work Conflict and What to Do about It* (Oxford: Oxford University Press, 2000), 1.

5. Dora L. Costa, "From Mill Town to Board Room: The Rise of Women's Paid Labor." *Journal of Economic Perspectives*, Fall 2000, 101–22, http://www.econ.ucla.edu/costa/jeppaper.pdf (accessed 20 July 2013).

6. Williams, *Unbending Gender*, 1.

7. Mitra Toossi, "A Century of Change: The U.S. Labor Force, 1950–2050," U.S. Bureau of Labor Statistics, *Monthly Labor Review*, May 2002, 15–28, http://www.bls.gov/opub/mlr/2002/05/art2full.pdf (accessed 1 November 2013).

8. Costa, "From Mill Town," 116.

9. Kate Lorenz, "10 Dead-End Jobs," Experience.com, 2008, https://bowdoin.experience.com/alumnus/article?channel_id=career_management&source_page=career_development&article_id=article_1156446477449 (accessed 20 October 2013).

10. US Bureau of Labor Statistics, *Women in the Labor Force: A Databook* (Rep. no. 1040), February 2013, 1, 36, http://www.bls.gov/cps/wlf-databook-2012.pdf (accessed 20 July 2013).

11. Susan J. Douglas and Meredith W. Michaels, *The Mommy Myth: The Idealization of Motherhood and How It Has Undermined Women* (New York: Free Press, 2004), 18–19.

12. US Bureau of Labor Statistics, *Women in the Labor Force*, 1, 36.

13. Costa, "From Mill Town," 101.

14. Shonda Rhimes, "A Hard Day's Night," *Grey's Anatomy*, television series (American Broadcast Company, 2005).

15. Rhimes, "A Hard Day's Night," 2005.

16. Godfrey Hodgson, *More Equal than Others: America from Nixon to the New Century* (Princeton, NJ: Princeton University Press, 2004), 126.

17. Rhimes, "As We Know It," 2006.

18. Lesley Goldberg, "'Grey's Anatomy's' Shonda Rhimes on Sandra Oh's Exit: 'This Feels Different,'" *Hollywood Reporter*, 13 August 2013, http://www.hollywoodreporter.com/live-feed/greys-anatomys-shonda-rhimes-sandra-602868 (accessed 16 September 2013).

19. Rhimes, "Death and All His Friends," 2010.

20. Rhimes, "Wishin' and Hopin'," 2007.

21. Rhimes, "Free Falling," 2011.

22. Douglas and Michaels, *The Mommy Myth*, 26.

23. Rhimes, "Walk on Water," 2007.

24. Douglas, *Enlightened Sexism*, 15.

25. US Bureau of Labor Statistics, *Women in the Labor Force*, 1.

26. Rhimes, "Thanks for the Memories," 2005.

27. Douglas and Michaels, *The Mommy Myth*, 23.

28. Williams, *Unbending Gender*, 147.
29. Paula Nicolson, "The Myth of the Maternal Instinct," *Psychology, Evolution & Gender* 1, no. 2 (1999): 167.
30. Douglas and Michaels, *The Mommy Myth*.
31. Wendy Wang, "Mothers and Work: What's Ideal?" Pew Research Center, 19 August 2013, http://www.pewresearch.org/fact-tank/2013/08/19/mothers-and-work-whats-ideal (accessed 1 November 2013).
32. Costa, "From Mill Town," 118.
33. Williams, *Unbending Gender*, 147.
34. Rhimes, "Lay Your Hands on Me," 2008.
35. Rhimes, "Lay Your Hands on Me," 2008.
36. Douglas and Michaels, *The Mommy Myth*, 137.
37. Douglas and Michaels, *The Mommy Myth*, 326.
38. Rhimes, "The First Cut Is the Deepest," 2005.
39. Yue Wu, "Model Minority Stereotypes of Asian American Women in American Media: Perceptions and Influences among Women of Diverse Racial-Ethnical Backgrounds," (master of science thesis, Kansas State University, 2010), http://krex.k-state.edu/dspace/bitstream/handle/2097/4172/YueWu2010.pdf?sequence=1 (accessed 1 November 2013).
40. Rhimes, "The First Cut Is the Deepest," 2005.
41. Rhimes, "Much Too Much," 2005.
42. Rhimes, "As We Know It," 2006.
43. Rhimes, "Deterioration of the Fight or Flight Response," 2006.
44. Rhimes, "From a Whisper to a Scream," 2006.
45. Rhimes, "Desire," 2007.
46. Rhimes, "Free Falling," 2011.
47. Douglas and Michaels, *The Mommy Myth*, 50.
48. Douglas and Michaels, *The Mommy Myth*, 326.
49. Williams, *Unbending Gender*, 16.
50. Rhimes, "Free Falling," 2011.
51. Williams, *Unbending Gender*, 1.
52. Girlguiding, "Equality for Girls," 2013, http://girlsattitudes.girlguiding.org.uk/pdf/2013_GirlsAttitudes_EqualityForGirls.pdf (accessed 1 November 2013).

BIBLIOGRAPHY

Barnet, Elizabeth. "Dissecting the Medical Drama: A Generic Analysis of *Grey's Anatomy* and *House, M.D.*" Department of Communication, Boston College, 2007.
Braunstein, Peter, and Michael William Doyle. *Imagine Nation: The American Counterculture of the 1960s and '70s.* New York: Routledge, 2002.
Costa, Dora L. "From Mill Town to Board Room: The Rise of Women's Paid Labor." *Journal of Economic Perspectives*, Fall 2000, 101–22. http://www.econ.ucla.edu/costa/jeppaper.pdf (accessed 20 July 2013).
Douglas, Susan J. *The Rise of Enlightened Sexism: How Pop Culture Took Us from Girl Power to Girls Gone Wild.* New York: St. Martin's Griffin, 2011.
Douglas, Susan J., and Meredith W. Michaels. *The Mommy Myth: The Idealization of Motherhood and How It Has Undermined Women.* New York: Free Press, 2004.
Girlguiding. "Equality for Girls." 2013. http://girlsattitudes.girlguiding.org.uk/pdf/2013_GirlsAttitudes_EqualityForGirls.pdf (accessed 1 November 2013)
Goldberg, Lesley. "'Grey's Anatomy's' Shonda Rhimes on Sandra Oh's Exit: 'This Feels Different.'" *Hollywood Reporter*, 13 August 2013. http://www.hollywoodreporter.com/live-feed/greys-anatomys-shonda-rhimes-sandra-602868 (accessed 16 September 2013).
Hodgson, Godfrey. *More Equal than Others: America from Nixon to the New Century.* Princeton, NJ: Princeton University Press, 2004.

Lorenz, Kate. "10 Dead-End Jobs." Experience.com, 2008. https://bowdoin.experience. com/alumnus/article?channel_id=career_management&source_page=career_ development&article_id=article_1156446477449 (accessed 20 October 2013).

Nicolson, Paula. "The Myth of the Maternal Instinct." *Psychology, Evolution & Gender* 1, no. 2 (1999): 161–81.

Rhimes, Shonda. *Grey's Anatomy*. Television series. American Broadcast Company, 2005–2013.

Toossi, Mitra. "A Century of Change: The U.S. Labor Force, 1950–2050." US Bureau of Labor Statistics *Monthly Labor Review*, May 2002, 15–28. http://www.bls.gov/opub/ mlr/2002/05/art2full.pdf (accessed 1 November 2013).

US Bureau of Labor Statistics. *Women in the Labor Force: A Databook*. Rep. no. 1040. February 2013. http://www.bls.gov/cps/wlf-databook-2012.pdf (accessed 20 July 2013).

Wang, Wendy. "Mothers and Work: What's Ideal?" Pew Research Center, 19 August 2013. http://www.pewresearch.org/fact-tank/2013/08/19/mothers-and-work-whats-ideal (accessed 1 November 2013).

Williams, Joan. *Unbending Gender: Why Family and Work Conflict and What to Do about It*. Oxford: Oxford University Press, 2000.

Wu, Yue. "Model Minority Stereotypes of Asian American Women in American Media: Perceptions and Influences among Women of Diverse Racial-Ethnical Backgrounds." Master of science thesis, Kansas State University, 2010. http://krex.k-state.edu/dspace/bitstream/handle/2097/4172/YueWu2010.pdf?sequence=1 (accessed 1 November 2013).

EIGHT

"There Is No Genius"

*Dr. Joan Watson and the Rewriting of Gender and
Intelligence on CBS's* Elementary

Helen H. Kang and Natasha Patterson

Riding the successes of the *Sherlock Holmes* film franchise as well as the
hit BBC show *Sherlock*, which is a modern interpretation of the classic
stories of Victorian era author and physician Sir Arthur Conan Doyle,
Elementary hit the North American prime time television schedule in the
fall of 2012 with its own unique twists—it was to be set in New York and
the character of Dr. John Watson was to be played by Lucy Liu as Dr.
Joan Watson. The plot and character developments in *Elementary* go beyond simply playing a numbers game of representational politics. What
Elementary does, and does very well, is not only ascribe intelligence to a
female lead character and a woman of color but also interrogate the very
concept of intelligence through the figures of Joan Watson and Sherlock
Holmes, and through the gender dynamics in the personal and working
relationship between them. Ultimately, *Elementary* challenges the gendered politics associated with cultural binaries such as intelligence/emo-
tion, personal/professional, success/failure, and teacher/student, and in
the process demonstrates that there is space for representations of intelligent and complex (racialized) women as well as for representations of
intelligent and emotional men on mainstream television.

Through a textual analysis of the first season of *Elementary*, in this
chapter we demonstrate how Joan Watson embodies both emotion and
logic, thus blurring lines between femininity and masculinity as well as
redefining the parameters of the intelligent (racialized) woman in North

American popular culture. We also suggest that her professional journey complicates contemporary notions of success and failure in the workplace, raising questions about what counts as legitimate work for intelligent women. We also explore the character of Sherlock Holmes (played by white British actor Jonny Lee Miller), who complicates the fictional archetype of the logical and unfeeling detective by demonstrating emotional vulnerability and engaging in platonic intimacy with Watson. We also examine Watson and Holmes's relationship to Moriarty, the notorious villain in the Sherlock Holmes mythology who, like Watson, is reimagined as a woman in *Elementary*. We argue that in *Elementary* new kinds of femininities and masculinities emerge that subvert gendered understandings of intelligence.

A NEW KIND OF WOMAN OF COLOR: DR. JOAN WATSON

The character of Dr. Joan Watson, as played by Lucy Liu, is not only a stark departure from the original Dr. John Watson in Sir Conan Doyle's stories but she also does not adhere neatly to preexisting models of female detectives in recent popular culture. In feminist criticism of crime television shows, particularly detective dramas, much of the focus has been on charting how the image of women has changed—often in response to Second Wave feminism—from primarily the victim of crime to an investigator of crime (although this is still a common criticism of formulaic series like *Law and Order SVU*).[1]

The shift in the genre is reflected in the centralization and growing prominence of lead female characters as investigators of crime, resulting in narratives that are characterized by "a negotiation of femininity in a 'masculine' genre."[2] These female detectives on television who find themselves in the male-dominated workplace of police work are often strong, independent, and capable (white) women as in the cases of Olivia Benson in *Law and Order SVU* and Clarice Starling in *Silence of the Lambs*, or they are feminist trailblazers who face tragic demise as in the case of Jane Tennison in *Prime Suspect*.

Not only do these shows and films feature women who cross over into a male-dominated workplace, the narrative format and visual styling can also bend genre conventions. For example, Danae Clark notes that the 1970s show *Cagney & Lacey* redefined crime television not only by casting two female actors as buddy cops but also by dealing with feminine narratives in a traditionally masculine genre, thereby integrating the soap opera with crime television.[3] More recently, *Veronica Mars* centered on a female teen amateur sleuth in a noir, a type of narrative and visual genre that has traditionally featured male lead characters.

Dr. Joan Watson brings yet another perspective on the female detective in crime television. Her role is not to provide an emotional dimension to the otherwise strictly rational and logical world of Holmes, thereby reinforcing the gendered binary between rationality (coded as masculine) and emotions (coded as feminine). Instead, she challenges the notion of intelligence as a gendered, racialized, and classed concept and presents a new way of imagining an intelligent woman and female detective in popular culture.

GENDER, CLASS, RACE, AND INTELLIGENCE

Watson is a trained surgeon who leaves surgery after a patient dies at her operating table and becomes a sobriety counselor, which is a live-in counselor for people who have recently completed rehabilitation for addiction. Her privileged middle-class access to higher education differentiates her from most other detectives, police work being a predominantly working-class line of work.[4] Hence, Watson has considerable intelligence that is linked to formal education, which is in turn connected to her class-based privilege. She is also a woman of color who succeeded in a field that has historically been the domain of middle-class white men. Watson's medical knowledge and skills become useful and even pivotal in many cases that the duo encounters. When we meet her in the pilot episode, she is strong, smart, independent, and assertive. The banter between Watson and Holmes is a major source of entertainment in *Elementary*, and Watson is able to hold her ground and parry Holmes's attacks on her intellect.

However, Watson is also attuned to people's feelings, communication cues, and interpersonal dynamics, forms of aptitude that are subject to debate as to whether or not they can truly be thought of as intelligence (incidentally, they are necessary in emotional work that is associated with the caring professions in which women are overrepresented).[5] In Watson, reasoning and deduction, which are culturally coded as masculine, and emotional intelligence, which is culturally coded as feminine, come together to form a coherent whole. Throughout the first half of the season, Watson is patient and suffers through Holmes's insults and succeeds in reading him very accurately—that he is indeed capable of emotional intimacy and that he has suffered a painful loss recently. Her command of both analytic skills and emotional intelligence allows her to excel in her job as a sobriety counselor and eventually as a detective consultant.

Not only does Watson challenge the definition of intelligence and its gendered construction, but she also challenges the sexism and misogyny in a major intellectual institution—science. On one occasion, Holmes refers to Watson's menstrual cycle in order to assess her mood, to which Watson counters sarcastically, "Couching it as a scientific observation totally negates the misogyny."[6] On another occasion, Holmes uses sexist criteria in order to search for a sex worker at a hotel lounge.

Watson: I just think your mouse hunt is a little misogynistic.

Holmes: Not misogynistic. Anthropological.[7]

Watson makes explicit the history of misogyny and sexism that underpins many scientific discourses. For example, nineteenth-century psychiatry diagnosed mental illness in women as hysteria, a disease that originates in the uterus, and it is a term that despite being scientifically refuted persists today in the popular vernacular.[8] Thus, when Watson explicitly names misogyny in Holmes's intellectual methods, she also calls attention to this historical legacy.

LEGITIMATE INTELLECTUAL WORK

In the capitalist labor market Watson is considered a failed elite professional: she left an illustrious career as a surgeon and took on an obscure and inferior job of sobriety counselor. When Watson prepares to meet her family for dinner, she is visibly nervous and Holmes points out that she is dressed for a job interview, not a family dinner. Holmes defends Watson in front of her family:

> She practices quite a unique specialty, your daughter. She rebuilds lives from the ground up. You can measure her success in careers restored, in my case criminals caught, and in lives saved.[9]

Later in private he admits to Watson that he "gave them some words that they would understand," words that sound like lines in a corporate report, because her family would not comprehend what she actually does, which is "outside the humdrum routine of ordinary life." The "ordinary life" in this case is a middle-class one in which one participates in intellectual labor that contributes directly and tangibly to the current financial economy. Watson says that she has not been able to explain to her family what she does as a sobriety counselor, most likely because the emotional work that she does is not readily translatable into measurable outcomes on financial reports.

When Watson accepts Holmes's proposal to become his apprentice in detective consulting, she encounters new social resistance against her career choice. In her first solo case, Watson confronts a male suspect whom she suspects has murdered his wife. The man lashes out by belittling her judgment as a woman: "You're just some woman with a crazy story. You want me to be guilty so you created this elaborate fiction to accommodate your theory."[10] Whether she is a trained police officer (e.g., Detective Kate Beckett in *Castle*) or an amateur sleuth (e.g., Veronica

Mars), women detectives in popular culture often contend with (male) suspects who challenge their expertise based on their gender, be it through sexual harassment, suspicions of mental instability, or accusations of having a man-hating vendetta. Watson faces a similar attack by a white middle-class male suspect. In response, she highlights the culture of sexism that makes the trope of the hysterical woman so familiar and readily available in the first place: "But don't take my word for it. I'm just a woman with a crazy story."[11]

Not only does Watson face sexism from hostile male suspects, she must also contend with the male-dominated world of policing that has historically been the domain of (masculine) physical strength.[12] During a particularly difficult and personal case for Holmes, Captain Gregson (Aidan Quinn), who invites Holmes and Watson as consultants on cases at the NYPD, attempts to put Watson out of harm's way by getting her to leave Holmes's side:

> Gregson: Guys like him, they walk around between raindrops. They don't get wet. People like you do, people like his ex-girlfriend do.

> Watson: So you're concerned for my safety? You're in the danger zone also.

> Gregson: I've been a cop for thirty years. I carry a gun.

> Watson: And a penis.

> Gregson: You think this is about you being a woman?[13]

While Gregson tries to deny Watson's claim that he is being sexist, he puts Watson in the same category as Holmes's ex-girlfriend, a (female) victim, rather than as Holmes's partner and equal on a case. Watson faces a similar plight of policewomen, who have historically been subject to cultural stereotypes of women as unable to meet the physical and gender ideal of police officers and relegated to lower-status tasks such as secretarial work and domestic cases.[14]

By the end of the first season, however, Watson emerges as a vital member of the police force as a detective consultant who is on par with Holmes. In "The Woman/Heroine," the final two-part episodes of the season, Watson leads the major case involving Irene Adler. Adler is Holmes's former lover, whom he believed was murdered by his notorious nemesis, Moriarty, but who is later revealed to be Moriarty herself. While investigating the crime scene, Watson uses Holmes's method and discovers a major clue. Detective Bell turns to Captain Gregson and says, "Feels just like having Holmes here, doesn't it?"[15] By the end of the episode and the season, Watson proves herself to be more than just a copy of Holmes. In a major plot twist and in a reversal of the roles of student and teacher, Watson coaches Holmes to trick Adler/Moriarty into revealing herself. Holmes says to Adler/Moriarty, "You know, she solved you,"[16] confirming that Watson has become his intellectual equal by defeating his nemesis.

ABSENT PRESENCE OF RACE

In the show's narrative, Watson's gender is a point of contention but not her racialization. She calls misogyny by name, but race and potential racism go unnamed. Watson's father is white and her mother is Chinese American, and despite being mixed raced, neither Watson nor her brother appears to have an ambiguous racial phenotype. We note the arguments in critical science studies that biological race is not a stable determinant of human difference, and that there are fluidities and ambiguities between supposedly pure racial categories.[17] However, feminist media studies literature suggests that women of color have been lumped together into one homogenous category of Other, with little regard for their racial, ethnic, or socio-historical specificities and differences, a representational practice that is a part of the colonial project.[18] Hence, the absence of visible mixed-racedness in Watson and in her brother supports this historical trend in popular culture in which all categories of nonwhiteness are rendered interchangeable with one another as a homogenous Other.

At the same time, however, Watson is a new kind of racialized woman on American television. In her analysis of Sydney Fox from the series *Relic Hunter*, Yasmin Jiwani argues that Fox is a reimagining of the racialized woman but one that still draws on an existing repertoire of colonial and Orientalist visual imagery, and that has been adapted to the new racial order.[19] Watson and Fox share many similarities: both have a white father and a mother who is a woman of color, and both have the class privilege that allows them access to higher education—Watson is a doctor and Fox is an archaeologist. Jiwani argues that Fox

> typifies the American Dream: the self-made woman whose professional and material success can be attributed to a combination of the innate race and class privilege imparted by her father and that certain je ne sais quoi afforded by her mother's cultural legacy. Sydney, in other words, epitomizes the liberal ideology of equality that is enshrined in the whole notion of the American Dream.[20]

However, Watson is not a poster child for the racial minority who attained the American Dream. She failed in the hierarchized capitalist labor market when she went from surgery, which is a profession of the upper middle class, to police work, which is predominantly the profession of the working class. Also, while Fox is hypersexualized, Watson is not. This is not only a departure from Fox and from previous representations of

Asian (American) women as dominatrix dragon ladies, sexually accessible geishas, and sexy martial arts masters, but it also marks a change for Liu who has often been typecast in these latter roles (e.g., in *Payback* and in *Charlie's Angels*). Hence, despite the show's shortcomings in representing mixed-racedness, Watson's character provides a new vocabulary for thinking about success and about successful women in the racial politics of immigration and the American Dream.

Finally, the dynamic between Watson and Adler/Moriarty presents a new kind of representation of the relationship between a woman of color and a white woman. In colonial iconography, the indigenous woman represents a danger to the empire: her exotic sexuality makes her an object of desire for the white male colonizer, and her fecundity can lead to miscegenation, which allegedly taints the pure European blood.[21] In contrast, the white middle-class woman represents future mothers whose racial purity and implied sexual innocence allow her to produce legitimate white children of the empire.[22] Hence, in the colonial iconography the relationship between the indigenous woman (who is later made synonymous with the postcolonial woman of color) and the white woman revolves around the figure of the white man. However, Watson and Adler/Moriarty's relationship to one another departs from this cultural script. Neither has a typical gendered relationship to Holmes: Adler/Moriarty was once Holmes's lover but is now his nemesis who rivals his intellect, and Watson is not romantically or sexually involved with Holmes but shares a very intimate platonic friendship with him. Subsequently, the dynamic between Watson and Adler/Moriarty is a battle of wits between two intelligent women, not a struggle for a man's attention.

While exceptionally intelligent women such as Adler/Moriarty are not common in popular culture, such characters do exist, for example, Dr. Temperance Brennan in *Bones*, Hermione Granger in the *Harry Potter* series, and Lisa Simpson in *The Simpsons*. However, a woman of color in a purely platonic yet close relationship with a white man based on shared intellectual curiosities is not a readily available cultural trope. Adler/Moriarty cannot figure out Watson's relationship to him: "You're like a mascot. . . . Do you want to sleep with him?"[23] Adler/Moriarty can only understand Watson in terms of existing cultural images of women of color—as a token racialized extra who has no personhood of her own and exists only to cheer on the main character. However, Watson turns out to be much more complex: she is intelligent without sacrificing empathy or morality, she is neither the demure geisha nor the dominatrix dragon lady, and she is neither the evil seductress nor the forgettable token extra. She is something new in the cultural iconography of racialized women, particularly of Asian (American) women, in popular culture.

CHALLENGING THE MALE GENIUS: SHERLOCK HOLMES

While Dr. Joan Watson presents us with an alternative image of the smart woman in popular culture, the character of Sherlock Holmes also plays an important part in this discussion about gender, emotion, and intelligence. Sherlock Holmes, as originally written by Sir Arthur Conan Doyle, is a "creature of science rather than emotion,"[24] and this aspect of his character has remained fairly consistent over the years despite the numerous adaptations, and even as Holmes has changed to reflect changing cultural constructions of masculinity where "brainy is the new sexy."[25] In many ways, *Elementary*'s Holmes builds upon Sir Conan Doyle's original vision but with a contemporary twist—he is still obsessed with the pursuit of scientific reasoning but he also reveals an emotional side that is more in tune with representations of the "new man."[26]

Although the popularization of feminist ideals has influenced the construction of female detectives in popular culture, according to Rebecca Feasey representations of masculinity in crime dramas have remained fairly consistent since the 1950s.[27] The male detective or agent's authoritative role is rarely questioned, and when men do face personal challenges, the work almost always takes priority over family and romance. In this way, she notes, contemporary crime dramas—even as they acknowledge that modern men also struggle with the work-life balance—ultimately reproduce distinctions between the public and the private. Using Jack from *24* to illustrate her point, Feasey shows how, in the interests of national security and upholding law and order, the male detective must eschew personal responsibilities and does so by neglecting his wife and daughter. What is more, viewers are invited to sympathize with these choices, rather than hold these men accountable for their actions. Thus, the failings of contemporary (white, middle-class, heterosexual) men are excused while reinforcing the idea that men's needs and roles are more important than those of women, thus pushing the latter to the margins of the public sphere.[28]

In a similar fashion, Holmes puts his work above all other facets of his life and takes what few relationships he does have for granted. For instance, Captain Gregson is often frustrated with Holmes's lack of sensitivity to those around him (e.g., Watson's safety) and his assumption that virtually everyone is his intellectual inferior. However, *Elementary*'s Holmes departs from Sir Conan Doyle's original characterization and also from the portrayal of masculinity in recent crime dramas: he is capable of emotional growth and a significant part of his character development in the first season is to learn the value of the people around him. In an episode where Holmes is kidnapped, Watson is forced to break her confidentiality agreement as a sobriety counselor and reveals Holmes's history of addiction and recovery to Gregson. To Holmes's surprise, Gregson already knows: "Do you honestly think I would let you consult for the NYPD without doing my homework?"[29] This is one of many key moments in the season where Holmes is confronted with the reality that he is not the only one with smarts and that other people have their own intellectual strengths and investigative strategies. Importantly, Holmes seems to have learned something from this encounter, as in the next episode he comments to a murder suspect, rather self-reflexively: "One of the dangers of brilliance, however, is that you sometimes fail to recognize the possibility that others are, at least in some respect, just as brilliant."[30]

On another level, we might also read this as a veiled critique of intellectualism as a classed concept. The claim that the upper middle class are naturally smarter than the working class is part of the discourse of class and economic inequality that has historically worked to exclude people of the working class from accessing postsecondary education, which in turn limits the latter's occupational options.[31] Such social perceptions also structure differences between working class and upper-middle-class men, which underpins the professional and personal dynamic between Holmes and Gregson.[32] Indeed, Captain Gregson's New York accent and profession as a civil servant mark him as different from Holmes, who comes from an old British family and old money, and has the socioeconomic privilege to work for free—for Holmes consulting is a rewarding intellectual passion. Gregson calls this privilege into question, reminding Holmes that he is not as special as he thinks, even poking fun at his so-called special abilities.

Holmes: I knew the Red Team's plan and then I told him that.

Gregson: How did you figure that out?

Holmes: I thought very quickly, very carefully.

Gregson: You mean you guessed?[33]

Thus, while Watson works to underscore the gendered dimension of intelligence, here Gregson reveals a classed distinction. When an upper-middle-class white British man of elite schooling makes a guess, he can claim to be using deductive reasoning, while a working-class man without access to such education does not have the privilege to make such claims.

HOLMES AND WATSON, AN EQUAL PARTNERSHIP

Elementary tackles gendered understandings of intelligence not only by questioning Holmes's intellectual credibility but by destabilizing the gender dichotomy that associates femininity with emotions and the private sphere, and masculinity with rationality and the public sphere. This plays out through the relationship between Holmes and Watson, and these tensions are evident in their work as detective consultants and in the way that Holmes responds to his addiction recovery. As his sobriety counselor, Watson shows Holmes that emotions have a place in both the world of work and in one's personal life.

At first, Holmes displays little understanding and interest in Watson's work as a sobriety counselor. In the first episode he refers to her as a "glorified helper monkey" and an "addict sitter,"[34] suggesting that he does not take her work seriously. Professional fields such as nursing and teaching, which tend to be female dominated and rely on a combination of emotional and intellectual labor, are similarly devalued in the public sphere.[35] Holmes's lack of understanding or appreciation for the place of emotions as another aspect of intelligence is also reflected in his unwillingness to be an active participant in AA (Alcoholics Anonymous) meetings, something that is a source of struggle between Holmes and Watson early on. Watson reminds him that their companionship is not one-sided and that he must be willing to open himself up to herself and others, to be vulnerable and trusting. Holmes proclaims that he finds the AA meetings tedious and refuses to empathize or connect with other recovering addicts. He refers to their narratives as "sob stories" comprised of "useless facts" that take up valuable brain space that he would rather use to solve cases.[36] However, later on in the episode, Holmes draws on his own sob story to confront a suspect about his drug use. Thus, his own experience with addiction becomes an important point of identification and empathy that allows him to reach out to the man, whom he gently but firmly encourages to get help. These moments of personal growth help to give Holmes a better appreciation of and respect for Watson's work.

Building on these experiences, Holmes eventually comes around to the idea that there is something useful in attending the meetings. This culminates in one of the most emotional episodes of the season for Holmes. He reveals a deeply personal secret as his one-year anniversary of sobriety looms—that he relapsed right after entering rehab and so his first day of sobriety actually begins a day later than he let on. As viewers, we are invited, through Watson's reaction, to feel compassion for Holmes, whose vulnerability is on full display, revealing to us that he is indeed more than a self-involved sleuth. We watch him struggle to deal with his emotions, which push the limits of cold, scientific logic and bodily control, and which cannot be easily solved through deductive reasoning. Sometimes, Holmes's intellectual tricks fail and he must contend with the pain of his past. Indeed, such transformative moments are integral to his recovery, painting a picture of a more complicated (and even messy) masculinity that challenges traditionalist discourses of masculinity that present men as unemotional, insensitive, and possessing a "tough mental attitude."[37]

BEYOND THE ROMANCE: NEW KINDS OF
MALE-FEMALE RELATIONSHIPS

The limits of Holmes's intelligence are called into question in his confrontation with Adler/Moriarty. When Holmes first met Adler/Moriarty, she was pretending to be Irene Adler, a painter and an occasional art thief. She seduced Holmes and then tricked him into believing that she was killed by a faceless enemy named Moriarty and that her death was Holmes's fault. The trauma of this event resulted in Holmes's depression and heroin addiction. In the scene where Adler/Moriarty's duplicity is revealed, she towers over Holmes, who has recently been shot and is extremely vulnerable. She explains to Holmes that she had to keep her true identity a secret due to gender bias in the criminal world: "As if men had a monopoly on murder."[38] She reveals that their romantic relationship was a way for her to maintain control over Holmes and to divert his attention from cases that involved her. In him she found someone who was her intellectual equal. She describes him as "a mind that rivalled [her] own" that she wanted to study "in [his] own environment,"[39] as though she is a biologist studying an animal in the wild. When Holmes tries to reclaim his dignity by asking whether she thinks that they are the same, she coolly and matter-of-factly contradicts him: "I'm saying I'm better. . . . You're a game that I will win every time."[40] Adler/Moriarty's physical and intellectual dominance over Holmes in this scene is completely devoid of sexuality and seduction: she wears a militaristic suit that comes up to her neck and her physical comportment is visibly masculine and domineering. Adler/Moriarty lists all the ways in which Holmes has disappointed her, that is, his depression and his heroin addiction. In calling attention to what she implies is a weakness in him, Adler/Moriarty also calls his masculinity into question—that he succumbed to his emotions and let his love for her override good sense.

Adler/Moriarty demands traditional masculine ideals of intelligence from Holmes, that is, to pursue rationality with single-mindedness, with brutality if necessary, and at all costs, be they human lives or jeopardizing one's relationships. Meanwhile, Watson pushes Holmes to synthesize empathy and emotional intelligence with his cerebral intelligence. While Holmes learns to be more trusting and open with his friends and colleagues, Watson in particular, his encounter with Adler/Moriarty and the revelation that their love was a fraud seem to refuel his emotional detachment, prompting him to disavow love altogether: "I am now and forever post-love."[41] At the same time that he abandons the ideal of romance, he fully embraces his friendship with his ally and partner, Watson, in whom he places his utmost trust and with whom he shares his methods and his love of knowledge. Early in their association he confesses to Watson that he is "sharper" and "more focused" with Watson.[42] However, as the season wears on it is evident that Holmes sees Watson as more than just a catalyst for his own intellectual process. Rather, she becomes his true partner—professionally, intellectually, domestically, and emotionally. However, *Elementary* stops short of suggesting that they will become romantically involved despite assumptions to the contrary, as some critics assumed rather harshly, that Lucy Liu was cast as the "love interest" [43] (events in the second season make this narrative conclusion even less of a possibility). Thus the closeness and respect they develop for each other is not a precursor to a stereotypical heterosexual romance but instead becomes the glue that binds them together as friends, peers, and consulting partners, and for once in his life Holmes is thinking about someone other than himself.

CONCLUSION

Elementary invites its audience to question the idea of intelligence by revisiting and reimagining the well-known stories of Sherlock Holmes, who is the ultimate archetype of the genius. Through Holmes and Watson, the show denaturalizes distinctions between men and women, instead offering more nuanced and elastic gender representations where women, particularly women of color, are unquestionably as capable and intelligent as (white) men, and where smart men are also emotionally vulnerable and imperfect. Also, Watson and Holmes are situated outside of heteronormative traditions: we are asked to accept them for who they are, as individuals and as domestic and intellectual partners, and not as potential wives, husbands, or parents, even if surely some viewers pine for this resolution. Holmes in particular explicitly rejects such gender scripts for men. Watson seems more comfortable juggling the personal with the professional (we see her go on dates) but, while she is not as critical of love, marriage, and family as Holmes, she also never openly discusses these things. Admittedly, as female fans of the program, we find it very refreshing to see a media representation of a woman that does not revolve around these stereotypical feminine concerns—indeed, Watson seems to be the antithesis of these other women.

When *Elementary* rewrote Dr. John Watson as Dr. Joan Watson, it accomplished much more than gender swapping or gender role reversal. The original stories with Dr. John Watson lent themselves to homoerotic interpretations, as we can see in the BBC's *Sherlock* and to a lesser degree in Guy Richie's *Sherlock Holmes* films that raise interesting questions about intimacy in male-male relationships. With Dr. Joan Watson, *Elementary* pushes the limits of female-male relationships beyond romance and sexual tension. We see two people—geeks, by today's cultural language—whose relationship is founded on a shared love for "the bizarre and unusual," [44] as Holmes puts it. However, the absence of romance or sex does not imply that their friendship is devoid of intimacy. They live together and they work together as partners. The entire storyline of *Elementary* is based on their individual emotional and intellectual developments and the development of their friendship. They are each a new kind of woman and man, and their partnership is a new kind of relationship between a woman and a man in which intelligence—in all its variations and diverse range—figures centrally.

NOTES

1. Heather Nunn and Anita Biressi, "Silent Witness: Detection, Femininity, and the Post-Mortem Body," *Feminist Media Studies* 3, no. 2 (2003): 193–206; Lisa M. Cuklanz and Sujata Moorti, "Television's 'New' Feminism: Prime-Time Representations of Women and Victimization," *Critical Studies in Media Communication* 23, no. 4 (2006): 302–21; Linda Mizejewski, *Hardboiled and High Heeled: The Woman Detective in Popular Culture* (New York: Routledge, 2004).

2. Nunn and Biressi, "Silent Witness," 194.

3. Danae Clark, "*Cagney and Lacey*: Feminist Strategies of Detection," in *Media Studies: A Reader*, ed. Sue Thornham, Caroline Bassett, and Paul Marris (Edinburgh: Edinburgh University Press, 1996), 211–20.

4. Mizejewski, *Hardboiled and High Heeled*.

5. Mary Ellen Guy and Meredith A. Newman, "Women's Jobs, Men's Jobs: Sex Segregation and Emotional Labor," *Public Administration Review* 64, no. 3 (May 2004): 289–98.

6. "A Giant Gun, Filled with Drugs," *Elementary* (New York: September 27, 2012); episode aired February 7, 2013.

7. "Dirty Laundry," *Elementary*.

8. Lisa Cartwright, *Screening the Body: Tracing Medicine's Visual Culture* (Minneapolis: University of Minnesota Press, 1995).

9. "The Leviathan," *Elementary*.

10. "A Déjà vu All Over Again," *Elementary*.

11. "A Déjà vu All Over Again," *Elementary*.

12. Jennifer M. Brown, "Aspects of Discriminatory Treatment of Women Police Officers Serving in Forces in England and Wales," *British Journal of Criminology* 38, no. 2 (1998): 265–82.

13. "Risk Management," *Elementary*.

14. Susan E. Martin, "'Outsider Within' the Station House: The Impact of Race and Gender on Black Women Police," *Social Problems* 41, no. 1 (1994): 383–400; Brown, "Aspects of Discriminatory Treatment of Women Police Officers."

15. "The Woman/Heroine," *Elementary*.

16. "The Woman/Heroine," *Elementary*.

17. Geoffrey C. Bowker and Susan Leigh Star, *Sorting Things Out: Classification and Its Consequences* (Cambridge, MA: MIT Press, 1999).

18. Yasmin Jiwani, "The Eurasian Female Hero(ine): Sydney Fox as the Relic Hunter," *Journal of Popular Film & Television* 32, no. 4 (2005): 183.

19. Jiwani, "The Eurasian Female Hero(ine)," 183.

20. Jiwani, "The Eurasian Female Hero(ine)," 188.

21. Jiwani, "The Eurasian Female Hero(ine)," 188.

22. Dorothy E. Chunn, "Sex and Citizenship: (Hetero)Sexual Offenses, Law and 'White' Settler Society," in *Contesting Canadian Citizenship: Historical Readings*, ed. Robert Adamoski, Dorothy E. Chunn, and Robert Menzies (Toronto, ON: University of Toronto Press, 2002), 359–84.

23. "The Woman/Heroine," *Elementary*.

24. Anissa M. Graham and Jennifer C. Garlen, "Sex and the Single Sleuth," in *Sherlock Homes for the 21st Century: Essays on New Adaptations*, ed. Lynnette Porter (Jefferson, NC: McFarland, 2012), 24.

25. Graham and Garlen, "Sex and the Single Sleuth," 24.

26. Rebecca Feasey, *Masculinity and Popular Television* (Edinburgh: Edinburgh University Press, 2008); Graham and Garlen, "Sex and the Single Sleuth"; Katie Milestone and Anneke Meyer, *Gender and Popular Culture* (Malden, MA: Polity Press, 2012).

27. Feasey, *Masculinity and Popular Television*, 86.

28. Feasey, *Masculinity and Popular Television*, 86.

29. "The Rat Race," *Elementary*.

30. "Lesser Evils," *Elementary*.

31. Helen Hyunji Kang, "Medical Disinterestedness: An Archaeology of Scientificness and Morality in the Canadian Medical Profession" (PhD diss., Simon Fraser University, British Columbia, Canada, 2013).

32. David Morgan, "Class and Masculinity," in *Handbook of Studies on Men and Masculinities*, eds. Michael Kimmel, Jeff Hearn, and R.W. Connell (Thousand Oaks, CA: Sage Publications, 2005), 165–77.

33. "The Red Team," *Elementary*.

34. "Pilot," *Elementary*. For the first part of the season, Holmes almost never refers to Watson by her official role, instead using generic work titles like "assistant" in order to retain his privacy. Later on, she becomes his "partner" reflecting the change in their professional relationship.

35. Guy and Newman, "Women's Jobs, Men's Jobs," 289–98.

36. "While You Were Sleeping," *Elementary*.

37. Milestone and Meyer, *Gender and Popular Culture*, 114.

38. "The Woman/Heroine," *Elementary*.

39. "The Woman/Heroine," *Elementary*.

40. "The Woman/Heroine," *Elementary*.

41. "We Are Everyone," *Elementary*.

42. "Details," *Elementary*.

43. Laura Prudom, "*Elementary* Aims to Update Sherlock Holmes with Dated Ideas: Is CBS Afraid to Go Gay?" *Huffpost TV: The Blog*, 29 February 2012, http://www. huffingtonpost.com/laura-prudom/elementary-cbs_b_1311340.html (accessed 2 November 2013).

44. "Possibility Two," *Elementary*.

BIBLIOGRAPHY

Bowker, Geoffrey C., and Susan Leigh Star. *Sorting Things Out: Classification and Its Consequences*. Cambridge, MA: MIT Press, 1999.

Brown, Jennifer M. "Aspects of Discriminatory Treatment of Women Police Officers Serving in Forces in England and Wales." *British Journal of Criminology* 38, no. 2 (1998): 265–82.

Cartwright, Lisa. *Screening the Body: Tracing Medicine's Visual Culture*. Minneapolis: University of Minnesota Press, 1995.

Chunn, Dorothy E. "Sex and Citizenship: (Hetero)Sexual Offenses, Law and 'White' Settler Society." In *Contesting Canadian Citizenship: Historical Readings*, edited by Robert Adomaski, Dorothy E. Chunn, and Robert Menzies, 359–84. Toronto, ON: University of Toronto Press, 2002.

Clark, Danae. "*Cagney and Lacey*: Feminist Strategies of Detection." In *Media Studies: A Reader*, edited by Sue Thornham, Caroline Bassett, and Paul Marris, 211–20. Edinburgh: Edinburgh University Press, 1996.

Cuklanz, Lisa S., and Sujata Moorti. "Television's 'New' Feminism: Prime-Time Representations of Women and Victimization." *Critical Studies in Media Communication* 23, no. 4 (2006): 302–21.

Elementary. New York: CBS, September 27, 2012.

Feasey, Rebecca. *Masculinity and Popular Television*. Edinburgh: Edinburgh University Press, 2008.

Graham, Anissa. M., and Jennifer C. Garlen. "Sex and the Single Sleuth." In *Sherlock Homes for the 21st Century: Essays on New Adaptations*, edited by Lynnette Porter, 24–34. Jefferson, NC: McFarland, 2012.

Guy, Mary Ellen, and Meredith A. Newman. "Women's Jobs, Men's Jobs: Sex Segregation and Emotional Labor." *Public Administration Review* 64, no. 3 (May/June 2004): 289–98.

Jiwani, Yasmin. "The Eurasian Female Hero(ine): Sydney Fox as the Relic Hunter." *Journal of Popular Film & Television* 32, no. 4 (2005): 182–91.

Kang, Helen Hyunji. "Medical Disinterestedness: An Archaeology of Scientificness and Morality in the Canadian Medical Profession." PhD diss., Simon Fraser University, British Columbia, Canada, 2013.

Martin, Susan E. "'Outsider within' the Station House: The Impact of Race and Gender on Black Women Police." *Social Problems* 41, no. 3 (1994): 383–400.

McClintock, Anne. *Imperial Leather: Race, Gender and Sexuality in the Colonial Contest*. New York: Routledge, 1995.

Milestone, Katie, and Anneke Meyer. *Gender and Popular Culture*. Malden, MA: Polity Press, 2012.

Mizejewski, Linda. *Hardboiled and High Heeled: The Woman Detective in Popular Culture*. New York: Routledge, 2004.

Morgan, David. "Class and Masculinity." In *Handbook of Studies on Men and Masculinities*, edited by Michael Kimmel, Jeff Hearn, and R.W. Connell, 165–77. Thousand Oaks, CA: Sage Publications, 2005.

Nunn, Heather, and Anita Biressi. "Silent Witness: Detection, Femininity, and the Post-Mortem Body." *Feminist Media Studies* 3, no. 2 (2003): 193–206.

Prudom, Laura. "*Elementary* Aims to Update Sherlock Holmes with Dated Ideas: Is CBS Afraid to Go Gay?" *Huffpost TV: The Blog*. 29 February 2012. http://www.huffingtonpost.com/laura-prudom/elementary-cbs_b_1311340.html (accessed 2 November 2013).

NINE

Stories Worth Telling

How Kerry Washington Balances Brains, Beauty, and Power in Hollywood

De Anna J. Reese

One of the most popular actresses in film and television, Kerry Washington possesses talent and success that mark a defining moment for black women in entertainment. A modern-day renaissance woman, Washington tackles the big screen, television, and politics with equal fervor. These days one is as likely to see her at a fundraiser in support of the arts or a forum on voting, as one would on the red carpet attending an awards show for her brilliant portrayal of the consummate Washington DC fixer Olivia Pope in the ABC primetime series *Scandal*. In 2013 she became the first black woman in almost twenty years to receive a nomination for a primetime Emmy Award for lead actress in a drama series.[1] Although Washington did not win, her portrayal of Olivia Pope is a radical departure from the types of roles in which black women are typically cast or for which they receive recognition.[2]

Rarely ever viewed as smart and competent on television or in film, black women are best known for their roles as cooks, maids, prostitutes, or abused women.[3] Despite stellar performances, the roles played by Oscar winners Hattie McDaniel, Halle Berry, Mo'Nique, and Octavia Spencer each reflect a society that has become far too comfortable with viewing poverty, domestic abuse, domestic work, and illegitimacy as the exclusive preserve of black women. In turn, many have asked whether a black woman can be taken seriously on prime-time television for her brains and leadership. The answer is yes, and perhaps this is why the character of Olivia Pope and the show *Scandal* have garnered so much attention. After a modest start in 2012, the much-tweeted-about drama is one of television's fastest-growing series.[4] Both speak to an important change underway for women of color on television and film; a change that would not be possible if not for the small but growing number of black female writers and producers, among them Shonda Rhimes, Suzanne De Passe, Tanya Hamilton, Mara Brock Akil, and Ava DuVernay.[5]

Consequently, these writers have been able to do something others have done only with limited success—tell the stories of black women in ways that are relevant and accessible. At a time when network executives have chosen to saturate the market with cheap, nonsubstantive reality television shows that far too often portray its female leads, especially African Americans, as bossy, manipulative, and belligerent, Kerry Washington gives new meaning to depictions of smart women on television. By examining *Scandal's* Olivia Pope, this chapter will show how the character builds on the legacy of other black professional women on television. It will also explore the ways in which stereotypical images of black women continue to impact acceptable notions of black womanhood on the small screen. Lastly, the chapter will highlight how the upbringing, education, and activism of Kerry Washington impact the grace and authenticity she brings to her role on *Scandal*.

Based on the real-life drama of crisis management adviser Judy Smith, *Scandal* shows the wit and charisma of Olivia Pope, who alongside her associates, "the gladiators," works to contain out-of-control, panic-driven situations while saving her high-profile clients from public disgrace.[6] The embodiment of confidence, class, and grace, Olivia Carolyn Pope is a smart independent woman whose gut-level instincts, pragmatism, and problem-solving skills enable her to protect and often remake the public image of her clients. However, what makes this role entirely different from that of other black professional women on television is the confidence and trust that Pope has earned from her peers.

At her quasi-law firm Pope and Associates, Pope's intellect does not appear to threaten those who work for her. On the contrary, her colleagues praise both her leadership and character to defend and protect the interests of her clients. In its debut episode, "Sweet Baby," Harrison Wright, played by Columbus Short, describes to new gladiator Quinn Perkins that Pope and Associates is not a law firm—they are lawyers who make problems (big or small) go away; they manage crisis and save reputations. With no commitment to finding justice or solving crimes, Pope is not only one of the "good guys," she is the best guy—a gladiator in a suit.[7]

What is striking about this scenario is the extent to which the gladiators concede to Pope's judgment about cases they would rather not take. Whether it's keeping ambassadors safe, defending gay war heroes, or protecting another mistress of the President, Pope's colleagues allow her a freedom few black women on television have historically ever had—the ability to set the rules and make decisions for the entire group. These are decisions the audience views as feasible given the exemplary job of *Scandal*'s production team in helping us believe Olivia Pope always knows what to do. Impeccably dressed each episode in designer suits while R&B artists like the Staple Singers, Sam Cooke, and Stevie Wonder play in the background, Pope commands respect from everyone she meets. And while she chooses to represent clients based on gut instinct, she is smart in how she leverages her power and reputation to assist the rich and powerful.

For example, in the episode "Hell Hath No Fury," Olivia reluctantly takes the case of a millionaire's son accused of rape. His mother desperately asks for Olivia's help even after there is evidence to suggest her son is guilty. In order to get dirt on the prosecutor, Olivia uses her love-hate relationship with US Attorney David Rosen (played by Joshua Malina) to make her case. She brings him coffee while he's on his morning run, and while he refers to her as "a stalker," Olivia insists they are "friends." Even though Rosen is unable to help her out, Olivia manages to get the prosecutor demoted, which is good because the prosecutor wants Rosen's job. After the millionaire's son is led away by the police, Rosen swings by long enough to tell Olivia that maybe they can be friends after all.[8]

ON THE ROAD TO *SCANDAL*

Long before Olivia Pope became the rapid-talking media relations consultant, there were others who attempted to create a more visible presence of African American women on television. Louise Beavers, well known for her roles in *Imitation of Life* and later *Beulah*, Hazel Scott, and Ethel Waters each had their own short-lived shows. Bereft of the support that would have enabled them to attract mainstream advertisers, most of the early shows featuring black stars failed. It was not until 1968 that Diahann Carroll changed the face of television when she became the first African American to star in her own television series, *Julia*.[9] This groundbreaking role was the first step in changing familiar ideas about black women, as it marked the first time a prime-time program featured a professional black woman in the starring role. Although Julia was a well-spoken nurse raising her only son after her husband's death in Vietnam, one major critique of the show was its inability to adequately address race and gender issues. In 1974, Teresa Graves would also star in her own series in *Get Christie Love*. Based on the pilot film with the same name, the show featured Graves as an undercover detective on the Los Angeles police force. Nonetheless, its blaxploitation references, stereotypical depictions, and time slot against Angie Dickinson's *Police Woman* ended the series after only one season.[10]

In the last forty years, shows featuring black professional women are still scarce. The 1980s brought a few other black women to television notably Debbie Allen, Phylicia Rashad, and daytime's Oprah Winfrey. In the 1990s, the sitcom *Living Single* was the only show that placed a spotlight on the pride and success of several black professional women. And in 2000, the sitcom *Girlfriends* was also about the lives of four smart and savvy women, although it focused much more on the personal drama of the characters rather than on their careers.[11] Over a decade later, *Scandal* has carved out a small but significant space for ethnic diversity on prime-time. Both self-identified feminists, Rhimes and Washington are eager to move away from portrayals of women as dim-witted, hyper-sexualized objects, to ones in which "women have the power."[12]

Washington has come to recognize this power. In one *Parade* magazine article, she states that she did not realize it had been almost forty years since a woman of color carried a network drama when she auditioned. "I knew that in my lifetime, I'd never seen it. But it didn't compute to me that I'd be making history. I just fell in love with the character."[13] *Scandal*'s success has also influenced competing networks such as NBC, which recently launched (and since cancelled) a new series starring Meagan Good. Originally titled *Notorious*, the show returned with the new title of *Deception* in which Good played detective Joanna Locasto. However, unlike the upper-middle-class background of Pope, Locasto was the daughter of the maid who grew up alongside a well-to-do family.[14]

Robert Entman and Andrew Rojecki, authors of *The Black Image in the White Mind*, discuss the longstanding racial divide in prime-time television and how major networks work at appealing to white audiences through segregated programming. They also note the relationship between stereotypical television and movie images and their link to human perception. In this sense, each member of a marginalized population bears the burden of representing his or her entire group. For some viewers, if a character conforms in any way to a negative stereotype, that is what they will notice and remember. Evidence suggests this is changing among younger viewers, and the success of shows like *Scandal* indicates this progression.[15] In doing so, *Scandal* has also done something most prime-time shows never do—create a black female lead character who is both smart and alluring.

With professional success, beauty, and social status, Pope is well respected by her gladiator team who would, as character Abby Wheelan mentions in the episode "Enemy of the State," go over a cliff for her.[16] Olivia's femininity is also an asset, but unlike most shows, which tritely objectify the sexuality of its female characters, *Scandal* downplays the sexuality of its women characters in order to emphasize their competence. For example, when Quinn interviews for the position with Pope and Associates, she is told first by Harrison and again upon meeting Olivia that she is showing too much cleavage.[17] With the help of award-winning costume designer Lyn Paolo, clothes are skillfully used to show-case Olivia's intellectual authority and femininity with styles that are slim cut and womanly, without revealing too much. The color white or cream is worn purposefully to symbolize her association with the good guys, but also her freedom from the constraints of the corporate world where staple colors like blue, gray, and an occasional red define the status quo.[18] These softer colors are worn to elicit Olivia's warmth and femininity in stark contrast to the harsh and cutthroat world of politics where she works.

Moreover, the success of characters such as Olivia Pope may be in part due to the visibility of more women in positions of power on television. The *Washington Post* reported that the participation of women in national politics has stagnated since the "year of the woman" (in 1992, when several female senators were elected),[19] possibly because of the rough and overtly sexist treatment of female candidates like Michele Bachmann, Sarah Palin, and Hillary Clinton. However, the one exception is fictional TV, where women in positions of power are now everywhere. A growing acceptance of women in politics has helped *Scandal*'s creator Shonda Rhimes develop smart and independent characters such as Pope, especially given the presence of powerful black women in national politics. Congresswomen such as Eleanor Holmes Norton (D-DC), Sheila Jackson Lee (D-TX), Maxine Waters (D-CA), Corrine Brown (D-FL), and Yvette Clarke (D-NY) have each made outstanding contributions on health care, education, universal human rights, and even Homeland Security even if there is little mention of their work or projects in the mainstream media.[20]

Moreover, the most visible public person to awaken the intellect and savvy of black women in politics is First Lady Michelle Obama. And while the family background of the First Lady can in no way be compared to the intrigue and dysfunction of Olivia Pope's life in DC, the two share a charismatic, confident, and graceful public persona, which enables them to inspire and motivate others. In turn, the power and presence of First Lady Michelle Obama in the last two national elections, coupled with that of other female leaders, have made television characters like Olivia Pope much more acceptable and realistic.

CONTROLLING IMAGERY, REALITY TV, AND OLIVIA POPE

Reality television has become a significant force in disseminating negative images about black women to the public. These shows often feature women who appear unreasonable, oversexed, violent, and lacking in self-esteem, reinforcing the worst stereotypes about the group. The popularity of shows such as *Love and Hip Hop, The Real Housewives of Atlanta,* and VH1's *Basketball Wives* are notorious in their depiction of "angry" black women. And while black women are abundant figures in these televised catfights, they remain, as earlier discussed, invisible on shows that deliver complex characters, well-written story lines, and top salaries. [21]

Offering characters that differ from the regular negative portrayals of black women on reality TV, Rhimes has been especially important in changing perceptions about women of color on television. Her two medical dramas—*Grey's Anatomy* and now-cancelled *Private Practice*—raised network ratings with their sexy plotlines and multicultural casts. She is also one of few African American producers with enough clout to get a network show written by, based on, and starring an African American. [22]

The portrayal of black women as stereotypical mammies, welfare recipients, and hot mammas has been essential to their oppression and domination. According to sociologist Patricia Hill Collins, controlling images are designed to make racism, sexism, and poverty appear to be a natural, normal, and inevitable part of everyday life. These images also make African American women appear as outsiders or strangers, enabling other groups to define what is normal. [23] Even as the smart, power-wielding, crisis management adviser of DC, Olivia Pope is unable to completely abandon the controlling images that dominate perceptions about the place of black women on television.

In turn, black career women like Pope encounter a curious repackaging of the controlling images generated for poor and working-class women such as the mammy and the jezebel. The loyal, nurturing female servant created under chattel slavery, the mammy symbolizes the ideal black female relationship to elite white male power. [24] In *Scandal*, Olivia is well respected with some authority over those around her, but she also has some of the qualities associated with the modern mammy. Driven by the needs and concerns of those in her circle, Olivia is the high-stakes fixer of everyone's problems except for her own. She is devoted to her clients no matter how difficult the case, or the toll it takes on her relatively nonexistent personal life. She also provides the perennial "shoulder" on which the gladiators depend to maintain their sanity and stability. In nearly every episode, there are constant references made to "Liv's fix-it skills." In one episode, First Lady Mellie Fitzgerald comments to her husband that if there is a serious problem, just call Olivia to fix it. [25]

In another episode, viewers witness the depth of Olivia's concern for one of her gladiators in which she is both boss and trusted adviser. Here Stephen Finch (played by Henry Ian Cusick) asks "to be talked into" a proposal to his girlfriend, Georgia. Pope tells him that he should propose because as opposed to the other women he has dated who were trashy, too young, or stupid, this woman is fun, old enough, and brilliant. [26] Mom-like Olivia has also organized every detail of the proposal including reservations at a fancy French restaurant and an expensive box of engagement rings for him; all he needs to do is choose one. Like a proud mother watching from a distance, Olivia comes to the restaurant to watch Stephen pop the question, but fights back her own anger and disappointment after learning that her lover, President Fitzgerald Grant or "Fitz," has lied about an affair with a young intern. Similar to the modern mammy who either has no family life or one that is second to her job, Olivia's concern for her "gladiator family" in the early episodes is more like a mother rather than close friend. When reminded by Stephen that she does not date, she replies that she is "not normal"; but regular people marry, so this is why he should propose and "get some normal." [27]

The modern mammy may also function as "the black lady." The black lady is known for her dignified public presence and strong work ethic. She typically works to maintain her status as part of the middle class and subscribes to middle-class notions (marriage and then motherhood) regarding her own sexuality. However, she is also part of the trope of controlling images that constrain the professional black woman. Similar to real-life public figures Oprah Winfrey and Condoleeza Rice, Olivia Pope is a prominent and powerful woman. Nonetheless, her affair with the President places her in a love triangle that makes her sexuality appear reckless and immoral—not only is she a home wrecker, she is a mistress with no regard for a standing marriage and three children.

As such, she has assumed the qualities often associated with the black woman as temptress or jezebel. While the details of the affair between Olivia and Fitz are not made public until nearly the end of season 2, there is an undercurrent of the sexual power dynamics during slavery that emerges when watching the sexual tension between Fitz and Olivia. In season 1, Olivia is presented to the audience as the good girl—hard working and confident, but guarded in reference to relationships. In season 2, the walls come down as viewers see a woman who is more comfortable with her sexuality. With season 3 now complete, revelations about Olivia's sexual past continue to highlight her character as a "good girl with bad tendencies"—one drawn to rich and powerful men who are unable to fully commit.

Affairs among the Washington elite, especially Presidents, are nothing new, but the fact that Olivia is involved with two white men (character Jake Ballard is the other) is a somewhat different twist. According to Rhimes, the fact that Fitz is white and Olivia is black is pretty much incidental to the story. Except for a brief but shocking Jefferson–Hemings reference in season 2, it has barely been acknowledged. [28] Viewers recognize that Olivia's love for Fitz is her major character flaw. Rhimes adds that most of the time on shows, the reason why characters are not together is internal. This is the opposite case for Fitz and Olivia. They want to be together, but their union would bring down his presidency. Fitz's marriage, revealed in more depth in season 2, remains key to his political career and an obstacle to the happiness of both him and Olivia. Rhimes also adds that she does not think the show is postracial: "I'm referring to race every time you see Kerry Washington being the person in charge and solving the crime and kissing the guy. Race is right there in your face."[29] Moreover television, like film, is an intricate site of cultural expression about race. Dominant perceptions about black women as caretakers who place their work above personal fulfillment, or sexual temptresses whose innate charm and beauty are believed to lure happily married men astray, are ones that continue to impact how even smart and empowered black women like Olivia Pope are understood and related to by mainstream audiences.

WASHINGTON INSIDER: KERRY'S PERSONAL POLITICS

Kerry Washington's personal standards of intellect, namely, her ability to tell good stories that deepen our understanding about the diversity of black women, begin with her childhood. Washington worked in both film and on Broadway before coming to television, giving her a background that perfectly fits her role on *Scandal*. A Bronx native and the only child of professional parents, Washington was fascinated by people as a child and admits to being quite sociable. "When I was about five or six, we'd take the train up to Amherst, where my mom was doing her dissertation, and I'd spend the whole trip going up and down the aisle asking people what they did."[30] She also commends her mother for channeling this energy into creative pursuits, acknowledging that whether it was children's theater, ballet class, or trips to the library, her mother always kept her actively engaged.

During her teen years, Washington commuted to Manhattan to attend the prestigious all-girls Spence School, the alma mater of Gwyneth Paltrow and Emmy Rossum. These years had a profound impact on helping Washington build her self-esteem and strengthen the value she placed on education over looks. They would also be the qualities Washington would draw from to better relate to and ultimately play other women. At the Paley Festival in New York, Washington told the audience,

> I was really lucky because I went to an all-girl school and that single sex education really helped me because I really learned to bond with women and to not compete with or compare myself as much because we were all allowed to be ourselves and be unique and kind of have our unique strengths. But I always felt like my value was much more in my intellect than it was in my appearance, and so that's what I spent time cultivating. And some of that I get from my mother, some of that comes from the schools that I went to, and some of that comes from probably insecurity.[31]

With greater emphasis placed on her education, Washington remembers acting as an enjoyable hobby. At age seventeen she made her television debut on the ABC Afterschool Special *Magical Make-Over*, but still thought she might become a psychologist or an educator like her mother. After participating in a summer conservatory program for actors in New York, she realized that she did not have to want fame to be an actor. In turn, her interest in acting was always more about the performance and bringing characters to life, rather than the superficial side of the business. Washington credits her parents with keeping her grounded especially in a business that places so much emphasis on the external. She recalls that the "looking pretty" part of the job was initially foreign and often intimidated her. Although she has now learned to embrace both aspects of the business, she refers to herself "as two different people: the real Kerry and the red carpet Kerry."[32]

Nevertheless, it was Washington's talent as an actress that would help pay for her college education. A graduate of George Washington University and member of Phi Beta Kappa, Washington returned to her alma mater where she gave the 2013 commencement address and received an honorary doctorate of Fine Arts. During her speech, Washington recalled developing a greater understanding for the value and importance of storytelling. Offered a scholarship in the Presidential Scholars in the Arts Program, she had to audition for every performance produced by the theater and dance department. Among them was the production of *Croak: The Last Frog*, for which she won the lead frog role. It was not a role she coveted, but it helped her grow as both a person and an actress.[33]

While acknowledging the praise received for her role on *Scandal*, Washington views herself as just an actor who plays pretend and "tells stories." Each has helped to prepare Washington for the powerful women she now plays, especially the role of Broomhilda von Shaft, the slave woman from *Django Unchained* (2012). Deeply affected by the events of the period, Washington said she barely survived *Django* emotionally, especially the violence and hearing the N-word every day. "It cost me a lot psychologically, but it was worth it to tell that story."[34] Having drawn inspiration from both characters she writes, "I'm grateful that these two women on opposite ends of history, on opposite ends of their experience, both strong women but in such different ways, can exist at the same time."[35]

Such stories continue to energize Washington's political activism and helped her to elect presidents both on and off screen. Even before President Obama's election in 2008, Washington was an ardent supporter. "I knew that he was the candidate we needed at the time, and I was inspired by the positive change he promised."[36] As the former co-chair for the Vote for Change initiative, Washington credits her socially conscious upbringing for her astute understanding of politics. At thirteen, she was taken to Yankee Stadium to see the newly freed Nelson Mandela speak,

and at eighteen she remembers celebrating her initiation into the electo-
rate with the same enthusiasm that other young women celebrate their
sixteenth birthday. As a teen, Washington began honing her acting skills
as part of an educational troupe at a local hospital that performed self-
written sex education sketches in schools and community centers. "It was
some of the best actor training I've ever had."[37] The sketches also taught
her the importance of really understanding one's character and the value
of improvisation.

Months before the 2008 election, the actress made her first trip to
Arkansas for Super Tuesday in February, where she hit the campaign
trail to build support for the Illinois senator. She admits that while some
may listen to her because she is a public figure, celebrity status is not
enough to get people to vote. Among the main points of her message was
to let people know that their voices mattered, that they had the power to
change this country for the better, and that it was important for different
voices to be heard. When asked by one reporter if she would like to run
for office, Washington replied that she would love to work in public
policy in DC someday, but did not know if stumping on the campaign
trail necessarily made one a good leader. Among her Hollywood role
models is Jane Alexander, an Emmy Award winner and acclaimed stage
and film actress who became the chairwoman of the National Endow-
ment for the Arts.[38]

In the 2012 presidential campaign, Washington continued her support
for the President's agenda while issuing her own advice on the role and
responsibility of everyday citizens to create change and continue the
democratic process. Although acknowledging the importance of voting,
especially for groups who have fought long and hard for this privilege,
she emphasized that having a voice in the political process was about
more than just voting. It was about participation and doing whatever one
could to elect progressive leaders. "If we want change and our voices
heard, we must ask ourselves: What more can I do?"[39] With this sentiment, Washington has shown how politically adept she has become at
urging fellow citizens to "find their voice" and think about the ways that
they and others can get more involved with the process. In her own
words, Washington reminded volunteers that their support for the campaign was a way to honor the sacrifices of those who have come before,
and a way to ensure a brighter future for those who will come after. She
celebrated those who worked on behalf of the President as a reminder of
the power and importance of the people in making our democracy work.
This, Washington believes, is one of the unique privileges we have as
Americans.[40]

With a penchant for choosing roles that showcase her talent to bring
smart, self-actualized black women to life on screen, Kerry Washington is
well on her way to making history. One of the most bankable black wom-
en in Hollywood, Washington committed to *Scandal* after being inspired

by the quality of the show's writing and the complexity of Pope's character: "I read the script and was sold from the first page. . . . Any actress wants a role that showcases a woman with power and smarts."[41] Yet, her role on *Scandal* is only one performance in an impressive body of work that began almost two decades ago. From *Our Song* (2000) and *Save the Last Dance* (2001), to more recent films such as *Ray* (2004), *The Last King of Scotland* (2006), *I Think I Love My Wife* (2007), *For Colored Girls* (2010), *Django Unchained* (2012), and *Peeples* (2013), Washington has played both wife and girlfriend. Yet, she also played a transgender person in *Life Is Hot in Cracktown* (2009), a sleek assassin in *Mr. & Mrs. Smith* (2005), and a Black Panther in *Night Catches Us* (2010). These roles show the range of Washington's talent and ability to move beyond the stereotypical roles assigned to "pretty women." Nonetheless, it is uncommon for actors to disrupt a successful film career and replace it with the rigors of shooting a weekly television show. This was the case for Washington, who mentions that while she toyed with the idea of doing a cable drama, she was not, initially, ready to let go of her film career. However, *Scandal* was different. The brainchild and creative genius of writer-producer Shonda Rhimes, Olivia Pope has a strength, work ethic, and desire to help others that she shares with the actress who plays her.

With a third completed season, *Scandal* may be on its way to becoming a cultural phenomenon with its fervent fan base, consistent ratings, and social media presence. A show about the tangled web of politics and the gladiators in suits who work to fix the problems of Washington power players, *Scandal* is rare in its depiction of a powerful black woman who fixes the problems of others, but is unable to handle her own. Yet, even with her flaws, Pope is a much-improved version of the stereotypical African American woman on prime time. From reality shows to ad campaigns, black women are more visible than ever; however, their presence on television is far too often derogatory. If one believes much of what they watch on TV, then black women live in extremes. They may be brilliant and iconic or belligerent and materialistic. Using her brains to help manage and help others rather than tear them down, Olivia Pope deviates from the stereotypical archetypes that many have come to associate with black women.[42] Still, there are elements of Pope's character that bear some resemblance to the controlling images that too often define black women on television. Olivia's single status, whole-hearted devotion to work, and nurturing sensibilities toward her gladiator family, share some similarity with Patricia Hill Collins' definition of the modern mammy. Moreover, her upper-middle-class status and independence relate to qualities inherent to *the black lady* or professional woman. Though not lewd or oversexed, Olivia's steamy affair with a married man and natural sensuality borrow upon stereotypical notions regarding the innate inclination of the black woman as "temptress."

Images aside, the aptly named Washington is a political powerhouse. Her upbringing inside a tight-knit professional family and stellar education, including a degree from George Washington University, has shaped her activism and attention to issues of social justice. This includes support for sustainable fabrics, fair trade, and American-made products.[43] She credits her childhood for starting her on this journey. Having stumped for President Obama in the 2008 and 2012 election cycles, Washington is a strong supporter of the Get Out the Vote campaign. She is also an appointee on President Obama's Committee on the Arts and Humanities Board. These positions have informed not only her personal politics, but also a body of work that frequently explores the nexus between politics, history, and morality. Such choices have made Kerry Washington a well-respected actress and role model. Drawing critical acclaim with a successful acting career and a new show that's changing the landscape on how audiences view black women, Kerry Washington is living proof that for a smart black woman in Hollywood, the road may not be easy, but the journey is always worth it.

NOTES

My sincere thanks to Dr. Delia Cook Gillis and Dr. Malik Simba for helping me think critically about why Kerry Washington's success in Hollywood is important.

1. Lynette Holloway, "Will Kerry Washington Be the 1st?" *The Root* September 21, 2013http://www.theroot.com/articles/culture/2013/09/will_kerry_washington_be_the_1st_black_actress_to_win_emmy_for_drama_lead.html (22 Nov. 2013).

2. From here on, the character of Olivia Pope will be referred to as either "Pope" or "Olivia." Kerry Washington was nominated for Best Actress in a TV Drama Series at the 2014 Golden Globe Awards, but she lost to Robin Wright of *House of Cards*.

3. After winning the first Academy Award by an African American, trailblazer Hattie McDaniel received criticism for her depiction of a slave in *Gone with the Wind*. Civil rights activists believed her role perpetuated Hollywood stereotypes and chided the actress for not becoming more politically active. For more information see Thomas Cripps, *Slow Fade to Black: The Negro in American Film, 1900–1942*, 363–64, and the account on McDaniel's missing Oscar by law professor W. Burlette Carter at http://www.law.gwu.edu/News/newsstories/Pages/TheCaseoftheMissingOscar.aspx (10 Dec. 2013). As the debate sharpens over images of African Americans on television, demeaning and single-minded portrayals of black women abound. In one case or another, they are repeatedly depicted as maids, prostitutes, drug addicts, unwed mothers, sapphires, welfare queens, or gold diggers. Tragically, the lives of such characters are still among the most accepted images of African Americans in television and film. Among popular shows that continue to show black women as one-dimensional characters, if at all, is *Saturday Night Live* (SNL). Ironically, a sketch featuring host Kerry Washington poked fun at the show's diversity challenges when it aired in early November 2013.

4. According to this article, *Scandal* was up 41% to 11.6 million viewers in its third season. "The 'Scandal Sheet': Meet Olivia's Men," *USA Today*, November 7, 2013, http://web.ebscohost.com.hmlproxy.lib.csufresno.edu/ehost/detail?vid=13&sid=7a3fdf9d-645b-41f1-b0ff-87aa87088642%40sessionmgr110&hid=112&bdata=JnNpdGU9ZWhvc3QtbGl2ZQ%3d%3d#db=a9h&AN=J0E281191206613 (15 Nov. 2013).

5. Arielle Loren, "10 Black Women Making Moves in Film," *Clutch* On-line Magazine 2011, http://www.clutchmagonline.com/2011/08/10-black-women-making-moves-in-film/ (27 Nov. 2013).

6. Judy Smith is the real-life muse behind Olivia Pope's character and the creator of Smith & Company, which has steered such high-profile clients such as Monica Lewinsky, Michael Vick, and Paula Deen through their public ordeals.

7. "Sweet Baby," *Scandal* (Season 1). Dir. Paul McGuigan, DVD. ABC Studios, 2012.

8. "Hell Hath No Fury," *Scandal* (Season 1). Dir. Paul McGuigan, DVD. ABC Studios, 2012.

9. Diahann Carroll, "From Julia to Cosby to Oprah: Tuning in to 60 Years of TV," *Ebony*, November 2005, 101-104, http://web.ebscohost.com.hmlproxy.lib.csufresno.edu/ehost/pdfviewer/pdfviewer?vid=6&sid=1daa9b99-f349-44e7-8658-943e933a6afa%40sessionmgr198&hid=119 (28 May 2013).

10. Richard Schickel, "Viewpoints," *Time*, October 21, 1974, 128, http://web.ebscohost.com/ehost/delivery?sid=be66b1ca-0292-468a-b5fc-5990f5a9 (28 May 2013).

11. For a brief description on the characters of *Living Single*, see http://www.commonsensemedia.org/tv-reviews/living-single (10 Dec. 2013).

12. David Kamp, "Scandal's First Lady," *Vanity Fair*, August 2013, 136 (print).

13. Benjamin Svetkey, "Kerry Washington's Scandal Role Breaks Rules, Makes History". *Parade Magazine* May 4, 2013, http://www.parade.com/11185/benjaminsvetkey/kerry-washingtons-scandal-role-breaks-rules-makes-history/ (17 June 2013).

14. Like Kerry Washington, Meagan Good is also a stand-out among young and successful black actresses in Hollywood. Good made her film debut in the hit movie *Friday*. She went on to appear in the movie *Eve's Bayou*, for which she earned her first NAACP Award nomination. Now a major box-office talent, Good appeared in *Jumping the Broom* (2011), the series *The Game, Think Like A Man* (2012), *Californication* (2012), *Deception* (2013), and *Think Like A Man Too* (2014).

15. Robert M. Entman and Andrew Rojecki, *The Black Image In The White Mind: Media and Race in America* (Chicago: University of Chicago Press, 2001), xiv–xv and 201. The authors also mention that those who associate a character with a commonly held stereotype often disregard the non-stereotypical qualities the same character may demonstrate.

16. "Enemy of the State" *Scandal* (Season One). Dir. Paul McGuigan, DVD. ABC Studios, 2012.

17. "Sweet Baby," *Scandal*.

18. Kamp, "Scandal's First Lady,"137.

19. The "Year of the Woman" was called such because never before had four women been elected to the Senate in a single year. This included now veteran politicians Dianne Feinstein and Barbara Boxer (CA), Carol Moseley Braun (IL), and Patty Murray (WA). For more information see http://www.senate.gov/artandhistory/history/minute/year_of_the_woman.htm.

20. "Women of the CBC," *A Voice: African American Voices in Congress*, http://www.avoiceonline.org/cbcwomen/ (accessed 28 Nov. 2013).

21. Allison Samuels, "Catfights, Ignorance, and Arguments: TV's Biggest Reality Stars Cash in on a Season's Worth of Fame" *Ebony*.com December 2011–January 2012, http://connection.ebscohost.com/c/articles/69627554/catfights-ignorance-arguments (8 July 2013).

22. Allison Samuels, "What Are They Hiding?: This Trio Is Keeping Politicians' Secrets—and Breaking Ground at the Same Time," *Newsweek* (12 Mar. 2012), 65, http://search.proquest.com.hmlproxy.lib.csufresno.edu/docview/927906209?accountid=10349 (8 July 2013)

23. Patricia Hill Collins, *Black Feminist Thought: Knowledge, Consciousness, and the Politics of Empowerment* (New York: Routledge, 1991), 71.

24. Collins, 71.

25. "Hell Hath No Fury" *Scandal* (Season 1). Dir. Paul McGuigan, DVD. ABC Studios, 2012.
26. "Sweet Baby" *Scandal.*
27. "Sweet Baby" *Scandal.*
28. Svetkey, "Kerry Washington's Scandal Role Breaks Rules, Makes History."
29. Svetkey, "Kerry Washington's Scandal Role Breaks Rules, Makes History."
30. Svetkey, "Kerry Washington's Scandal Role Breaks Rules, Makes History."
31. "Kerry Washington: 'I Was Really Lucky Because I Went to an All-Girl School': How Her Education Shaped Her as a Person," October 4, 2013, http://www. huffingtonpost.com/2013/10/04/kerry-washington-intelligence-over-looks_n_4043653. html (27 Nov. 2013).
32. Svetkey, "Kerry Washington's Scandal Role Breaks Rules, Makes History."
33. Brandon Wetherbee, "Kerry Washington's GWU Commencement Address: How A Frog Transformed Her Thinking," *Huffington Post*, 20 May 2013. http://www. huffingtonpost.com/2013/05/20/kerry-washington-gwu-commencement_n_3307512. html?view=print&comm_ref=false (30 Nov. 2013).
34. Svetkey, "Kerry Washington's Scandal Role Breaks Rules, Makes History."
35. Kevin Powell, "Kerry Washington: Woman On Top" *Ebony*, March 2013, http:// kerrywashington.com/kw/kerry-washington-ebony-march-2013-%E2%80%9Cwoman-on-top%E2%80%9D-by-kevin-powell/ (16 Dec. 2013).
36. Kerry Washington, "Kerry Washington: Volunteer, Because Voting Is Not Enough," *NewsOne for Black America* July 24, 2012, http://newsone.com/2026767/kerry-washington-volunteer-because-voting-is-not-enough/ (accessed 16 Nov. 2013).
37. Kamp, "Scandal's First Lady," 86.
38. Ursula Liang, "The Backstory: Kerry Washington Goes to Washington?" *The New York Times Style Magazine*, 4 January 2008, http://tmagazine.blogs.nytimes.com/ 2008/01/04/the-backstory-kerry-washington-goes-to-washington/?_php=true&_type= blogs&_r=0 (17 Nov. 2013).
39. Washington, "Kerry Washington: Volunteer, Because Voting Is Not Enough," 2.
40. Washington, "Kerry Washington: Volunteer, Because Voting Is Not Enough," 2.
41. Samuels, "What Are They Hiding?," 65.
42. Rhonesha Byng, "The Images of Black Women in Media Still 'Only Scratch the Surface,' *Essence* Study Finds," *The Huffington Post*, 15 October 2013. http://www. huffingtonpost.com/2013/10/15/the-images-of-black-women-in-media_n_4102322. html?view=print&comm_ref=false (23 Nov. 2013).
43. Liang, "The Backstory: Kerry Washington Goes to Washington?"

BIBLIOGRAPHY

Bogle, Donald. *Toms, Coons, Mulattoes, Mammies, & Bucks: An Interpretive History of Blacks in American Films.* New York, New York: Continuum, 1990.
Byng, Rhonesha. "The Images of Black Women in Media Still 'Only Scratch the Surface,' *Essence* Study Finds." *Huffington Post*, 15 October 2013. http://www. huffingtonpost.com/2013/10/15/the-images-of-black-women-in-media_n_4102322. html (accessed 23 November 2013).
Carroll, Diahann. "From Julia to Cosby to Oprah: Tuning in to 60 Years of TV." *Ebony*, November 2005.
Collins, Patricia Hill. *Black Feminist Thought: Knowledge, Consciousness, and the Politics of Empowerment.* New York: Routledge, 1991.
Cripps, Thomas. *Slow Fade to Black: The Negro in American Film, 1900–1942.* New York: Oxford University Press, 1977.
Entman, Robert M., and Andrew Rojecki. *The Black Image in the White Mind: Media and Race in America.* Chicago: University of Chicago Press, 2001.
Holloway, Lynette. "Will Kerry Washington Be the 1st?" *Root*, 21 September 2013. http://www.theroot.com/articles/culture/2013/09/will_kerry_washington_be_the_

1st_black_actress_to_win_emmy_for_drama_lead.html (accessed 22 November 2013).

Kamp, David. "*Scandal*'s First Lady," *Vanity Fair*, no. 636 (August 2013): 136.

Liang, Ursula. "The Backstory: Kerry Washington Goes to Washington?" *New York Times Style Magazine*, 4 January 2008. http://tmagazine.blogs.nytimes.com/2008/01/04/the-backstory-kerry-washington-goes-to-washington/?_php=true&_type=blogs&_r=0 (accessed 17 November 2013).

Loren, Arielle. "10 Black Women Making Moves in Film." *Clutch*, 22 August 2011. http://www.clutchmagonline.com/2011/08/10-black-women-making-moves-in-film (accessed 27 November 2013).

Poniewozik, James. "Color Crosses Over." *Time* 159, no. 8 (February 2002): 64.

———. "Leading Ladies," *Time*, April 2012.

Powell, Kevin. "I See Kerry Washington." *Ebony*, March 2013, 112. http://www.ebony.com/entertainment-culture/kerry-washington-woman-on-top-333#axzz2o3yIiJwO (accessed 16 December 2013).

Samuels, Allison. "Catfights, Ignorance, and Arguments: TV's Biggest Reality Stars Cash In on a Season's Worth of Fame." *Ebony* 67, nos. 2–3 (December 2011–January 2012): 124–27.

———. "What Are They Hiding?" *Newsweek*, 12 March 2012.

Scandal. Directed by Paul McGuigan. Los Angeles: ABC Studios, 2012. DVD.

Schickel, Richard. "Viewpoints." *Time* 104, no. 17 (October 1974): 128.

Svetkey, Benjamin. "Kerry Washington's *Scandal* Role Breaks Rules, Makes History." *Parade*, 4 May 2013. http://www.parade.com/11185/benjaminsvetkey/kerry-washingtons-scandal-role-breaks-rules-makes-history (accessed 17 June 2013).

Washington, Kerry. "Kerry Washington: Volunteer, Because Voting Is Not Enough." *NewsOne for Black America*, 24 July 2012. http://newsone.com/2026767/kerry-washington-volunteer-because-voting-is-not-enough (accessed 16 November 2013).

Wetherbee, Brandon. "Kerry Washington's GWU Commencement Address: How a Frog Transformed Her Thinking." *Huffington Post*, 20 May 2013. http://www.huffingtonpost.com/2013/05/20/kerry-washington-gwu-commencement_n_3307512.html (accessed 30 November 2013).

"Women of the CBC." A Voice: African American Voices in Congress. http://www.avoiceonline.org/cbcwomen (accessed 28 November 2013).

TEN

Postfeminism, Sexuality, and the Question of Millennial Identity on HBO's *Girls*

Margaret J. Tally

Recent writing on postfeminism has tried to assess the reaction of young women of the millennial generation (those who were born between 1980 and 2000) to the gains made by their mothers during the Second Wave of feminism in the 1970s. One media scholar in this area, Rosalind Gill, offers a way of thinking about postfeminism as not so much a reaction against the Second Wave of feminism of the 1970s, but as a "new kind of feminism for a new context of debate."[1] Another way of framing this that Gill offers, drawing on the work of Rachel Moseley and Jacinta Read, is to try and move beyond the debates of the mid-70s, where feminism was seen as antithetical to traditional notions of femininity.[2] Postfeminism is understood instead as an example of how these two ideas are not mutually exclusive. Speaking more generally of how postfeminist media representations try to, in a sense, have it both ways, Gill notes,

> Today's media culture has a distinctive post-feminist sensibility organized around notions of choice, empowerment, self-surveillance, and sexual difference, and articulated in an ironic and knowing register in which feminism is simultaneously taken for granted and repudiated.[3]

In this reading, cultural images of young women today, also known as Generation Y or the millennials, as somehow both "empowered" and sexually available as well as free to work in any occupation for the same pay as men are believed to characterize a kind of historical rewriting or

161

amnesia with respect to the hard fought gains of the women's movement of the 1970s.

It is within this cultural conversation over postfeminism that the television program *Girls* came onto the scene. *Girls* is a half-hour-long comedy on HBO that premiered in April of 2012. Lena Dunham, who is the creator, writer, and director of the show, as well as the main character, Hannah Horvath, wanted to depict the experiences of herself and her group of friends, postcollege. Hannah is a struggling writer who moves to Greenpoint, Brooklyn, with her three friends, two years after they graduate from Oberlin College. The friends—Marnie, Jessa, and Shoshonna, who are played, respectively, by Allison Williams, Jemima Kirke, and Zosia Mamet—struggle with trying to support themselves financially while also realizing themselves as artists and writers.

In terms of the question of postfeminism, one of the ways the show tries to speak to the experiences of twenty-something women is through chronicling the exploits of these young women as they pursue relationships with men, try to find creative work, and, particularly for Hannah, try to gain life experiences that can be used as material for her budding career as a writer. These experiences, particularly with men, are not always wholly positive, but *Girls* tries to show that it is this admixture of both positive and negative experiences that in fact characterizes this life stage for many twenty-something women.

For example, the sexual encounters that the girls have are both complicated and unsatisfying, and in fact, have led some writers to comment that the way sex is portrayed is "grim" and demeans the women on the show.[4] Dunham has responded to this charge by explaining that it isn't so much that the sex that the characters have is bad, as that it represents the kind of fumbling sense of being unformed that young women at this age oftentimes are. Contrasting the bad sex that is portrayed on *Girls* with that of a precursor on HBO to which *Girls* is often compared, *Sex and the City*, Dunham has observed,

> Well, the bad sex in *Sex and the City* was sort of like, "It was so bad he left his socks on." Our sex is like "It was really bad because we're not emotionally connected and he doesn't want to be here and I'm scared and alone." There are people, obviously, making ridiculous, fumbling sexual moves but the badness is sort of coming more from just a place of being unformed people trying to connect rather than like someone committing a specific sexual faux pas, if that distinction makes sense.[5]

This quote is instructive, because it reveals how *Girls* is trying to locate its understanding of twenty-something women in a supposedly postfeminist landscape, where young women are assumed to have the freedom to express themselves sexually, and that this openness somehow translates into uniformly positive sexual experiences. At the same time, I would argue that by showing the messiness and complexity of sex and relationships for these young women, *Girls* is able to reveal how postfeminism both represents a victory in terms of some of the goals of Second Wave feminism, in terms of calling for women's freedom to take ownership of their sexuality, and demonstrates that these goals are themselves oftentimes elusive, and at any rate, not a given for this group of young women.

The issue of feminism and postfeminism is further complicated, as will be shown, by the fact that these young women are highly intelligent and able to describe in precise detail the contradictions of being sexually active young women in this particular historical landscape. They are not typically nerdy, and thus their intelligence isn't used as a way of making them seem sexually naïve or unappealing. On the contrary, their intelligence is what they offer as their means of attracting the men in their lives. They often "overthink" their problems with men, as the character of Hannah is wont to do. More generally, their intelligence is not viewed as antithetical to their being sexually appealing. The fact that they are articulate, whether conventionally pretty or unconventionally attractive, is something that contributes to their being compelling characters.

In this chapter, then, I will try to locate where *Girls* is in terms of the recent descriptions of postfeminism as somehow regressive and a repudiation of Second Wave feminism. I will explore this question through the treatment of sexuality on the show, by analyzing scenes from several episodes where sexual encounters occur. I will demonstrate how each of these episodes challenges the assumption that we have somehow moved beyond the struggles of the Second Wave of the women's movement. Dunham, as both auteur and commentator on her generation, or as she has put it in her character Hannah's mouth in the pilot episode, "*a voice of a* generation," has very self-consciously created a forum where these questions are being debated, in the actions and reactions of the characters. In this way, *Girls* self-consciously offers a vital space to explore how millennials are making sense of the hopes and desires and realities of being a young women in this millennium, and how they may even be crafting a new sensibility that is post-postfeminist, by both acknowledging and moving beyond the assumptions of both feminism and postfeminism alike.

One of the primary ways that *Girls* tries to negotiate between the various generations of feminism is through leading with an explicit emphasis on the ability of the young women to be self-reflective about the implications of their sexual engagements with young men. Rather than mindlessly "acting out," these young women discourse endlessly about sex, and engage in protracted dialogues with each other and the men in their lives. The ability to use their minds, and their own reasoning, however tortured, to define their interactions with the opposite sex, is what provides the show with its sense of immediacy and freshness. These are thinking women, and their intellectual commitments to their work as artists, writers, and students is what they lead with and what informs all of their actions in the world, including their actions with young men.

Their empowerment, furthermore, to engage in sexual activity, is fueled by a sense that they are trying to live out the courage of their ideas as thinking young women. It is not simply a carnal lust driving them, or a sense that they are fulfilling either a cultural script of femininity or post-femininity, but rather being sexual for them is a way of realizing their assumptions about what it means to be free and young and in their twenties. Their intellect is the driving force, in other words, which informs all of their decisions in their lives, including and especially their actions with the male characters.

In fact, one of the tensions that the show reveals in the larger culture is that it opens up the assumption that thinking women are still not viewed as sexually engaging or attractive even. This is especially the case with the main character of Hannah, who is played by Lena Dunham. Dunham has explicitly tried to complicate the audiences' view of what is considered sexually attractive, by portraying herself as literally naked in several episodes and as the ambivalent object of lust by different men, including conventionally handsome men. The media has reacted with a firestorm of debate over the appropriateness of Dunham having her character be nude in several scenes throughout the first two seasons. In a recent interview, Dunham responded to a reporter's question about why she was showing her character naked, a criticism that wouldn't be launched against other HBO shows such as *Game of Thrones*, where the unrealistically beautiful actresses are nude in several scenes:

> It's a realistic expression of what it's like to be alive. . . . If you are not into me that's your problem and you are going to have to kind of work that out.[6]

As Caitlin Dickson, writing for the online journal the *Daily Beast* noted, Dunham is trying to offer a more realistic portrait of what real women look like undressed, rather than the fantasy naked women who are normally shown on cable shows or Hollywood films:

> It's only when faced with the fleshy body of a real life human being — one perhaps uncomfortably similar to the one they have (or are afraid of having)—that people start to freak out. The deluge of questions about Dunham's nudity conveys the message that imperfect bodies should be hidden in shame.[7]

Dunham, on the contrary, isn't afraid to complicate these images of young women with realistic bodies who are able to speak about their relative desirability with intelligence and wit, both in real life as well as through her character. Her mind and her body are meant to demonstrate to the audience that she is a realistic young woman, intelligent, vibrant, insecure, and at the same time, sometimes her own worst enemy. As she explains to her shrink concerning the burden of her intelligence in "Women's Only," the first episode of the third season, "My only limitation is my own mind. Like, I hold the keys to the prison that is my mind." It is this limitation, as well as gift, that Dunham is trying to portray in her characters through representing their struggles at this period of their lives.

WHY BAD SEX IS GOOD[8]

In a recent article on *Girls* on the online dating site called DatingReport.com, the author Chiara Atik tallied up the numbers on the amount and kinds of sex that was portrayed in the first two seasons of the series.[9] Interestingly enough, this online magazine, devoted to dating issues for millennial females, has a kind of regressive feel to it, in the sense that the word *dating* might sound like a quaint term for the kinds of ways that young women today get together with men in heterosexual encounters, where the term *hookups* has become the more prevalent description. Similarly, the term *girls*, which was eventually chosen for the title of the series, is also meant to connote, in a somewhat ironic tone, the phase of life Dunham wanted to capture for her generation of young women, who are no longer girls, but are also not quite grown up, at least in terms of the traditional markers of adulthood. Speaking more generally, Dunham has commented on why she wanted to capture this period of life in her series:

> Well, something I feel about being in your 20s, which is different than—you know, *Sex and the City*, was a show about women in their 30s who had successful careers, pre-recession, the best, most supportive friends. They didn't have—I mean they had little friend tiffs, but the characters on our show are tortured. It's sort of impossible to get through your 20s without—it's like if you as a girl in her 20s, "Are you a happy person?" I think she can say, "I have happy moments," but I don't think it's possible—maybe I'm—maybe people will radically disagree with me, but I don't really think it's possible to be sort of an at-peace human when you are between 22 and 30. . . . And now, people today—it seems like young people, they think they have more time to figure it out. They're turning 25 and they really don't have that picture in focus.[10]

While the term *girls*, then, as well as *dating*, would seem to be somewhat prefeminist in their connotations, what *Girls* actually portrays in the series is arguably anything but prefeminist. For, just as this dating online magazine takes for granted that the "dates" or hookups young twenty-something women have will oftentimes involve casual sex, so too does the show portray, with a fair amount of frequency, the pervasiveness of sexual encounters for this group of women.

In the first two seasons, for example, Atik found that the total number of sex scenes was 29; the total number of orgasms was 8.5, out of which the total number of orgasms of the male characters was 7 and the total number of orgasms of the female characters was 1.5. This tally for the women includes .5 for the character of Marnie, who achieved climax after meeting a minor character, Booth Jonathan, in season 1, episode 3, and Hannah who, off-camera, has an orgasm with Adam, her on-again, off-again lover, in the season 1 premiere episode. Atik also found that Adam was the character with the most frequently depicted orgasms (3), while Hannah was shown having the most sex scenes (10), followed closely by Adam (8) and Marnie (7). Interestingly enough, the supposedly most free-spirited character, Jessa, in fact has the fewest sex scenes (2). Other relevant findings include the relatively even number of times when the sex was initiated by a male (8) versus a female (9), and overall, there were an almost identical amount of sex scenes in seasons 1 (15) and 2 (14), while the episodes that contained no sex scenes were far less frequent (5).[11]

While simply quantifying the presence, frequency, and kind of sex that the characters have on *Girls* is not necessarily revealing of the ways in which these characters experience these sexual encounters, they do, nevertheless, offer an inventory of some of the assumptions that are embedded in the show, including the fact that young women are having sex on a routine basis outside of marriage, and that frequently they are the ones who initiate these encounters. While these facts would suggest that these young female characters are indeed living in a postfeminist world where they are free not only to engage in but even initiate sex outside of marriage, the frequency of orgasms, or lack thereof, for the girls suggests that there may be some ways in which the sexual revolution has been incomplete. In this way, it may be that *Girls* is trying to portray how, even in a postfeminist culture, there are still some taboos for these millennial women in terms of being direct and vocal about how to articulate their sexual needs.

The discussion of the unstated sexual needs and desires of the female characters can be viewed in several episodes of the first two seasons of the series. There is a noteworthy scene, for example, in the pilot episode of the show, that portrays Hannah in uncomfortable and compromising positions with her would-be boyfriend, Adam.[12] This discomfort is both literal, in terms of the positions he wants her to take when they make love, as well as symbolic, in terms of her confusion over the status of their relationship. Hannah is shown at Adam's apartment, for example, having sex, but then he doesn't return her texts. When she shows up at his apartment subsequently, without having heard back from him, they again have sex and then she leaves, with no better sense of what the terms are of their casual relationship.

In this and subsequent episodes in the first season, Adam initially seems to be the one who controls the dynamics of the relationship as he orchestrates how the sex will be played out, and asks Hannah to do various things that appear on the surface, at least, of putting her in a passive position. In the first episode, Hannah is lying face down on a dirty couch in Adam's apartment, struggling to remove her tights while lying in this awkward position.[13] Adam tells her he will be back in a moment, as he is just going to grab the "lube," and Hannah continues to babble on nervously, because she is afraid that he is readying himself to enter her from behind. Adam finally tells Hannah to play "the quiet game," so he can concentrate on his own pleasure rather than have to answer her. At other points in the episode, Adam seems to be both delighting in as well as taking swipes at Hannah's body, which is pudgy and has tattoos, as he asks her if she was going to try to "lose some weight."

Though these and many other scenes are played for laughs, many commentators have criticized the graphic sex scenes that Hannah has with her partner Adam, showing how casual sex for young women can be not only sexually unsatisfying but even debasing and dehumanizing. Whereas this terrain was broached in *Sex and the City*, for example, and explicitly talked about in terms of a power dynamic between men and women, in *Girls*, the abstract nature of the conversation is replaced with a real-world scenario, with Hannah, "trying to get some reassurance that he's not heading in the wrong direction."[14] Frank Bruni, writing for the *New York Times*, has wondered aloud whether *Girls* represents a backlash against the ideas of the women's liberation movement of the 1970s:

> You watch these scenes and other examples of the zeitgeist-y, early-20s heroines of *Girls* engaging in, recoiling from, mulling and mourning sex, and you think: Gloria Steinem went to the barricades for *this*? Salaries may be better than in decades past and the cabinet and Congress less choked with testosterone. But in the bedroom? What's happening there remains something of a muddle, if not something of a mess.[15]

In this reading, *Girls* offers a sober assessment for these young twenty-something women in a postfeminist landscape where women's power is viewed in terms of her ability to have hookups, or casual sex without emotional attachments. Dunham herself describes her amazement that she had so many friends who were trying to feel empowered by disconnecting sex from emotions, or as she explained to Bruni in an interview, "I heard so many of my friends saying, 'Why can't I have sex and feel nothing?' It was amazing: that this was the new goal."[16]

This sense of trying to attain the same attitude as young men in casual hookups is reinforced in the second episode of the first season, titled "Vagina Panic."[17] After first being told by her parents that they no longer want to support her "groovy lifestyle," and then being told by Adam that she's "not that fat anymore," Hannah is shown again having another awkward sexual encounter with Adam. The scene begins with Adam and Hannah having sex, and he is breathing hard while thrusting in a violent way. This kind of violent thrusting is juxtaposed with him questioning Hannah whether she "likes that." Then, he goes on to ask her what she likes, and she replies, "I like everything; I like what you're doing." It was revealed earlier that Hannah has only had sex with two "and a half" partners in her life, so her admission that she "likes everything," seems more like an attempt to sound more experienced than she is. Adam then moves ahead, constructing his own fantasy that he found Hannah on the street, and she was only eleven years old, and she was carrying a Cabbage Patch lunchbox. Hannah, though confused, plays along, and takes on the role of an eleven-year-old girl.

Very soon after the role play, Adam pulls out of Hannah and takes off his condom, as if ready to ejaculate, and offers Hannah the option of having him ejaculate on any body part she chooses, "Face? Tummy? Those little tits of yours?" to which she replies, "It seems like you want to come on my tits, so I think you should come on my tits because I want you to come, and it seems like you're going to do it." After Adam ejaculates, Hannah tells him that the sex was good, and "that was so good. I almost came." In another scene in the same episode, Adam reveals to Hannah that he has been having other sexual encounters with girls and without using condoms. This admission makes Hannah panic that she might have contracted AIDS or another STD from Adam, because there were a few seconds where Adam was not wearing a condom and was inside of her. Hannah rushes home and immediately begins to google "diseases that come from no condom for one second."

In the next episode of season 1, episode 4, titled "Hannah's Diary," Hannah attempts to break it off with Adam, after being given a pep talk by older, female employees at the law firm where she is working as a temporary secretary.[18] The women encouraged her to end things with him, after she revealed that Adam sent her a picture of his penis by text, and then apologized because he meant to send it to another girl, saying "SRY that wasn't for you." Hannah attempts to break it off with Adam, but later in the same episode, goes back and has sex with him again. As she is leaving his apartment, she has the following dialogue with him:

Hannah: I'm not asking you for anything. I'm really not asking you for anything. I've never asked you for anything, and I don't even want anything. I respect your right to see and do whoever you want. I don't even want a boyfriend.

Adam: What do you want?

Hannah: I just want someone who wants to hang out all of the time, who thinks I'm the best person in the world and wants to have sex with only me. And it makes me feel very stupid to tell you this because it makes me sound like a girl who wants to, like, go to brunch. And I really don't want to go to brunch, and I don't want you to sit on the couch while I shop or even meet my friends. I don't even want that.

At the end of the conversation, she finally says to him, "I care about you, and I don't want to anymore because it feels too shitty for me."

This episode would seem, at least on the surface, to be a clear indictment of the claim that this Generation Y of millennial females are postfeminists who are completely liberated in their sexual relations with young men. Far from feeling empowered by her sexual encounters with Adam, Hannah is reduced to awkward, confusing, and painful moments as she works hard to make Adam happy by playing out his fantasies; in addition, she is humiliated when she realizes that Adam is having sex with other women, sending them texts of his genitals, and essentially asking her to put up with it and "play the quiet game." Hannah, in turn, is struggling with her own desires to have more connection to Adam emotionally, to have him love her and to be together.

At one level, the episode reveals that, even as young women are now able to have sex outside of marriage and to be free to have casual hookups, the reality is that young men and women today still have difficulties breaking out of these earlier roles where the man is taking the lead and defining the sexual encounter. That so many young men today are watching pornography and using this as their measure for the kinds of sexual scenarios they want to play out with women, and that young women, in turn, are trying to be that woman for the young men, suggests that there is a disconnect between the millennial men and women in their levels of intimacy, honesty, and pleasure that they are getting from these encounters. Another way of putting this is to say that whatever confusions this generation has over their status as adults, the young men, at least, seem to have some more agency in saying what they want sexually. The young women, by contrast, are less able to articulate what they want, with the ensuing complications that arise when there is this kind of asymmetry.

On the other hand, it could be argued that by portraying the awkwardness of these encounters, and the messiness of the ways in which Hannah hasn't learned how to be more proactive in articulating her desires to Adam, she is in fact offering a cultural space for the audience to themselves reflect on these power dynamics. Second, the fact that she is verbalizing her sense that she is being treated poorly reflects her ability to analyze the situation and describe exactly what is wrong about it and how it makes her feel. Her intelligence, in other words, is as powerful a mechanism for her character as the behaviors she is enacting with Adam.

Furthermore, her intelligence is what also allows her to renegotiate why this relationship isn't working for her. As she observes, "I realize I'm not different. I want what everyone wants. I want what they all want. I want all the things. I just want to be happy."[19]

It should be noted that for the young women, even when they do find themselves in a long-term relationship, there is still the lingering problem of not asking for or perhaps being fully aware of what they want, which also creates a space for the audience to further reflect on why it is that these young women are initially unable to state their needs. For example, in *Girls*, the character of Marnie is in a long-term relationship with her boyfriend, Charlie; they met in college and are still seeing each other. While Charlie seems completely committed to Marnie, Marnie can't tell him that she is ambivalent about him, and in fact, wants to end the relationship. Instead, she crawls into bed with Hannah, for example, pretending to want to watch old episodes of *The Mary Tyler Moore Show*, but in reality, wanting to get away from Charlie.[20] In another scene, Marnie asks Charlie to have sex in different positions rather than face to face, because she doesn't want to have to look at him when they have sex. Madeleine Gyory, writing for the Women's Media Center, has noted that, as seemingly different as Marnie and Hannah's situations are with respect to the men in their lives, the two women share a common problem, namely, "both women are dissatisfied."[21] These vastly different scenes both depict women not getting what they want. At the same time, the two young men, however different they are as people, don't express ambivalence, but in fact aggressively pursue their desires.

DISCUSSION

Thinking about the trajectory of the first as well as much of the second season of *Girls*, it appears that the ways in which the young women form relationships with men embody a kind of postfeminist sensibility where the goals of the women's movement are simultaneously taken for granted and repudiated. The part where some of the goals are taken for granted is demonstrated in their casual attitude toward having sex with different partners. At the same time, there is also a kind of repudiation of the women's movement, as evidenced by the young women seeming to rely quite heavily on young men to make them happy. For example, though Hannah espouses her desire to be free of the idea of having a boyfriend, it is clear that her feelings for Adam are very strong, and she is portrayed as continually waiting for him to call or text her. Hannah and her friends share a belief that the "markers of adult life," that is, having a committed sexual relationship with a man, is how they will be happy. That the young women on *Girls* don't fully interrogate this idea, or don't understand that, as Dunham notes, "you have to pick the right one and spend a little time floundering. It's not just about the *having* of the thing,"[22] means that their relationships will be complicated by this unexamined view of what having a man in their life can offer them.

These ideas about finding a man, and thinking about their own needs, also ties into a larger problem on *Girls* in that the characters are often portrayed as not necessarily being fully aware of their own emotions and needs, or as Dunham notes, "Hannah and Marnie and Jessa are doing so much posing. There's a certain amount of post-modern distance from their own emotions."[23] This kind of postmodern irony ties into the post-feminist sense that there isn't a need to really reflect on the role of men in their lives. There is a lack of honesty that the characters exhibit about their own motives, and it may be that the reality they find themselves in is a lot more messy than the "You go girl!" attitudes that postfeminism was supposed to bring.

Having said this, it should be noted that *Girls* tries to move forward from this initial sense that the female characters lack agency in terms of expressing their own desires, sexual and otherwise. Hannah begins to communicate more openly with Adam in later episodes, and she is even shown having an orgasm with him. This suggests that *Girls* is trying to move beyond its earlier focus solely on "bad sex," to allow their characters to develop and move forward.

The transition from being passive to having increasing agency is much more fully developed in the second season's fifth episode, titled "One Man's Trash,"[24] where Hannah has a two-day sexual interlude with an older man, played by Patrick Wilson. In the episode, Hannah has been throwing away the trash for the café where she works in another person's trash can. When the owner of the brownstone where she has been placing her trash comes to the café to confront the owner, played by Alex Karpovsky, Hannah goes to the brownstone to apologize. After she apologizes for throwing the trash into his cans, Joshua, the forty-two-year-old doctor and owner of the brownstone, and Hannah begin to flirt with each other and end up in a passionate embrace, which then turns into a two-day sexual interlude. In the two days, Hannah and Joshua, in addition to having sex, also laugh, cavort, play Ping-Pong (with Hannah being in the nude), and eat meals together. Hannah is awed by the beauty and wealth of Joshua's house, including the 400-thread-count sheets, and while the end of the two-day tryst is awkward and somewhat painful, the overall sense is that it was a blissful and dreamy moment in Hannah's life. The playfulness of the characters, and the ways in which it is taken for granted that she would be enjoying a two-day interlude with a handsome stranger, speaks to the show's assumption that young women are now able not only to acknowledge their sexuality, but indeed, to initiate and enjoy this kind of spontaneous connection with another person, without guilt or remorse.

Interestingly enough, when commentators have written about this episode, it was viewed as somehow implausible and counter-intuitive that a wealthy, handsome, forty-two-year-old doctor would want to have a sexual relationship with Hannah. Dunham herself has commented on this controversy, and views it as a kind of misogyny in the larger culture:

> That was the only argument I heard: "It feels weird to me." And I'm like, "Dude, I get it. It felt weird to kiss an actor that looked like Patrick Wilson." I get so tired of having to cry out "misogyny," but that's what's going on in this situation. People questioning the idea that a woman could sleep with a man who defied her lot in the looks bracket hews so closely to these really outdated ideas about what makes a woman worth spending time with. Really? Can you not imagine a world in which a girl who's sexually down for anything and oddly gregarious pulls a guy out of his shell for two days? They're not getting married. They're spending two days [having sex], which is something that people do.[25]

In this way, it could be said that the sort of postfeminist celebration of one's sexuality as a young woman who has been freed from the constraints imposed by earlier eras is undercut by the cultural reception of the episode itself, which reinforces a very stereotypical understanding of what makes a woman "worth spending time with." In this way, the reception of the show by some critics raises the question that, whatever gains women have made as a result of the women's movement, there are still lingering attitudes that continue to measure women by how they look.

While the reception of the show, then, may reveal that sexism still exists in the larger culture, even as young women like Dunham get to tell their stories, it may be that by finally being able to write narratives from these young women's point of view, Dunham is offering a way to illustrate the gains made by the women's movement. Writing the life stories of *Girls* not only creates a cultural vehicle to depict these struggles, but also allows these struggles to be represented from a young woman's point of view. This distinguishes the show not only from *Sex and the City*, but from just about everything else on HBO, where the conventional viewpoint of their "quality" programs is that of a fifty-year-old male.[26]

This point of view from the perspective of a female twenty-something also ties into another aspect of *Girls* that is arguably unique, and that has to do with its portrayal of young women's sense of their bodies. Lena Dunham has often shown her character nude on the show, and willingly offers up this nonglamorous and "chubby" body for her viewers to react to. This kind of self-exposure from a young woman's point of view is rarely seen on television, much less in contemporary cinema. Her intelligence, furthermore, isn't held up as a substitute for this imperfect body, but rather is part of a whole "package" that she carries with her and asks her viewer to similarly take as a whole.

There are other ways in which *Girls* offers a radical departure from conventional television in general, and HBO in particular, including its portrayal of one of the characters going for an abortion, Jessa, without much fanfare.[27] Again, as the women's movement fought for women's right to freedom of choice, this postfeminist take on the way in which the ability to have an abortion is taken for granted may seem regressive on one level. However, on another, it represents a victory for women's rights that young women today can be viewed as going for an abortion and having it be a difficult, but not the most difficult, decision of their lives.

As season 2 progresses, it is clear that, just as the young women continue to struggle and are confused about who they are and how they should be relating to young men, Dunham in the end offers no easy answers. This is especially evident in a very dark episode, episode 9 of season 2, "On All Fours." In this episode, Hannah and Adam have been broken up and Hannah is in a state of deep anxiety over not being able to write the kind of story that her editor was hoping she could produce.[28] Her editor asks her, "Did your hymen grow back?" referring to the e-book pages of her draft, and he then asks, "Where's the pudgy face slicked with semen and sadness?" Adam, meanwhile, has started dating a woman, Natalia (played by Shiri Appleby), who he met through the woman's mother, when they were both attending AA (Alcoholics Anonymous) meetings. At first, it seems as if Adam is having a more conventional relationship with Natalia, in terms of being responsive and asking her out. In the early part of the episode, in addition, we see them making love, and as if by contrast, Natalia is full of really clear directives: "I'm ready to have sex now," she explains, and then elucidates a list of details of what she likes in bed. Adam responds by saying, "I like how clear you are with me," as if to counterpose his reaction to Hannah's inarticulateness about what she likes in bed.

The episode quickly turns dark, however, when they have sex a second time. The scene begins with Adam having a drink, after being sober and in AA for a long period. He is clearly trying to get drunk, at least in part, so it seems, because he accidentally bumped into Hannah on the street and was upset at seeing her. He then proceeds to get really drunk with Natalia, and they dance provocatively for hours. They then go back to his place, which Natalia remarks is dark and dirty. Adam then orders her to crawl to his bedroom on her hands and knees, and she reluctantly does so, even as she tells him that there are nails on the floor from his carpentry work. He then roughly picks her up and throws her on the bed, and it is clear from her expression that she is upset by this turn in his behavior. She even tells him, "no," but then he tells her to "relax," and flips her over and penetrates her from behind. He then flips her over again, and asks her where she wants him to ejaculate and she tells him not to ejaculate on her dress, at which point he ejaculates on her breasts.

The scene is graphic and disturbing. Visually, it is one of the only scenes on television where a man's sperm is actually shown. The visual and verbal reactions of the female character, however, are even more jarring, as she tells him almost in tears that, "I, like, really, didn't like that." Adam then claims that he didn't even know "what came over him." The debate about the scene, which occurred on both online and print media, was whether what viewers saw was a "gray rape," that is, not consensual, but not rising to the level of legal sexual assault. Writing for an online young women's magazine *XO Jane*, Marianne offered the following analysis:

> Gray rape can be a problematic term—some people use it as a label for rape that they don't consider "real" or "as bad as real" rape. That is totally bogus. I use the term here to mean the kind of encounter that people sometimes have where consent is not given but it is assumed; it's a term used to describe "nonstandard" sexual assault and, in some ways, it is a weasel term to cover the conflict we feel about consent. . . . Because that is the kind of thing that happens all the time in our culture. Our rape culture. And it's the kind of thing that leaves women (not just women) uncomfortable and unsure, both about their own experiences and when they are watching something like the scene between Adam and Natalia.[29]

In many ways, whether Dunham intentionally set out to portray an "actual" rape or a "gray" rape, or even a "misunderstanding," between the two characters, what was revealed by the episode is that the terms of sexual engagement between millennial men and women are by no means fully equal. There are still entrenched areas where young women's agency and autonomy in sexual encounters not only cannot be fully articulated, but also can be in fact contravened, to the point where deeply problematic sexual encounters can occur. And whether Dunham self-consciously set out to portray a gray rape or simply a deeply uncomfortable "bad" sexual encounter, the scene itself could be read as a further indication that young women still have many sexual experiences that don't address their stated and unstated needs, and indeed arguably constitute a form of sexual assault. In either event, these scenes in *Girls* reveal the ways that, as far as young women have come in gaining a sense of freedom to realize their sexual and emotional needs, they have not fully won the battle for equal rights to be free from coercion and assertions of power that can occur in certain instances.

ALL ADVENTUROUS WOMEN DO!

While it is tempting to believe that the narratives of *Girls*, which assume that young women's reproductive freedom is assured or that their freedom to have sex outside of marriage is a given, are evidence of the victory of the women's movement of the 1970s for women's rights, *Girls* also tries to ultimately complicate this message, by showing how precarious these freedoms are. In addition to the sexual encounters described here, there is also still sexism that the female characters encounter in the workplace, as when Hannah works at a job where it is taken for granted by the other women that the boss would ogle and fondle their breasts.[30] Dunham herself has tried to talk about the ways in which her generation still has to deal with this sexism and, at the same time, has to disavow it as something that was in the past and that is no longer an issue. Speaking to this kind of double consciousness on the part of young women today, of both wanting to distance themselves from being feminists and, at the same time, still having to deal with remaining areas of sexism (not the least of which occur in the film and television industry), Dunham has offered this assessment of her generation's ambivalence about feminism:

> I feel exactly like that—where people are kind of like, "Our moms handled this, and we really have nothing to complain about anymore." It's amazing how not true that is, and yet I feel like every time I make a claim of misogyny, I always sort of apologize for it first, which is itself not very feminist. I'm always like, "I'm sorry to be the girl who wants to talk about feminism, but that person is sexist." So the idea that the feminism conversation could be cool again and not just feel like some granola BS is so exciting to me. It is really funny how even cool chicks are sort of like, "Our moms covered the feminism thing and now we're living in a post-*that* world," when that just isn't true.[31]

In addition, it can be argued that the negative responses to *Girls* in general, and to Dunham in particular, may themselves be part of a larger cultural war that is uncomfortable with the kinds of "inconvenient truths" that have been raised by Dunham, specifically from a young woman's point of view. Perhaps one clue can be found in Dunham's assessment of the hostile response to her show:

> If there were ever a moment where I thought sexism is dead in this country—like our moms had done the work for us—seeing the kind of mini-tornado that was the response to the show certainly showed me that that was not the case. And it made me more determined; the more people were like "shut up about this!" You know that Dixie Chicks lyric "shut up and sing"? I have a real shut-up-and-sing response to a lot of the criticism of the show, but not to others.[32]

For Dunham, the kind of firestorm the show has generated, and the way in which critics, many of whom are male, have tried to paint the program as regressive because the sex is painful or awkward, is itself evidence of a kind of sexism that assumes that women either make "intelligent" or "foolish" choices in terms of their sexual encounters. This either/or sensibility reduces young women's sexuality, which is the opposite of the liberation that the Second Wave women's movement was supposed to bring. As Dunham concludes in a recent interview,

> Then there's a dialogue about whether or not the show is feminist or whether it's irresponsible to show women engaging this way sexually. Or whether this is something that will advance or arrest the cause of women—those are the things where I'm just like, *get it together*.[33]

In conclusion, by reflecting on the narratives of writers such as Dunham, who are ashamed of neither their intelligence nor their ability to create equally intelligent, if confused, young women, it may be more helpful to move beyond the dichotomies left by arguments of whether we have fulfilled the goals of the women's movement and have moved on to a postfeminist cultural landscape. By following these stories that *Girls* tries to tell, we may be able to hear how there is a new sensibility beginning to emerge for millennials, one that honors both the gains made by the women's movement and the hopefulness of those who have proclaimed that those struggles are now over. That sensibility, which *Girls* offers in such a powerful narrative, and in a half-hour comedy format no less, is in the end nothing to take lightly.

NOTES

1. Rosalind Gill, *Gender and the Media* (Malden, MA: Polity Press, 2007), 270.
2. Rachel Mosley and Jacinta Read, "Having It *Ally*: Popular Television and (Post-) Feminism," *Feminist Media Studies* 2, no. 2 (2002): 231–50.
3. Gill, *Gender and the Media*, 270.
4. Frank Bruni, "The Bleaker Sex," *New York Times*, Sunday Magazine Section, 31 March 2012, http://www.nytimes.com/2012/04/01/opinion/sunday/bruni-the-bleaker-sex.html?_r=0 (accessed 26 November 2013).
5. James Poniewozik, "Dead Tree Alert: Brave New Girls," *Time Magazine*, 5 April 2012, http://entertainment.time.com/2012/04/05/dead-tree-alert-brave-new-girls (accessed 26 November 2013).
6. Caitlin Dickson, "Hate Lena Dunham's Naked Body on 'Girls'? Show Us Yours," *Daily Beast*, 10 January 2014, http://www.thedailybeast.com/articles/2014/01/10/hate-lena-dunham-s-naked-body-on-girls-show-us-yours.html (accessed 20 January 2014).
7. Dickson, "Hate Lena Dunham's Naked Body On 'Girls'?"
8. Madeleine Gyory, "Why Bad Sex Is Good," *Women's Media Center*, 4 May 2012, http://www.womensmediacenter.com/feature/entry/why-bad-sex-is-goodon-hbos-girls (accessed 26 November 2013).
9. Chiara Atik, "A Complete Breakdown of the Sex Scenes in *Girls*," The Date Report, 13 March 2013, http://www.thedatereport.com/dating/pop-culture/a-complete-breakdown-of-the-sex-scenes-in-girls (accessed 26 November 2013).

10. Lena Dunham, "Interview with Lena Dunham," *Here's the Thing*, 21 January 2013, http://www.wnyc.org/story/263094-lena-dunham/transcript (accessed 26 November 2013).

11. Atik, "A Complete Breakdown of the Sex Scenes in Girls."

12. Lena Dunham, "Pilot," *Girls* (New York: HBO, 15 April 2012). DVD.

13. Dunham, "Pilot," *Girls*.

14. Emily Nussbaum, "It's Different for 'Girls,'" *New York Magazine*, 25 March 2012, http://nymag.com/arts/tv/features/girls-lena-dunham-2012-4 (accessed 26 November 2013).

15. Bruni, "The Bleaker Sex."

16. Bruni, "The Bleaker Sex."

17. Dunham, "Vagina Panic," *Girls*.

18. Dunham, "Hannah's Diary," *Girls*.

19. Dunham, "One Man's Trash," *Girls*.

20. Dunham, "Pilot," *Girls*.

21. Gyory, "Why Bad Sex Is Good."

22. Frank Bruni, "Naked in New York," *Frank Bruni*, 31 March 2012, http://bruni.blogs.nytimes.com/2012/03/31/naked-in-new-york (accessed 26 November 2013).

23. Frank Bruni, "Naked in New York," *Frank Bruni*, 31 March 2012, http://bruni.blogs.nytimes.com/2012/03/31/naked-in-new-york (accessed 26 November 2013).

24. Dunham, "One Man's Trash," *Girls*.

25. Glenn Whipp, "Lena Dunham Analyzes Three Episodes of *Girls*," 6 June 2013, http://www.latimes.com/entertainment/tv/showtracker/la-et-st-lena-dunham-girls-20130606,0,3395164.story (accessed 26 November 2013).

26. Poniewozik, "Dead Tree Alert."

27. Dunham, "Vagina Panic," *Girls*.

28. Dunham, "On All Fours," *Girls*.

29. Marianne, "A Culture without Consent: On All Fours with Adam and Natalia in Girls," *XO Jane*, 12 March 2013, http://www.xojane.com/entertainment/girls-adam-natalia-rape-scene (accessed 1 December 2013).

30. Dunham, "Vagina Panic," *Girls*.

31. Megan O'Rourke, "A Conversation with Lena Dunham," *Slate*, 15 June 2012, http://www.slate.com/articles/arts/interrogation/2012/06/girls_creator_lena_dunham_interviewed_by_meghan_o_rourke_.html (accessed 26 November 2013).

32. O'Rourke, "A Conversation with Lena Dunham."

33. O'Rourke, "A Conversation with Lena Dunham."

BIBLIOGRAPHY

Atik, Chiara. "A Complete Breakdown of the Sex Scenes in *Girls*." The Date Report, 18 March 2013. http://www.thedatereport.com/dating/pop-culture/a-complete-breakdown-of-the-sex-scenes-in-girls (accessed 26 November 2013).

Baldwin, Alec. "Interview with Lena Dunham." *Here's the Thing*, 21 January 2013. http://www.wnyc.org/story/263094-lena-dunham/transcript (accessed 26 November 2013).

Bruni, Frank. "The Bleaker Sex." *New York Times*, Sunday Magazine Section, 31 March 2012. http://www.nytimes.com/2012/04/01/opinion/sunday/bruni-the-bleaker-sex.html?_r=0 (accessed 26 November 2013).

———. "Naked in New York." *Frank Bruni* (blog), 31 March 2012. http://bruni.blogs.nytimes.com/2012/03/31/naked-in-new-york (accessed 26 November 2013).

Danes, Clare. "Lena Dunham." *Interview Magazine*, 2012. http://www.interviewmagazine.com/film/lena-dunham-1 (accessed 26 November 2013).

Dickson, Caitlin. "Hate Lena Dunham's Naked Body on 'Girls'? Show Us Yours." *Daily Beast*, 10 January 2014. http://www.thedailybeast.com/articles/2014/01/10/

hate-lena-dunham-s-naked-body-on-girls-show-us-yours.html (accessed 20 January 2014).

Dunham, Lena. "Pilot." *Girls*. New York: HBO, 15 April 2012. DVD.

———. "All Adventurous Women Do." *Girls*. New York: HBO, 29 April 2012. DVD.

———. "Hannah's Diary." *Girls*. New York: HBO, 6 May 2012. DVD.

———. "One Man's Trash." *Girls*. New York: HBO, 10 February 2013. DVD.

———. "Vagina Panic." *Girls*. New York: HBO, 22 April 2012. DVD.

Gill, Rosalind. *Gender and the Media*. Malden, MA: Polity Press, 2007.

Gyory, Madeleine. "Why Bad Sex Is Good." *Women's Media Center*, 4 May 2012. http://www.womensmediacenter.com/feature/entry/why-bad-sex-is-goodon-hbos-girls (accessed 26 November 2013).

Holmes. Anna. "The Age of Girlfriends." *New Yorker*, 6 July 2012. http://www.newyorker.com/online/blogs/books/2012/07/the-age-of-girlfriends.html (accessed 25 November 2013).

Marianne. "A Culture without Consent: On All Fours with Adam and Natalia in Girls." *XO Jane*, March 12, 2013. http://www.xojane.com/entertainment/girls-adam-natalia-rape-scene (accessed 1 December 2013).

Mosley, Rachel, and Jacinta Read. "Having It *Ally*: Popular Television and (Post-)Feminism." *Feminist Media Studies* 2, no. 2 (2002): 231–50.

Nussbaum, Emily. "It's Different for 'Girls.'" *New York Magazine*, 25 March 2012. http:/ /nymag.com/arts/tv/features/girls-lena-dunham-2012-4 (accessed 26 November 2013).

O'Rourke, Meghan. "A Conversation with Lena Dunham." *Slate*, 15 June 2012. http://www.slate.com/articles/arts/interrogation/2012/06/girls_creator_lena_dunham_interviewed_by_meghan_o_rourke_.html (accessed 26 November 2013).

Poniewozik, James. "Dead Tree Alert: Brave New Girls." *Time*, 5 April 2012. http://entertainment.time.com/2012/04/05/dead-tree-alert-brave-new-girls (accessed 26 November 2013).

Whipp, Glenn. "Lena Dunham Analyzes Three Episodes of *Girls*," *Los Angeles Times*, 6 June 2013. http://www.latimes.com/entertainment/tv/showtracker/la-et-st-lena-dunham-girls-20130606,0,3395164.story (accessed 26 November 2013).

ELEVEN

I Can't Believe I Fell for Muppet Man!

Female Nerds and the Order of Discourse

Raewyn Campbell

"I'm not ashamed, it's the computer age. Nerds are in! . . . They're still in, right?"[1] This observation came from Buffy's best friend, Willow, in 1997 in the first season of the cult television series *Buffy the Vampire Slayer*. Eight years later, in 2005, American fantasy author and contributor to *Time* magazine Lev Grossman noted,

> Over the past few years, an enormous shift has taken place in American culture, a disturbance in the Force, a rip in the fabric of space-time. What was once hopelessly geeky—video games, fantasy novels, science fiction, superheroes—has now, somehow, become cool. . . . Rappers and athletes trick out their Hummers with Xboxes. Supermodels insist in interviews that they used to be losers in high school. Jon Cryer—Jon Cryer? Duckie from *Pretty in Pink*?—has a hit TV show. Did we lose a war with Nerdistan?[2]

This comment from Grossman was made two years before nerd centric texts such as *The Big Bang Theory* and *Chuck* premiered on US television. Since then, nerds have arguably only grown in prominence and visibility in countries such as the United States, the United Kingdom, and Australia. Today it seems that nerds are everywhere: it's not possible to turn on the TV, pick up a book, or watch a movie without bumping into a nerd. It seems that, nine years on from Grossman's observations, Nerdistan continues to reign.

Nerds have gone from social marginalization to culturally visible and powerful within a remarkably short period of time. People are claiming, not just the label *nerd*, but the attributes encompassed within the label: unselfconscious enthusiasm, intelligence, pursuit of knowledge, obsessive interest, dwelling in the imaginary. It is not merely the case of a new term gaining attention; it is that what *nerd* represents is being seen in a new light. Nerd identity—that is, attributes the nerd label encompasses—is undergoing a process of coolification.

This is enough to constitute a threat to deeply ingrained worldviews, to the legitimacy of power, to what constitutes masculinity, and even to the increasing cultural presence of technology and those who deal with it. There are material conditions, such as the reliance on, and the ordinariness of computers in everyday life, that make people who fall under the *nerd* signifier indispensable. These conditions make it impossible for the story of nerds to be reorganized into its old, negative shape. A new story is required in order to make sense of the dissidence that has occurred between the old understanding of *nerd* and the emerging identity, a story that rectifies the new culturally credible positions nerds currently occupy throughout society despite previously having been culturally ostracized.

It is significant, however, that although discourses surrounding nerd identity have changed shape dramatically over the past two decades, not all self-identifying nerds fare equally within this new discursive regime. One of the most notable and consequential discrepancies in nerdom relates to gender. Men continue to be privileged within the world of nerdom over women. In *Hanging Out in the Virtual Pub*, cultural theorist Lori Kendall argues that shifts in attitudes toward nerds are due to the partial incorporation of nerd identity into hegemonic masculinity. She writes,

> The growing pervasiveness of computers in work and leisure activities has changed many people's relationship to this technology and thus has also changed the meaning of the term "nerd." Since the 1980s, the previously liminal masculine identity of the nerd has been rehabilitated and partly incorporated into hegemonic masculinity.[3]

This suggests that Western society's acceptance of nerds did not come through any intrinsic appreciation of their "nerdiness" and is not indicative of an approval of their obsessive or eccentric behavior. Instead, it seems to suggest that society—rather than beginning to see scholarly aptitude, fiddling with the minutiae of computers, or playing video games as acceptable, "normal," or valid behavior for its own sake—sees nerdy behavior as validated through its ability to fulfill certain requirements of "real" masculinity, and more importantly to reinforce patriarchal legitimacy. This reincorporation protects longstanding male-dominated power positions by impeding major shifts within gender paradigms. Interestingly, however, this leaves females, and particularly female nerds, in an untenable position. As male nerds are largely validated through conforming to notions of hegemonic masculinity, female nerds are unable to sit comfortably within this paradigm.

While the dominance of males is apparent in many "suburbs" of nerdom (such as science and technology industries), this chapter will focus on gendered power imbalances in the media—both textually and extratextually. Nerds currently occupy positions in the media where they can shape and spread narratives regarding nerd identity. Using Michel Foucault's theory on the author function, this chapter will consider how nerds can infiltrate the order of discourse and reshape narratives on nerdom by taking on the roles of author and commentator.[4] Alan Sinfield's theory on the plausibility also provides an apt perspective through which to investigate how nerds (both male and female) are able to infiltrate the order of discourse by gaining legitimacy as authors and through commentary.[5]

In his work "Politics of Plausibility," cultural materialist Alan Sinfield discusses the issue of what he calls cultural "fault lines" and the role of cultural narratives when dissidence occurs. One way dissidence can occur, I suggest, is when belief and practice threaten to split apart, such as when previous outsiders, like nerds, become powerful and central within mainstream society. This exposes cultural fault lines that need to be bridged—society tends to be very uncomfortable if the fault lines are not dealt with. If, as Sinfield argues, bridging is done through the creation and telling of stories, we can see how the entertainment industry can be instrumental in the bridging of cultural fault lines. These bridging stories need to fit conditions of plausibility to be most effective. Conditions of plausibility, Sinfield suggests, are "crucial" as they "govern our understandings of the world and how to live in it, thereby seeming to define the scope of feasible political change."[6] That aspects of nerdom have merged with hegemonic masculinity can be seen to provide these crucial conditions of plausibility.

Narratives are deemed plausible if they fit with dominant discursive regimes. In "The Order of Discourse," Foucault stresses that discourse is not continuous; it is not smooth, organic, or even. Rather discourse is "a violence which we do to things."[7] It is through the use of regulatory procedures such as authorship and commentary that the "chance" elements and "events" of discourse "find the principle of their regularity."[8]

The title *author* (and I would suggest *producer* or *show runner* could be added to this category), although constructed, evasive, and intangible, works institutionally through being granted, no matter how tenuous, a status and authority, allowing those who retain such a title to speak with legitimacy on behalf of many and to many. In "The Order of Discourse," Foucault explains,

> The author is asked to account for the unity of the texts which are placed under his name. He is asked to reveal or at least carry authentification of the hidden meaning which traverses them. He is asked to connect them to his lived experiences, to the real history which saw

their birth. The author is what gives the disturbing language of fiction it unites, its nodes of coherence, its insertion in the real.[9]

Foucault suggests that it is not the historical person behind the author who is of most import, but rather the way the title of "author" functions that is worthy of consideration. As poststructuralist theorists such as Roland Barthes have argued, it is impossible to fully know an author's intention, and even if it were possible would be of little importance as audiences consign their own meaning and understanding onto the texts they encounter.[10]

However, whether arbiters of meaning or not, the notion of the author continues to function effectively in our society. Foucault argues that this is because the title is imbued with a sense of authority and almost deity like status. He argues in "What Is an Author?" that, even when critical theorists moved toward recognizing the importance of the conditions in which a text was created and read, the god-like status of the author was still maintained. He says,

> This concept of *écriture* sustains the privileges of the author through the safeguard of the *a priori*; the play of representations that formed a particular image of the author is extended within a grey neutrality. The disappearance of the author—since Mallarmé, an event of our time—is held in check by the transcendental.[11]

In this quote, Foucault appears to suggest that when emphasis of meaning is placed on works rather than the author, the author sustains power in that she or he invisibly anchors a text in certain conditions; conditions that, if taken into consideration, are believed to shed light on "hidden meanings" within a text. Even when emphasis is placed on works rather than author, the author continues to be used as a link between the text and the "real." This renders the author godlike, or at least of prophetic status in which he or she is allowed to speak with greater legitimacy and where the words espoused are assumed a deeper, more essential significance to that of the ordinary layperson. This means that, whether justifiable or not, authors play a significant role in the defining, creation, and circulation of certain narratives.

Self-identifying nerd producers are no exception and play a hugely important role in the defining of nerd identity and the creation and maintenance of discourses surrounding what it means to be a nerd. By identifying themselves as nerds, producers claim authenticity and therefore legitimacy as constructors of nerdom. It is increasingly evident that nerd producers feel the need, and are in fact required, to prove authentication of their nerdity. Indeed, their very status and success seems to rely upon it. However, as mentioned earlier, male nerds have been granted legitimacy in the order of discourse by meeting plausible conditions of hegemonic masculinity, a condition that females are, quite frankly, unable to satisfy.

The intersection of nerd identity, and the author function in the creation, dissemination, and regulation of discourses surrounding nerdom, is evident particularly in the Anglo-American media landscape of the last decade. The majority of texts that depict nerds as protagonists and that have achieved mainstream success and/or cult status with predominantly nerd audiences generally have at least one of two things in common: first, they have been written/produced/directed by men, and second the title characters and/or central nerd figure is male. Television programs such as *Chuck, The Big Bang Theory, Community, The IT Crowd,* and *Doctor Who* are notable examples of this trend. So too are films such as the *Iron Man* franchise, *The Amazing Spiderman,* and *Star Trek into Darkness,* and books such as the Harry Potter series. No matter the treatment of female characters within these texts, men continue to be privileged over women in nerdom, merely through the latter's absence from the central roles.

However, even in several of the preceding examples, female nerds *are* present in recent/current popular media. In some texts, such as the Harry Potter series, the *Iron Man* franchise, and *The Big Bang Theory,* female nerds occupy significant positions within the narrative. Yet despite this, female nerds are typically relegated to supportive roles. Often they are conduits for the development of male characters, enabling heroism and/ or their incorporation into hegemonic masculinity. For example, the introduction of series mainstays Amy and Bernadette into *The Big Bang Theory* during the third season provides entertaining narrative complications for preexisting nerd characters Sheldon and Howard, respectively. Both of these men escape the potential for their characters to stale as Amy and Bernadette allow for different and unseen aspects of these characters to be explored; asexual Sheldon becomes involved in an unconventional relationship with Amy that is based on both intellect and romance, while the sleazy perpetually single Howard enters a long-term monogamistic relationship with Bernadette culminating in their marriage.

In the same vein, Hermione Granger from the Harry Potter series is integral to Harry's success and heroism. Harry's feats of daring would be much more difficult and the pace of the adventure significantly protracted had the intelligent and swotty Hermione not been there to disperse knowledge, utter incantations, and make sure the banal necessities of everyday responsibilities had been remembered and dealt with. Similarly, the inclusion of Pepper Potts in the three *Iron Man* films allows Tony Stark/Iron Man to become a "better" man. The fact that he settles down with kind and intelligent Pepper reflects well on Tony. It indicates that he has given up his playboy ways, that he has matured enough to privilege intellectual compatibility above mere sensual experience, and that he is far less self-centered. Moreover, threats to Pepper's safety frequently provide Tony with opportunities to perform his heroism.

In addition to serving the purpose of providing a channel for male development, female performance of nerdom is often subtly criticized as female nerds are cast as socially incongruous, inept, or deviant; in other words, they are presented as unnatural. A notable example of this is the character Temperance (Bones) Brennan from *Bones*. Though an exemplar in her field of forensic anthropology, she subverts traditional binaries of femininity by being scientifically minded, rational, and socially reserved. While highly successful by broader cultural standards and in her profession, she is nevertheless represented as unnatural, as lacking, due to her extreme social ineptitude. This infantilizes Bones as those around her—and particularly her professional and personal partner, Seeley Booth—are required to explain simple social cues and niceties. Extreme social incompetence is a trait commonly associated with male nerds (Sheldon from *The Big Bang Theory*, Steve Urkle from *Family Matters*, even Sherlock Holmes). Such behavior has, in recent years, increasingly been diagnosed as Asperger's syndrome. Indeed, a leading researcher on Asperger's syndrome, Simon Baron-Cohen, has posited that autism (the spectrum on which Asperger's syndrome lies) is an extreme form of the male brain. Therefore, despite her intelligence, not only does Bones come across as immature and socially inappropriate, the way these characteristics are represented as pathological binds her to hypermasculinity. Significantly, however, the policing/apologetic actions of other regular characters in *Bones* demonstrate that hypermasculine traits are far less legitimate in someone with a vagina instead of a penis.

Textual representations of female nerds are additionally prone to being sexualized, and again, infantilized. Female nerds become characters who male characters can objectify and/or patronize, and through identification with the protagonists, audiences are also invited to participate in this objectification. Annie, from the television program *Community*, is a particularly potent example of this. Annie shares many traits in common with Hermione from the Harry Potter books; she is an enthusiastic student who is intelligent, strives to top tests and assignments, and longs to impress the teachers. Annie, along with Troy, is one of the youngest members of the study group that forms the focus of *Community*. Her youth is a defining feature of her character; indeed, Annie's behavior and inexperience often comes across as childish. Certainly, while childishness might also be attached to the actions of two nerdy male characters, Troy and Abed, Annie is the only of the three to be overtly sexualized. This is exemplified in an episode titled "Regional Holiday Music" in which Annie dresses in a skimpy Santa outfit and sings to Jeff in an exaggerated baby voice, "teach me how to understand Christmas." Although this number is clearly a satire of the characterization of Annie and her relationship with the older Jeff, it brings to the fore a preexisting and underlying dynamic within the show. This song demonstrates an awareness on the part of the writers of *Community* that Annie is both infantalized and sexualized, yet simultaneously highlights that this is a deliberate creative decision. Indeed, in an interview with *DigitalSpy*, series creator, Dan Harmon states,

> I [also] do try many times a season to put Alison [Brie] in a situation, wardrobe-wise, that I know is going to end up as an animated GIF file! I observe that stuff and the way people are consuming it, because I'm a nerd too and I love to obsess about my favorite TV shows. [12]

The GIFs Harmon is referring to take moments from the show where Annie's cleavage is particularly prominent. It is telling that Harmon self-identifies as a nerd and knowingly makes creative decisions with consideration for his audience—an audience with whom he feels an affinity. Harmon takes for granted that part of his nerdy audiences' practice is to objectify female characters.

These examples of popular media texts support Foucault's notion that not everyone is deemed legitimate as participants in certain discursive regimes:

> There is a rarefaction, this time, of the speaking subjects; none shall enter the order of discourse if he does not satisfy certain requirements or if he is not, from the outset, qualified to do so. To be more precise: not all the regions of discourse are equally open and penetrable; some of them are largely forbidden (they are differentiated and differentiating), while others seem to be almost open to all winds and put at the disposal of every speaking subject, without prior restrictions. [13]

The authenticated claims of authors exert significant pressure on the shape of discourses concerning what it means to be a nerd. This pressure works to place restrictions, not only on what nerd identity is, but also on who is able to participate in nerdom, and on who is allowed to call themselves a nerd. Consequently, this influences and directs the ripple effects nerd identity has within societies in countries such as Australia, the United States, and the United Kingdom. Unfortunately, Foucault's claim that "none shall enter the order of discourse if *he* does not satisfy certain requirements" (emphasis mine) can be taken quite literally when it comes to the role of gender in discourses surrounding nerd identity. It is significantly more difficult for females to satisfy taken-for-granted requirements for entry into the nerd sphere—female participation and involvement in nerdom, as well as female identification as nerd, is met with amplified scrutiny, surprise, and even hostility compared with their male counterparts.

However, it is important to recognize that the representations of female nerds in mainstream media discussed earlier are rife with ambivalence. Dominant discourses are not fixed or stable. Sinfield points out that once a story is accepted—once it meets conditions of plausibility—it can be used by, and to the advantage of, those who are marginalized by it. He asserts,

> In fact, a dissident text may derive its leverage, its purchase, precisely
> from its partial implication with the dominant. It may embarrass the
> dominant by appropriating its concepts and imagery. . . . Deviancy
> returns from abjection by deploying just those terms that relegated it
> there in the first place. A dominant discourse cannot prevent "abuse"
> of its resources.[14]

Once nerdom wins consent and legitimacy—even if it does maintain sexist paradigms—those who share in the signifier, albeit on the margins, can ride the coattails of that which *is* accepted. In this manner female nerds can gain some purchase on the more positive aspects of the label.

Perhaps a helpful analogy for the way the politics of plausibility work is Muppet Man. There is a trope associated with the Muppets in which, in order to gain access to people and places from which they, as a motley group of animals and monsters, were barred, they would disguise themselves as a man. They would balance on top of one another, cover themselves in a large coat with only one of the Muppets' heads protruding from the collar, a hat (maybe sunglasses, maybe a fake mustache) adorning their head, and walk into a space they were forbidden to enter under the guise that they were one ordinary person. In this analogy, the single person "ordinary man" disguise is the condition of plausibility, while the Muppets represent the marginalized/exempt/deviant/subordinate who are given a chance at incorporation into the dominant through concealing themselves under the conditions of plausibility. The signifier *nerd* gained cultural legitimacy, in a large part, through incorporation into preexisting aspects of hegemonic masculinity, and this entailed an exclusion of female nerds.

I suggest, however, that female participants in nerdom are currently in the process of successfully reclaiming the label and the status that this label now affords, through the Muppet Man strategy. Let us return to the examples mentioned earlier. The very introduction of Bernadette and Amy into *The Big Bang Theory*, albeit as addendums to the long-standing male characters, has provided female characters with the opportunity to develop into funny fleshed-out characters in their own right, simultaneously exemplifying the diverse and varied embodiment and performance of nerd identity. Their inclusion also provides moments within a previously male-dominated narrative for females to interact and engage with one another, separate from the male cast. This might be seen to subtly challenge viewer expectations regarding female-driven narratives, but in an unintimidating fashion. Likewise in the Harry Potter series, though Hermione does play a supportive role, both to Harry and within the narrative at large, she does provide an example of a nerdy, intelligent female who is also a heroine. The very fact that she is highly valued both within and outside this highly successful text subverts the idea that femininity, intelligence, eccentricity, and heroism are mutually exclusive. In the case of *Bones*, though her nerdity sits uncomfortably, Bones reveals that while a female character might be socially incompetent and intimidatingly intelligent, she can also be the title character in an enduring prime-time drama, winning admiration from characters within the text and from the viewing audience. Finally in *Community*, though Annie does bear the brunt of sexist stereotypes regarding young sexually inexperienced women, within the context of the program she is one of an ensemble cast, each of whom is also satirized, parodied, and exaggerated. While Annie is undeniably and deliberately objectified, it is equally telling that she is accepted and highly valued by her fellow characters for characteristics beyond her perky cleavage, particularly by nerdy Troy and Abed, who invite her to be their housemate.

Each of the preceding examples of female nerds in popular media can be read in multiple ways. This demonstrates the flexibility and unevenness of discourse. Although representations of female nerds can be problematic, the fact that these characters exist as valued members within their respective narrative contexts, suggests that discourses surrounding nerdom are beginning to be infiltrated by Muppety she-nerds. In conjunction with the Muppet Man strategy, the discursive regime surrounding nerdom has also been destabilized by a crescendo-ing chorus of commentary on the issue. Commentary's role is to say "this is what the text says" without merely repeating the text itself, and as such is able to sew new ideas in with preexisting discursive formations. As Foucault explains,

> Commentary's only role, whatever the techniques used, is to say at last what was silently articulated "beyond," in the text. By a paradox which always displaces but never escapes, the commentary must say for the first time what had, nonetheless, already been said, and must tirelessly repeat what had, however, never been said. [15]

Commentary's power resides in a perception that it is able to explain the hidden truths within a text that the text itself is not at liberty to divulge. In this way, commentary contains and limits discourse by claiming to address once and for all the essential meaning and contents of a text:

> Commentary exorcises the chance element of discourse by giving it its due; it allows us to say something other than the text itself, but on condition that it is this text itself which is said, and in a sense completed. [16]

Commentary works very similarly to the Muppet Man strategy in that its assertions or interpretations have more chance at being granted legitimacy; they appear supported by the text on which it is commenting. It is almost as though commentary, at its most successful, has sprouted organically out from the text; that it is the text itself pointing back to itself saying "This is what I say." But it is crucial to remember that commentary is not the text. They are separate entities. And this is where discursive infiltration is made possible. Indeed, Foucault argues that commentary simultaneously contains and liberates discourse. This is because there is no one commentary on any given text. Paradoxically, commentary completes a text, yet at the same time there exists a multitude of commentaries; commentaries that draw out different (and sometimes conflicting) exegesis of a text, and commentaries that emerge across time and place. Foucault states that this generative aspect of commentary is due to its relationship to the primary text. This relationship

> allows the (endless) construction of new discourses: the dominance of the primary text, its permanence, its status as a discourse which can always be re-actualised, the multiple or hidden meaning with which it is credited, the essential reticence and richness which is attributed to it, all this is the basis for an open possibility of speaking.[17]

The thing that has arguably had the most significant impact on commentary, and by extension on nerdom, is the Internet. Digital media has facilitated a much freer creation and dissemination of commentary, making it a more accessible and interactive process than ever before. Many who have previously been culturally muted are now, through the Internet, able to talk back. And every now and then, an idea, someone's commentary, can gain mass. It can be heard, circulated, discussed, commented upon, and used. It is through moments like these that the excluded have an opportunity to enter the order of discourse.

American actress, writer, comedian, and web entrepreneur Felicia Day is a pertinent example of an individual who has successfully participated in this process, with the effect of disrupting the borders of nerdom. In an interview with *Forbes* magazine, Day reveals, "Hollywood typecast me as the secretary. . . . I could have worked as the quirky secretary for the rest of my life, but I decided not to do that."[18] Resisting traditional entry and advancement points within the entertainment industry, Day decided to create her own content online. She began with a web series called *The Guild* in 2007 and has since expanded her involvement into a range of other web-based projects—most notably the YouTube channel Geek and Sundry in 2012. Geek and Sundry initially hosted six new video series, and has grown to include a second channel, Geek and Sundry Vlogs, which, as of December 2013, hosts eighteen individual vloggers. In another *Forbes* interview, Day explains that the appeal of bypassing traditional industry channels and setting up her own space online lies in her ability to customize her content for her audience. She says,

> I think the seamless connection between viewers and content might make very specific niche programming more successful more quickly than on the walled garden of the cable box. . . . I'm personally excited to be able to make content that is tailored specifically for the audience I've worked with for four years now on *The Guild*.[19]

By publicly acknowledging the importance of her audience in her creative process, Day also improves her chances of winning audience loyalty. She also does this through the manner in which the Geek and Sundry enterprise is set up, through branding, and through her own commentary on the state of Geek and Sundry. Emphasis is consciously placed on authenticating Day as an author/producer of content, on affirming that Day is just like her viewers, that she is one of them; she is a geek. By including eighteen vloggers on the second channel, ten of whom were voted for by the audience via an open audition call, Day not only shows that she is willing to share the limelight; she also demonstrates her dedication to her audience by selecting new talent from within her viewership, then paying and mentoring them in the construction of her business. The importance of mutual engagement and community through Geek and Sundry is also reinforced through the channel's branding. The "About" page on Geek and Sundry's website simply states,

> We are an internet community centered around web videos with shows about comics, games, books, hobbies, and more. We want our audience to connect with each other through common interests online and in real life.[20]

Again, this mission statement removes the focus away from Day herself and places it instead on the audience. This statement suggests that the aim of the channel is not merely to provide Day and her colleagues with a platform from which they can gain recognition and success; rather it asserts that Geek and Sundry's true purpose is to facilitate community and friendships for like-minded people. It eschews conventional hierarchy by insinuating that even those behind the enterprise are a part of the community.

Additionally, Day's own commentary about Geek and Sundry (interestingly often hosted on Geek and Sundry) works to affirm in a very direct and personal way that Day's central role in current nerdom is legitimate. In a vlog titled "State of the Sundry," Day pontificates,

> What is a geek? . . . I realized that in the six years I've been doing this that word became something else. We've been using it so much that it's kind of lost meaning. Geek has become a cliché; it's become a label; it's become something to monetise, to market, to pigeonhole, to brand, to exploit. It's become something to describe a person who is defined solely by liking comics or games or movies or TV. And it's like we've become these consumer badgers that will eat anything that you put a zombie or a superhero on and look just stop. Just stop! That is not what geek means to me. We are more than the hobbies that we do, or the things that we like. We are not mash-up T-shirts (don't get me wrong I love a good mash-up T-shirt). But that is just like the superficial stuff. To me geek means an outsider, a rebel, a dreamer, a creator—whether it's with our own world or someone else's. It's a fighter. It's a person who dares to love something that isn't conventional. The mantra of

geek to me is "Your judgment is not my problem." You think comics are dumb, fine. You think I may not be a real gamer, whatever, that's your problem. I think we need to re-own geek. And that's what I want to do with Geek and Sundry in season 2.[21]

In the course of this speech, Day uses both the author function and the Muppet Man strategy to insert herself into, and solidify her position in the order of, discourse surrounding nerdom. She establishes her credentials as a geek, cloaks herself as being like her audience, she is one of them, and once authenticated and affiliated, she steps through the gap between text and commentary and grabs nerdom by the balls. Through these processes, Day legitimizes herself as an active agent in nerd discourse. And possibly more revolutionary still, Day demonstrates that nerdom is not only the domain of men.

This is not to say that Day's participation and even the participation of women generally in nerdom has been universally accepted, nor does it mean that discourses surrounding nerdom and gender have stabilized. Discourse is always necessarily in a process of contestation. But at this particular time in regard to this particular issue, positive progress seems to be taking place regarding the inclusion of women in nerdom. More encouraging still is the increasing number of examples of female nerds infiltrating the order of discourse via traditional institutional channels. Tina Fey and Gail Simone in the United States, Miranda Hart in the United Kingdom, and Debra Oswald in Australia are only a few of the growing number of female content creators writing intelligent nerdy female characters within traditional media industries.

NOTES

1. Joss Whedon, "Prophesy Girl," _Buffy the Vampire Slayer_, television program (Burbank, CA: WB Television Network, 2 June 1997).

2. Lev Grossman, "The Geeks Shall Inherit the Earth," _Time_, 25 September 2005, http://content.time.com/time/magazine/article/0,9171,1109317,00.html.

3. Lori Kendall, _Hanging Out in the Virtual Pub: Masculinities and Relationships Online_ (Berkeley: University of California Press, 2002), 261.

4. Michel Foucault, "The Order of Discourse," in _Untying the Text_, ed. Robert Young (Boston: Routledge and Kegan Paul, 1970), 48–78.

5. Alan Sinfield, "Cultural Materialism, Othello, and the Politics of Plausibility," in _Literary Theory: An Anthology_, ed. Julie Rivkin and Michael Ryan (Oxford: Blackwell, 1992), 804–26.

6. Sinfield, "Cultural Materialism," 807.

7. Foucault, "The Order of Discourse," 67.

8. Foucault, "The Order of Discourse," 67.

9. Foucault, "The Order of Discourse," 58.

10. Roland Barthes, "The Death of the Author," _Image-Music-Text_, ed. Stephen Heath (New York: Farrar, Straus and Giroux, 1967), 142–48.

11. Michel Foucault, "What Is an Author?" _Screen_ 20, no. 1 (1969): 17.

12. Morgan Jeffery, "'Community' Dan Harmon Q&A: 'Our Fans Influence the Show,'" DigitalSpy, 9 November 2011, http://www.digitalspy.com.au/ustv/s222/

community/interviews/a349824/community-dan-harmon-qa-our-fans-influence-the-show.html.
13. Foucault, "The Order of Discourse," 61–62.
14. Sinfield, "Cultural Materialism," 48.
15. Foucault, "The Order of Discourse," 58.
16. Foucault, "The Order of Discourse," 58.
17. Foucault, "The Order of Discourse," 57.
18. David M. Ewalt, "Felicia Day: Mogul in the Making," *Forbes*, 8 March 2011, http://www.forbes.com/sites/davidewalt/2011/08/03/felicia-day-dragon-age-redemption.
19. David M. Ewalt, "Felicia Day's 'Geek and Sundry' Could Be the Future of TV," *Forbes*, 4 February 2012, http://www.forbes.com/sites/davidewalt/2012/04/02/felicia-day-geek-and-sundry.
20. http://www.geekandsundry.com/about.
21. Geek and Sundry, "State of the Sundry," YouTube video, 25 March 2013, http://www.youtube.com/watch?v=WUU4L0QzA0E.

BIBLIOGRAPHY

Abrams, J. J. *Star Trek into Darkness*. Film. Los Angeles: Bad Robot Productions, 2013.
Baron-Cohen, Simon. "Autism, Sex and Science: Simon Baron-Cohen at TEDxKingsCollegeLondon." YouTube video, 2013. http://www.youtube.com/watch?v=eEYy1GXaNNY
Barthes, Roland. "The Death of the Author." In *Image-Music-Text*, edited by Stephen Heath, 142–48. New York: Farrar, Straus and Giroux, 1967.
Basilone, Steve, and Annie Mebane. "Regional Holiday Music." *Community*. Television Program. Burbank, CA: NBC, 2013.
Bickley, William, and Michael Warren. *Family Matters*. Television Program. Los Angeles: ABC, 1989.
Black, Shane. *Iron Man 3*. Film. Burbank, CA: Marvel Studios, 2013.
Davies, Russell T., and Steven Moffat. *Doctor Who*. Television Program. London: BBC, 2005 and 2009.
Day, Felicia. *The Guild*. Web Series. USA, 2007. http://www.watchtheguild.com
Doyle, Sir Arthur Conan. "A Study in Scarlet." In *Beeton's Christmas Annual*, 1867.
Ewalt, David M. "Felicia Day: Mogul in the Making." *Forbes*, 8 March 2011. http://www.forbes.com/sites/davidewalt/2011/08/03/felicia-day-dragon-age-redemption
———. "Felicia Day's 'Geek and Sundry' Could Be the Future of TV." *Forbes*, 4 February 2012. http://www.forbes.com/sites/davidewalt/2012/04/02/felicia-day-geek-and-sundry
Favreau, Jon. *Iron Man*. Film. Burbank, CA: Marvel Studios, 2008.
Favreau, Jon. *Iron Man 2*. Film. Burbank, CA: Marvel Studios, 2010.
Fedak, Chris, and Josh Schwartz. *Chuck*. Television Program. Burbank, CA: NBC, 2007.
Foucault, Michel. "What Is an Author?" *Screen* 20, no. 1 (1969): 13–34.
———. "The Order of Discourse." In *Untying the Text*, edited by Robert Young, 48–78. Boston: Routledge and Kegan Paul, 1970, 48–78.
Geek and Sundry. YouTube channel, 2012. http://www.youtube.com/user/geekandsundry
———. "Geek and Sundry Launches New Channel!" 19 May 2013. http://www.geekandsundry.com/view/geek-sundry-launches-new-channel
———. "State of the Sundry." YouTube video, 25 March 2013. http://www.youtube.com/watch?v=WUU4L0QzA0E
Geek and Sundry Vlogs. YouTube channel. 2013. http://www.youtube.com/user/geekandsundry
Grossman, Lev. "The Geeks Shall Inherit the Earth." *Time*, 25 September 2005. http://content.time.com/time/magazine/article/0,9171,1109317,00.html

Hanson, Hart. *Bones*. Television Program. Los Angeles: Fox, 2005.

Harmon, Dan. *Community*. Television Program. Burbank, CA: NBC, 2009.

Jeffery, Morgan. "'Community' Dan Harmon Q&A: 'Our Fans Influence the Show.'" DigitalSpy, 9 November 2011. http://www.digitalspy.com.au/ustv/s222/community/interviews/a349824/community-dan-harmon-qa-our-fans-influence-the-show.html

Kendall, Lori. *Hanging Out in the Virtual Pub: Masculinities and Relationships Online*. Berkeley: University of California Press, 2002.

Linehan, Graham. *The IT Crowd*. Television Program. London: Channel 4, 2006.

Lorre, Chuck, and Prady, Bill. *The Big Bang Theory*. Television Program. Los Angeles: CBS, 2007.

Rowling, J. K. *Harry Potter and the Philosopher's Stone*. London: Bloomsbury Publishing, 1997.

———. *Harry Potter and the Chamber of Secrets*. London: Bloomsbury Publishing, 1998.

———. *Harry Potter and the Prisoner of Azkaban*. London: Bloomsbury Publishing, 1999.

———. *Harry Potter and the Goblet of Fire*. London: Bloomsbury Publishing, 2000.

———. *Harry Potter and the Order of the Phoenix*. London: Bloomsbury Publishing, 2003.

———. *Harry Potter and the Half-Blood Prince*. London: Bloomsbury Publishing, 2005.

———. *Harry Potter and the Deathly Hallows*. London: Bloomsbury Publishing, 2007.

Sinfield, Alan. "Cultural Materialism, Othello, and the Politics of Plausibility." In *Literary Theory: An Anthology*, edited by Julie Rivkin and Michael Ryan, 804–26. Oxford: Blackwell, 1992.

Webb, Marc. *The Amazing Spiderman*. Film. New York: Marvel Entertainment, 2012.

Whedon, Joss. "Prophesy Girl". *Buffy the Vampire Slayer*. Television Program. Burbank, CA: WB Television Network, 2 June 1997.

TWELVE

Brains, Beauty, and Feminist Television

The Women of The Big Bang Theory

Amanda Stone

The remarkably popular show *The Big Bang Theory* on CBS features four male self-identified "nerds" who revel in their knowledge of science, technology, and various science fiction universes. In the pilot episode they meet the "hot girl" who lives next door, and thus a classic American sitcom is born.[1] There has been criticism heaped on the creators and writers of the show not only for their depiction of nerd and geek culture but also for their one-dimensional views of females in relation to their intelligence, specifically scientific intelligence.[2] I argue just the opposite: the multitude of female characters depicted on the show represent a realistic spectrum of female intellectual experiences and that these female characters collectively destabilize the image of the "normal" woman portrayed in most American television shows. Penny (played by Kaley Cuoco), Bernadette Rostenkowski (Melissa Rauch), and Amy Farrah Fowler (Mayim Bialik), along with the many female recurring and guest characters, are fully formed people in their own right. They are fighting against popular assumptions that science, and by extension, knowledge as a whole, "is a masculine endeavor"[3] and that intellect and sexuality are mutually exclusive. As the show evolves, the female characters not only showcase their intelligence with more freedom and expression but also discover and exhibit their sexual identities, oftentimes by way of their intellectual experiences.

I also assert that shows like *The Big Bang Theory*, where there is a distinct and realistic range of female intellect and agency, represent a subtle change in attitude and a trend toward a contemporary generation of "feminist sitcoms." Lauren Rabinovitz argues that feminist sitcoms "help construct powerful everyday knowledge about political and cultural feminism."[4] While the female characters within *The Big Bang Theory* never use the term *feminism*, they are constructing unique views about the mental, and physical, capabilities of women through their interactions amongst themselves and with the male characters. Critically engaging with *The Big Bang Theory* is "crucial for understanding television's role in modern culture"[5] as well as discovering how a new generation of television shows is responding to previous (mis)representations of women. While *The Big Bang Theory* certainly has problems, it represents a step in a positive direction for female representation.

The show features women in careers that are otherwise largely ignored on mainstream television. Amy and Bernadette (as well as various female guest stars) are scientists, specifically in a research capacity. Admittedly, the roles for women on television have progressed over the years from stay-at-home mothers and secretaries to women in power. In modern American culture, it is now common to see women as lawyers, doctors, and owners of small businesses. The one field that has been neglected, however, is the role of scientific researcher, a career choice that is usually misunderstood by the public at large anyway. Shows like *The Big Bang Theory* fill that role.[6] As Lorna Jowett explains, "All representations of science on television or in other popular media explore our relationship as humans with science and technology . . . depictions of women scientists can influence or shape ideas about gender and science."[7] In one episode, the male characters brainstorm ways in which the scientific community could be less gender biased and subsequently foster more female involvement. One character astutely points out that it has to begin when women are young girls—media and academia have to illustrate and encourage young girls that they can enter and thrive in the sciences.[8] Characters like Amy and Bernadette portray two highly intelligent women who have the power to change the public discourse about science away from the masculine—Jowett calls this power "subversive," and rightly so.[9]

When the show first premiered in 2007, it revolved around the comedic lives of four scientists and the blonde, beautiful neighbor across the hall. Sheldon Cooper (Jim Parsons) and Leonard Hofstadter (Johnny Galecki), both physicists at Caltech, are roommates. Sheldon is an asocial scientist who enjoys comic books and video games much more than he does the company of other humans. He is analytical and finds it difficult to understand basic human emotions and needs. Leonard is more adept at handling social situations; he interacts with the outside world with more finesse than Sheldon, a fact that forms one of the show's core comedic threads. Their two friends, Rajesh Koothrappali (Kunal Nayyar), an Indian astrophysicist who cannot speak to women unless he is drinking alcohol (an absurdity that is corrected in later seasons), and Howard Wolowitz (Simon Helberg), an oversexed engineer who makes inappropriate comments to women, are constant fixtures in the apartment.

During season 3, we meet both Bernadette Rostenkowski, a microbiologist love interest for the perpetually inappropriate Howard, and Amy Farrah Fowler, a companion for Sheldon.[10] Amy proves to be the female equivalent to Sheldon and her idiosyncrasies match his throughout the show, although her character makes much social progress in terms of human interaction and sexual expression. I will argue that even though these female characters were created as complements to the men, the writers of the show have side-stepped degrading stereotypes of women by portraying a full range of female personalities, intelligences, and life experiences.

WOMEN AND THE SCIENCES

The lack of representations of female scientists within the history of American television reflects how gendered science and technology have become and explains why, in turn, there are few women who pursue

Shown from left: Penny (Kaley Cuoco), Bernadette Rostenkowski (Melissa Rauch), Raj Koothrappali (Kunal Nayyar), and Amy Farrah Fowler (Mayim Bialik). From season 6, "The Santa Simulation."

careers in these fields. In October 2013, Eileen Pollack from the *New York Times* wrote "Why Are There Still So Few Women in Science?" In this piece, she illuminates a study at Yale that found that "physicists, chemists and biologists are likely to view a young male scientist more favorably than a woman with the same qualifications."[11] If, as she claims, only one-fifth of physics PhDs are awarded to women, there is a problem within the field of science. The author herself graduated from Yale with a bachelor of science degree in physics, but "not a single professor—not even the advisor who supervised my senior thesis—encouraged me to go to graduate school."[12] While it can hardly be said that her problems would have been completely eradicated had there been more women physicists on television, the constant masculinization of a particular field within popular culture reflects a widespread social consciousness. Seeing female characters, like those from *The Big Bang Theory*, exceed expectations and thrive within the sciences undermines that gendered association.

Unfortunately, public opinion holds onto the belief that women are genetically predisposed to dislike science, technology, and math. In 2005, Lawrence Summers, the president of Harvard University at the time, argued that men outperform women in science because of a biological difference.[13] These comments, made at a private conference, were certainly not an isolated incident. In November 2013, Fox News Business host Stuart Varney asked the guests on his show, and his viewers, "Is there something about the female brain that is a deterrent for getting on board with tech?"[14] This supposition, that men and women are biologically dissimilar when it comes to understanding math, science, and technology, begins a cycle where fewer young girls are encouraged to study these particular fields. Sherrie Inness claims that American culture at large "has a deeply rooted fear of brilliant women"[15] that manifests in negative stereotypes of the brainy woman and her abilities. The more brilliant the woman, the more agency she has over the trajectory of her own life, including the decision to marry or have children.

Pollack acknowledges that since 1979, "the climate has become more welcoming to young women who want to study science and math"[16] but that the struggle is still evident. Interestingly, she specifically criticizes *The Big Bang Theory* for its role in this problem: "What remotely normal young woman would want to imagine herself as dowdy, socially clueless Amy rather than as stylish, bouncy, math-and-science-illiterate Penny?"[17] This criticism reveals that Pollack had, at best, only a perfunctory and superficial engagement with the women featured in the show. Natalie Angier from the *New York Times* explores how the rise of the "geek chic" and "smart is the new cool" image of the last five years has positively impacted how we as a culture interact with science and technology, and more specifically how women engage with these fields.[18] This enthusiasm, most certainly fostered by television and film, can reject the speculation that women are biologically incapable of succeeding in science.

The unintended backlash of geek chic, however, is a new phenomenon of shaming what are perceived as "fake" geek girls. Kaite Welsh writes that now more than ever, "women are watching, writing, acting in and making sci-fi and fantasy films" but the advent of the "fake geek girl" label has eviscerated those women who take part in Comic-Con and fandoms.[19] Welsh explains that when men take part in dressing up as a character, it is considered normal fandom behavior but when women do it, it is a way to attract male attention rather than an expression of a personal relationship with a cultural text.[20] We can expand this to include more than just those interested in science fiction—the same sentiment is found within the scientific community. The male scientist has been normalized in American popular culture, but the female scientist seems to us to be an exotic creature.

There is a bright spot on the horizon for women interested in science and technology, however. The Internet, specifically the prominence of blog culture, has allowed women to become vocal about their interests in traditionally "male" activities. In 2006, an anthology titled *She's Such a Geek! Women Write about Science, Technology and Other Nerdy Stuff* was published that contains personal stories from various contributors. They divulge not only how they were discouraged from their interests but also how they actively resisted this gendering. There are scores of websites where women can gather together and discuss interests without fear of misogyny and gender persecution.[21] *The Big Bang Theory* represents a leap forward from these specialized blogs to a mainstream discourse. As we shall see, *The Big Bang Theory* does not show one type of woman as with the incredibly successful and unrealistically beautiful scientist sought by Pollack. Instead, the success of the show lies in the fact that the viewers are introduced to a wide assortment of female intellectual experiences, from the nonacademic waitress Penny to the highly successful microbiologist PhD Bernadette. It would be difficult for a television series to succeed if it attempted to pigeonhole the full range of female intelligence into one, carefully crafted character, and certainly, the same can be said about representations of male intelligence.

FEMALE INTELLIGENCE IN *THE BIG BANG THEORY*

The women featured on the show can be loosely divided into three groups. The first is the down-to-earth Penny, who struggles to understand basic science and technology. Second, there is the female equivalent of Sheldon, Raj, and Howard found in the socially naïve genius character of Amy; and finally there are the socially skilled and well-adjusted intellectuals Bernadette and Leslie Winkle (Sara Gilbert).

Penny keeps the show grounded in a sense; she serves as a buffer between the highly specialized, difficult technical language of the scientists and the common vernacular of the average viewer. Penny is also the stereotypical girl next door: the thin, blonde, energetic aspiring actress. What she lacks is academic intelligence—a perceived "flaw" that bothers Sheldon to no end. She is confused whenever scientific topics are discussed in depth and is easily bored with their preoccupation with *Star Wars*, *Star Trek*, and various other science fiction franchises.

Penny's intelligence, however, while not strictly academic, grows and shifts as the show progresses. Her constant interaction with others involved in academia proves to be a catalyst for her own desire to learn, culminating in enrollment in a community college.[22] She is open with her sexuality and is (mostly) unapologetic about her sexual conquests. One of the running gags throughout the show is her knowledge of sex that far outstrips that of Leonard, Sheldon, Raj, and Howard. While Sheldon and Leonard comment often that they cannot afford to live without the other, Penny lives alone across the hall, leaving us with the assumption that she is more financially independent than her male neighbors. She frequently goes out dancing or has friends over for parties while Sheldon and Leonard are highly insulated and very rarely gather in social areas outside of comic book stores and Comic-Con.

When we first meet Penny in the pilot episode, Leonard falls immediately in love, telling Sheldon, "Our babies will be smart and beautiful," meaning of course that he will provide the brains and Penny the beauty. The fact that Penny keeps repeating, "Hi! I'm Penny. I work at The Cheesecake Factory," exemplifies the chasm between her reality and that of the men, all of whom work in a university. The male characters believe that her looks somehow prevent her from entering their world and understanding their interests. For example, due to a lack of a fourth player, Penny is forced to play in their Halo tournament and does surprisingly well. Sheldon responds to this by exclaiming, "I don't know how, but she's cheating. No one can be that attractive and this skilled at a video game."[23] This belief that attractive women cannot possibly be good at anything else other than being attractive perpetuates the image of the "unattractive female nerd." Penny realizes how little she understands of Leonard's world and attempts to correct this ignorance. Eventually, Penny asks Sheldon to teach her basic physics in an attempt to surprise Leonard. While she only learns enough to impress Leonard with one conversation, we see Penny attempting to expand her mind under the influence of others.[24]

Penny is certainly open to intellectual experiences more and more as the show advances. After she and Leonard break up for the first time in "The Lunar Excitation," Penny acknowledges that knowing Leonard and his friends has opened her eyes to a whole new world unknown to her before. She laments the fact that now Leonard and his friends have ruined "dumb men" for her:

Penny: Zach was a perfectly nice guy and then you ruined him!

Leonard: How did I ruin him?

Penny: Cause in the olden days, I never would have known he was so stupid . . . you have destroyed my ability to tolerate idiots!

Penny can no longer go back to the life she had before she met the four male characters. Once they have repaired their relationship, Penny visits Leonard in his lab. As Leonard explains his theoretical work to Penny, he becomes aroused and they have sex. Leonard is, in effect, seducing Penny with science.[25] Leonard's knowledge does not necessarily intimidate Penny. In fact, she goes out of her way many times to understand his work because she loves him.

While Penny is often characterized as the "dumb blonde" by most of the characters in the show, she possesses physical and social abilities that far surpass the men. In "The Zarnecki Incursion," Sheldon wanted to confront the man who hacked his World of Warcraft account.[26] When he discovers that the hacker is bigger and more intimidating than he is, Sheldon employs Penny to threaten the bully. Penny's considerable strength in comparison to the men is mentioned multiple times throughout the show. This challenges what "dumb blondes" are capable of doing. Rather than being the meek and mild damsel in distress, Penny is able to protect the men.

Conversely, Amy Farrah Fowler, the Sheldon of the female group, is virginal, mousy, and highly intelligent. She is, in most ways, the opposite of Penny. When the audience meets Amy at the end of season 3, she is meant to be a match for Sheldon, having responded to an online dating profile created by Raj and Howard.[27] She mimics Sheldon's awkward body language and condescending tone and understands his idiosyncrasies in a way that no other character does. She is also a successful neurologist who forms an unlikely friendship with Penny and Bernadette. Slowly, Amy discovers and develops her sexual nature, much to the consternation of Sheldon. She possesses not only a high intelligence but also recognition of her femininity and sexuality, a combination of traits that are sorely missing from mainstream American television.

Amy refuses to devalue her own work as a neurologist in light of Sheldon's assumptions about her abilities. When Amy and Sheldon have their first fight, Sheldon attempts to diminish Amy's work, believing that physics is far superior to other sciences:

Shown, from left: Penny and Amy Farrah Fowler, from the season 5 episode, "The Skank Reflex Analysis."

Amy: I'm sorry, was I being too subtle? I meant compared to the real-world applications of neurobiology, theoretical physics is, what's the word I'm looking for? Hmm, cute.

Sheldon: Are you suggesting the work of a neurobiologist like Babinski could ever rise to the significance of a physicist like Clarke-Maxwell or Dirac?

Amy: My colleagues and I are mapping the neurological substrates that subserve global information processing, which is required for all cognitive reasoning, including scientific inquiry, making my research ipso facto prior in the ordo cognoscendi.

Amy, although lacking in many things, refuses to apologize for her own success in light of Sheldon's.[28] In many sitcoms, women's successes take a backseat to the primary accomplishment of the male characters. Later in the series, Sheldon is forced to go on vacation from Caltech and invites himself to work in Amy's own lab. He invades her workspace, criticizing how she completes her experiments. Instead of altering how she functions to suit Sheldon's needs, Amy forces him to step out of her way and clean beakers.[29]

Where Penny lacks academic knowledge, Amy lacks the ability to understand social cues. Amy is unable to function in what most people would consider "normal" social situations. For example, Amy has to consult the Internet to determine what constitutes a successful sleepover.[30] She admits frequently that she had few friends growing up and that she was more often than not the social outcast. Throughout the show's run, Penny and Bernadette have to teach Amy basic "feminine" activities: how to paint nails, apply makeup, and wear heels, activities that American culture assumes that all women understand. Lauren Sele believes that Amy's personality, specifically her lack of "feminine" knowledge, is an example of a negative portrayal of women in the sciences. Apparently, the fact that Amy dresses "frumpily" and is "jovially pragmatic to the point of annoying the other characters" means that she has made it seem "socially unnatural" for a female to exist in the masculine world of science and technology. Because Amy exists outside of Sele's perceived notion of what *feminine* means, she becomes "seemingly genderless."[31] The problem with this critique is that it assumes that there is only one accepted version of "feminine," when in reality, femininity is as varied as any other personality trait.

Arguably, the most intriguing female characters in *The Big Bang Theory* are Bernadette and Leslie Winkle. Both women are successful in their respective careers but unlike Amy can easily function in a group and with members of the opposite sex. Bernadette is petite and blonde—two main requirements for a ditzy, popular female front-runner. However, she also is a successful microbiologist with a doctorate degree who is the primary breadwinner in her marriage to Howard. When Bernadette is introduced as a possible romantic match for Howard, her choice of feminine dress and long blonde hair combined with her research interests places her as an odd juxtaposition to Penny.[32] In her critique of *The Big Bang Theory*, Lauren Sele believes that Bernadette's appearance is not the answer "girl nerds" are actually looking for because of her "ultra-conformity to the norms of femininity."[33] Somehow, Sele denounces Bernadette's scientific abilities because she is "sickeningly feminine." This discounts what could be reality—Bernadette is not allowed to be ultra-feminine because this somehow takes away from her role as female nerd. Not only is this misguided, but also it assumes that all female nerds must fit one particular mold that Sele has created. To Sele's mind, Amy is somehow not feminine enough, while Bernadette occupies the other end of the spectrum.

Bernadette admits openly that she does not necessarily enjoy children, and she can be rude and acerbic at times—traits that successful, beautiful women are not usually allowed to possess in American mainstream television. Her high-pitched voice seems to encapsulate the "little girl" image that is in need of saving by the domineering male character, but that stereotype is eradicated as we see her change from a background character to one of the driving forces of the entire show. Bernadette is confident in her intellectual abilities, admitting to Penny and Amy in "The Alien

Shown, from left: Bernadette and Raj from the season 5 episode, "The Skank Reflex Analysis."

Parasite Hypothesis" that she is "much smarter" than Howard but that it is "important to protect his manhood."

Bernadette's relationship with Howard reveals much about her character, specifically how she defies Sele's label of "sickeningly feminine." In what is probably the most important episode for the scope of this research, season 4's "The Roommate Transmogrification" features Bernadette defying expectations of the workingwoman. She reveals to the group that her dissertation has been accepted and she now has a PhD, while Howard has only a master's degree. She has been headhunted by a pharmaceutical company and is now going to make a "butt load" of money. Howard is obviously uncomfortable with the fact that Bernadette is now the breadwinner. This is most obvious when Bernadette buys him a Rolex and tells him, "You let me worry about the money. I just want my baby to have pretty things." She has now taken over what is considered the "man's role" as moneymaker and now has the ability to give expensive gifts to Howard. Similarly subversive, Bernadette exposes her dislike of children, defying the normal standards of the young female character in sitcoms:

Bernadette: I know it makes me sound like a bad person, but I just don't like children.

Howard: Yeah, no, we all got that. But don't you think it'll be different when the child is ours?

Bernadette: Right, when it's our kid that's ruined my body and kept me up all night and I've got no career and no future and nothing to be happy about for the next twenty years, sure, that'll be completely different.

Superficially, Bernadette seems as though she would be the warm, nurturing, and maternal woman, not only because of her high-pitched voice and her choice of dress but also because that is what we expect young women to want. The end of the episode sees Bernadette and Howard reach a compromise about children; in the event they decide to have children, she will give birth but Howard will stay home to care for them.[34] This gender reversal reveals as much about our associations with men's roles as it does about women's. The natural assumption in American culture is that the woman will leave her job and stay home with the children, but *The Big Bang Theory* turns this on its head.

When the audience first meets Leslie Winkle, she is using a "500 kilowatt oxygen iodine laser," establishing her as the intellectual equal to the men to whom we have already been introduced. She moves within the same space and has the same abilities as the male geniuses. When Leonard asks her on a date, Leslie counters by asking, "Would you agree that the primary way we would evaluate either the success or failure of the date would be based on the biochemical reaction during the goodnight kiss?" This showcases her understanding of the scientific (and male) language within the show. She clearly expresses what she wants out of Leonard, and when the practice kiss produces "no arousal" on her part, she turns Leonard down for the date.[35]

When Penny is introduced to Leslie, she is immediately impressed that there is a "girl scientist," to which Leslie responds, "Yep, come for the breasts, stay for the brains."[36] Leslie is unapologetic about her intelligence and in fact chooses to openly flaunt it. This is most obvious in her involvement with the Physics Bowl competition. When Sheldon proves intolerable to work with in a competition, Leonard, Raj, and Howard approach Leslie to replace him:

Leslie: Wait, you're going up against Sheldon Cooper?

Howard: Yes.

Penny in season 6, "The Santa Simulation."

Leslie: That arrogant, misogynistic east Texas doorknob that told me I should abandon my work with high-energy particles for laundry and child bearing?

Leonard: She's in.

She refuses to bow down to the "genius" of Sheldon Cooper and actively participates in proving to him that female scientists are capable of the same levels of intelligence that he himself possesses.[37]

FEMALE SEXUALITY, ROMANCE, AND *THE BIG BANG THEORY*

Penny is the most sexually experienced of all the female characters. In the pilot episode, Penny is able to manipulate Leonard into confronting her ex-boyfriend because of his immediate attraction to her. The directors of the show constantly show Penny dressed in provocative clothing, especially tight, low-cut shirts. While this ostensibly objectifies Penny, she is unapologetic in her dating and sexual life. Unlike Leonard, who is eager to jump into a serious relationship with Penny and displays multiple times throughout the show his desire to be romantic and thoughtful, she is resistant to a monogamous relationship. Although popular culture, and this of course includes the long history of television programming, typically portrays women as "centrally concerned with and in need of love, romance and relationship,"[38] Penny defies this label. She dates (and subsequently has sex with) quite a few men throughout the course of the show. She and Leonard date throughout the third season but break up when Leonard tells Penny he loves her. She tells him, "You don't get to decide when I'm ready to say I love you."[39] These words are quite powerful and portray a young woman who actively resists assumptions about what she is supposed to want. When they attempt a second relationship later in the show, Penny and Leonard agree to undergo a "beta test" in their relationship. They each have the power to list their grievances about the other and attempt to "correct" said behavior. Agreements like these set up an equal power exchange between Penny and Leonard.[40]

She only doubts herself when others point out her promiscuity as something shameful. Sheldon uses a complex equation to figure out that Penny has dated "approximately 171 different men" during her lifetime. When he narrows it down to thirty-one sexual partners, Amy is fascinated and asks Penny, "This is very interesting. Cultural perceptions are subjective. Penny, to your mind, are you a slut?" While Amy is certainly not shaming Penny into admitting that she is too promiscuous, Penny begins to doubt her own sexual identity.[41] Interestingly, Penny acts as a type of sexual "mentor" for both Amy and Leonard. They lack experience with sex, and Penny is able to impart advice. She holds the sexual power in her relationship with Leonard and is able to teach him how to pleasure her.

Likewise, Leslie Winkle openly expresses her sexual experience multiple times in her appearance in the show. After initially turning Leonard down for a date because his kiss did not arouse her, Leslie later admits that she is sexually attracted to him after witnessing Leonard play the cello: "Just so we're clear, you understand that me hanging back to practice with you is a pretext for letting you know that I'm sexually available."[42]

This exchange establishes Leslie as sexually active, and able to express her desires openly to men, oftentimes quite explicitly. After sleeping with Leonard, Leslie turns him down in his pursuit of a romantic relationship:

Leslie: Listen, Leonard, neither of us is a neuroscientist but we both understand the biochemistry of sex, I mean, dopamine in our brains is released across synapses causing pleasure. You stick electrodes in a rat's brain, give him an orgasm button, he'll push that thing until he starves to death.

Leonard: Who wouldn't?

Leslie: Well, the only difference between a rat and us is that you can't stick an electrode in our hypothalamus. That's where you come in.

At this point in the show, Leslie is uninterested in a romantic relationship and admits that all she was looking for was sexual arousal and satisfaction. Her intelligence and sexuality exist together, rather than as mutually exclusive aspects of her femininity. When Leslie and Leonard attempt an actual relationship, we see Leslie take over the "male" role in a heterosexual relationship:

Leslie: Your place, we'll order Chinese, you'll rent a movie, artsy but accessible, then light petting, no coitus.

Leonard: Sounds fun.

Leslie: I'll leave the details up to you; I think it's better if you assume the male role.

Leslie takes charge and sets the rules and regulations for her romantic and sexual relationships in ways that are unusual for mainstream television.[43] Her later sexual relationship with Howard uncovers more of this personality trait.

Howard and Leslie begin a "friends with benefits" association based solely on sexual fulfillment. She desires nothing further in terms of commitment. She offers gifts to Howard as "rewards" for sexual pleasure. She effectively becomes the stereotypical "man"—seeking only sexual fulfillment with no lingering amorous obligation.[44] When Leslie actively decides to breaks off this relationship, Howard is visibly upset, prompting Sheldon to ask, "If you were in a nonemotional relationship, why are you having what appears to be an emotional response?" Howard is now the stereotypical "woman"; he is unable to separate sex and emotions although it was made perfectly clear that a romantic relationship was never going to happen.[45] Lauren Sele characterizes Leslie as "consistently cold and unfeminine" who "callously" ends her sexual relationship with Howard, "breaking his heart" in the process.[46] This criticism exposes our biases about sexuality. Had it been Howard who initiated the sex-only relationship, only to break it off later, we would admonish Leslie for being gullible enough to fall for that line. The fact that it was Leslie who suggested that they "scratch" each other's backs subverts our associations of sex and emotion.

Interestingly, like Amy, Leslie refuses to compromise her intellectual beliefs for a man. During Leslie's very short-lived romance with Leonard, Sheldon makes it clear that he disagrees with her work with loop quantum gravity, believing that his work with string theory is far superior. When Leonard refuses to take a side in this particular argument, Leslie storms out, exclaiming, "I'm sorry, I could have accepted our kids being genetically unable to eat ice cream or ever get a good view for a parade, but this? This is a deal breaker."[47] Leslie would rather end a relationship than continue in one where she is not intellectually stimulated.

Amy Farrah Fowler's burgeoning sexuality is a running theme throughout the show. When she first meets Sheldon, Amy is quick to note, "Now before this goes any further, you should know that all forms of physical contact, up to and including coitus, are off the table," a stipulation that Sheldon is more than happy to accommodate.[48] However, Amy's attitude changes dramatically in later episodes. As she interacts with Penny and Bernadette, Amy begins to recognize the desire to explore her sexuality with Sheldon. Amy reveals that she only dates once per year, per an agreement with her mother and that she has volunteered an astounding 129 times for experiments "in which orgasm was achieved by electronically stimulating the pleasure centers of the brain." This confession uncovers that Amy has only explored sexual pleasure through scientific experiments, rather than with human contact.[49] She is obviously open to sexual pleasure but is uncomfortable around other human beings. When Amy meets Penny's cute but hopelessly dumb ex-boyfriend Zach, she is immediately sexually attracted to him but is unable to identify what is happening to her body:

Amy: I'm suddenly feeling flushed. My heart rate is elevated. My palms are clammy, my mouth is dry. In addition, I keep involuntarily saying the word "hoo."

Penny: Oh, we know what's causing that, don't we?

Amy: It's no mystery. I obviously have the flu coupled with sudden onset Tourette's Syndrome.

While she and Sheldon are attempting to uncover her "illness," Amy comes to the realization that sexual attraction is only natural: "I have a stomach, I get hungry. I have genitals, I have the potential for sexual arousal."[50] This moment of clarity represents a turning point in Amy's sexual life. Later, we see the first hint of sexual interaction between Amy and Sheldon. They go out for "girl's night" with Penny and Bernadette and Amy consumes too much alcohol, thereby lowering her inhibitions. She admits her attraction to him—calling him a "sexy toddler" because he smells like baby powder (an uncomfortable admission that exemplifies how little both Amy and Sheldon understand about flirting). When Amy drunkenly kisses Sheldon, he is taken aback but does not immediately reject her advances. While the kiss is interrupted by Amy's need to vomit, we see that she is willing to explore her urges in ways she has never done before.[51]

As Amy comes to terms with her sexuality, she has to turn to trickery to get Sheldon to physically interact with her, relying on his inability to understand sexual and emotional needs. In "The Fish Guts Displacement," Amy relies on Sheldon to nurse her back to health. When Sheldon suggests rubbing medicine on her chest, Amy becomes visibly interested and excited. She clearly has a sexual response as he touches her. Even after she recovers, Amy decides to manipulate Sheldon into believing that she is still unwell in order to continue the physical contact. Unfortunately, Amy is discovering her own sexual needs with a man who rejects all form of sexual interaction. The most remarkable change in their relationship occurs at the end of season 6. We see Sheldon admit that a sexual relationship with Amy is "possible."[52] This admission, after years of sexual denial, exemplifies an awakening in both Sheldon and Amy.

CONCLUSION

As we have seen, the female characters of *The Big Bang Theory* are all markedly diverse, both intellectually and emotionally. These differences create a complicated and credible look at how female intelligence manifests in popular culture. By providing these realistic depictions, the writers of the show are de-gendering science and technology. Unlike what some of the show's critics argue, the female characters of *The Big Bang*

Theory are fighting cultural and social assumptions about the intellectual and romantic capabilities of women. In effect, they are clearing a path for easier entry for young girls interested in these masculinized fields. Introducing extremely intelligent women as attractive and sexual eradicates the image of the socially inept and awkward nerd and instead places value on women in all of their varied realities.

NOTES

1. At the time of writing, *The Big Bang Theory* was in its seventh season and had been renewed for an eighth installment.

2. Sam Lowry, "Is 'Big Bang Theory' Bad for Science?" *Discover Magazine*, 3 February 2009, http://bit.ly/184WN9s, and Meghan Neal, "Stereotype and 'The Big Bang Theory' Are Keeping Women Out of Science?" *Vice*, 29 June, http://bit.ly/17tGT4x.

3. Lorna Jowett, "Lab Coats and Lipstick: Smart Women Reshape Science on Television," in *Geek Chic: Smart Women in Popular Culture*, ed. Sherrie A. Inness (New York: Palgrave Macmillan, 2007), 31.

4. Lauren Rabinovitz, "Ms.- Representation: The Politics of Feminist Sitcoms," in *Television, History, and American Culture: Feminist Critical Essays*, ed. Mary Beth Haralovich and Lauren Rabinovitz (Durham, NC: Duke University Press, 1999), 145.

5. Mary Beth Haralovich and Lauren Rabinovitz, "Introduction," in *Television, History, and American Culture: Feminist Critical Essays*, ed. Mary Beth Haralovich and Lauren Rabinovitz (Durham: Duke University Press, 1999), 3.

6. See also the *CSI* franchise, *Bones*, and *NCIS*.

7. Jowett, "Lab Coats and Lipstick," 31.

8. "The Contractual Obligation Implementation," *The Big Bang Theory* (Burbank, CA: Warner Home Video, March 7, 2013).

9. Jowett, "Lab Coats and Lipstick," 35.

10. "The Creepy Candy Coating Corollary," *The Big Bang Theory*.

11. Eileen Pollack, "Why Are There Still So Few Women in Science?" *New York Times Magazine*, 3 October 2013, http://nyti.ms/156YTSw (accessed 3 November 2013).

12. Pollack, "Why Are There Still So Few Women in Science?"

13. Suzanne Goldenberg, "Why Women Are Poor at Science, by Harvard President," *Guardian*, 18 January 2005, http://bit.ly/184ruvs (accessed 3 November 2013).

14. Katie McDonough, "Fox Business Host Wonders If Women Have Weird Brains," *Salon*, 18 November 2013, http://bit.ly/1bW50Kn (accessed 23 November 2013).

15. Sherrie Inness, "Who Remembers Sabrina? Intelligence, Gender and the Media," in *Geek Chic: Smart Women in Popular Culture*, ed. Sherrie A. Inness (New York: Palgrave Macmillan, 2007), 2.

16. Pollack, "Why Are There Still So Few Women in Science?"

17. Pollack, "Why Are There Still So Few Women in Science?"

18. Natalie Angier, "In 'Geek Chic' and Obama, New Hope for Lifting Women in Science," *New York Times*, 19 January 2009, http://nyti.ms/19bUqMU (accessed 1 October 2013).

19. Kaite Welsh, "Does Misogyny Lie at the Heart of 'Fake Geek Girl' Accusations?" *New Statesman*, 8 August 2013, http://bit.ly/13IC1Zf (accessed 15 November 2013).

20. Welsh, "Does Misogyny."

21. For example, GirlGeeks, http://www.girlgeeks.org; TheMarySUe, http://www.themarysue.com; GirlGeekCon, http://www.geekgirlcon.com; and GeekGirl, http://geekgirlcamp.com.

22. "The Extract Obliteration," *The Big Bang Theory*.

23. "The Dumpling Paradox," *The Big Bang Theory*.

24. "The Gorilla Experiment," *The Big Bang Theory*.
25. "The Holographic Excitation," *The Big Bang Theory*.
26. "The Zarnecki Incursion," *The Big Bang Theory*.
27. "The Lunar Excitation," *The Big Bang Theory*.
28. "The Zazzy Substitution," *The Big Bang Theory*.
29. "The Vacation Solution," *The Big Bang Theory*.
30. "The 21-Second Excitation," *The Big Bang Theory*.
31. Lauren Sele, "Talking Nerdy: The Invisibility of Female Computer Nerds in Popular Culture and the Subsequent Fewer Number of Women and Girls in the Computer Sciences, *Journal of Integrated Studies* 1, no. 3 (2012): 4.
32. "The Creepy Candy Coating Corollary," *The Big Bang Theory*.
33. Sele, "Talking Nerdy," 4.
34. "The Shiny Trinket Maneuver," *The Big Bang Theory*.
35. "The Bran Hypothesis," *The Big Bang Theory*.
36. "The Hamburger Postulate," *The Big Bang Theory*.
37. The Bat Jar Conjecture," *The Big Bang Theory*.
38. Katie Milestone and Anneke Meyer, *Gender and Popular Culture* (Cambridge: Polity Press, 2012), 87.
39. "The Spaghetti Catalyst," *The Big Bang Theory*.
40. "The Beta Test Initiation," *The Big Bang Theory*.
41. "The Robotic Manipulation," *The Big Bang Theory*.
42. "The Hamburger Postulate," *The Big Bang Theory*.
43. "The Codpiece Topology," *The Big Bang Theory*.
44. "The Cushion Saturation," *The Big Bang Theory*.
45. "The Vegas Renormalization," *The Big Bang Theory*.
46. Sele, "Talking Nerdy," 3.
47. "The Codpiece Topology," *The Big Bang Theory*.
48. "The Lunar Excitation," *The Big Bang Theory*.
49. "The Robotic Manipulation," *The Big Bang Theory*.
50. "The Alien Parasite Hypothesis," *The Big Bang Theory*.
51. "The Agreement Dissection," *The Big Bang Theory*.
52. "The Love Spell Potential," *The Big Bang Theory*.

BIBLIOGRAPHY

Angier, Natalie. "In 'Geek Chic' and Obama, New Hope for Lifting Women in Science." *New York Times*, 19 January 2009. http://nyti.ms/19bUqMU (accessed 1 October 2013).
Brown, Mary Ellen, ed. *Television and Women's Culture: The Politics of the Popular*. London: Sage Publications, 1990.
Goldenberg, Suzanne. "Why Women Are Poor at Science, by Harvard President." *Guardian*, 18 January 2005. http://bit.ly/184ruvs (accessed 3 November 2013).
Haralovich, Mary Beth, and Lauren Rabinovitz, eds. *Television, History, and American Culture*. Durham, NC: Duke University Press, 1999.
Inness, Sherrie. "Who Remembers Sabrina? Intelligence, Gender and the Media." In *Geek Chic: Smart Women in Popular Culture*, edited by Sherrie A. Inness, 1–9. New York: Palgrave Macmillan, 2007.
Jowett, Lorna. "Lab Coats and Lipstick: Smart Women Reshape Science on Television." In *Geek Chic: Smart Women in Popular Culture*, edited by Sherrie A. Inness, 31–48. New York: Palgrave Macmillan, 2007.
Lorre, Chuck, and Bill Prady. *The Big Bang Theory*. Burbank, CA: Warner Home Video, 2008–2013. DVD.
Lowry, Sam. "Is 'Big Bang Theory' Bad for Science?" *Discover Magazine*, 3 February 2009, http://bit.ly/184WN9s

McDonough, Katie. "Fox Business Host Wonders If Women Have Weird Brains." *Salon*, 18 November 2013. http://bit.ly/1bW50Kn (accessed 23 November 2013).

Milestone, Katie, and Anneke Meyer. *Gender & Popular Culture*. Malden, MA: Polity Press, 2012.

Neal, Meghan. "Stereotype and 'The Big Bang Theory' Are Keeping Women Out of Science?" *Vice*, 29 June 2013, http://bit.ly/17tGT4x

Pollack, Eileen. "Why Are There Still So Few Women in Science?" *New York Times Magazine*, 3 October 2013. http://nyti.ms/156YTSw (accessed 3 November 2013).

Sele, Lauren. "Talking Nerdy: The Invisibility of Female Computer Nerds in Popular Culture and the Subsequent Fewer Number of Women and Girls in the Computer Sciences." *Journal of Integrated Studies* 1, no. 3 (2012): 1–14.

Welsh, Kaite. "Does Misogyny Lie at the Heart of 'Fake Geek Girl' Accusations?" *New Statesman*, 8 August 2013. http://bit.ly/13IC1Zf (accessed 15 November 2013).

THIRTEEN

Too Smart for Their Own Good?

Images of Young Jewish Women in Television and Film

Rachel S. Bernstein

In the first season of the Fox cable network television show *Glee*, the handsome, bad-boy football player Noah "Puck" Puckerman discusses the ambitious and brainy Rachel Berry saying, "That Rachel chick makes me want to light myself on fire, but she can sing."[1] Here Puck is praising Rachel's singing talent while rebuking her personality. One important aspect of this scene is the pairing of these two characters—Puck and Rachel, both Jewish characters on the show—highlighting the differing images of Jewish male characters and Jewish female characters present in television and film today. Such a double standard has existed in images of Jews since their first representation on screen;[2] however, images of Jewish women and men since 2000 have evolved and changed over the decades to reflect contemporary demographic and social concerns relevant to the twenty-first century. Young, unmarried Jewish women like Rachel Berry are portrayed as ambitious intellectuals and artists who often choose their talent and careers over interpersonal relationships, while Jewish men like Puck are presented as approachable slackers who ultimately get rewarded with popularity and acceptance in their relationships with non-Jewish partners. This example represents a trend evident in at least five instances from television and film released since the year 2000 in which the young, Jewish female characters are portrayed as smart and creative individuals, yet their intelligence and talents are shown to trump and ruin their personal lives.

Rachel Berry and young Jewish women in television and film like her display a broad range of talents and intelligence; however, these potentially positive images of Jewish women still carry a stigma inherited from characterizations of previous generations of Jewish characters. In the history of Jews on screen, the location and concerns of the American Jewish community have impacted the representation of Jewish characters, both men and women.[3] From the tension over assimilating to American cultural norms coinciding with the increasing acceptance of minorities and cultural and ethnic distinctiveness following the social movements of the 1960s and 1970s, in conjunction with the rising affluence of American Jews, images of young Jewish men and women in the 1960s through the 1990s reflected the communal anxieties over fitting in and succeeding in American culture. As anthropologist Riv-Ellen Prell argues, Jewish women were particularly burdened with the discomforts of the Jewish community in their increasing affluence and move toward acceptance in the American middle class. The Jewish American Princess (JAP) image created within the Jewish community in literature, film, and material culture in the 1960s through the 1990s served as a scapegoat for the Jewish community's, and especially Jewish men's, concerns over overt consumerism as part of American middle-class culture and the process of assimilation, which was hindered by overt Jewishness and ostentatious consumption.[4] As these signifiers of assimilation—the move into the middle class and consumption—began to morph into accepted communal norms of achieving high levels of education and career success, images of young Jewish women have evolved beyond the JAP, but these images still demonstrate a concern over Jewish women. Following in the footsteps of earlier film and television representations of the young Jewish woman, especially images of the JAP stereotype, today's images of young Jewish women similarly reflect corresponding anxieties in the Jewish community over the community's demographic trends and place in American society.

To contextualize today's images of brainy and creative Jewish women, I begin first with some background on the JAP and the broader communal concerns that fed that image. Next I outline the current demographic trends and concerns in the American Jewish community, for just as anxieties in the Jewish community helped produce the JAP image, contemporary communal trends are also reflected in images of young Jewish women today. These trends provide demographic background for these images, and such trends parallel several characteristics of images of young Jewish women in television and film. I then discuss the five films and television series distributed in the twenty-first century that feature young, unmarried Jewish women as central characters in contemporary environments. While there are Jewish creators behind each of these examples who have contributed to these images of Jewish women and men, the main concern is the resulting images and how they parallel current trends and their consequences. To better understand the particular characteristics of young Jewish women and the consequences of these images, I then compare these images of Jewish women to young Jewish men. It is clear in this comparison that images of Jewish men—once presented as overly ambitious and neurotic—have evolved into approachable characters with mediocre ambitions who are rewarded with successful relationships and productive sexuality. Jewish women, however, are often represented as alienating their friends and romantic partners with their intelligence and ambitious creative pursuits. The continued pairing of the American Jewish community's demographic trends and images of Jews in television and film demonstrates that young Jewish women are still marginalized in these images when compared to the successes of Jewish men.

IMAGES OF THE JEWISH AMERICAN PRINCESS

In investigating the intersection of concerns in the Jewish community with images of Jews in television and film, and how these images portray and impact young Jewish women, it is important to start with its widely known predecessor, the Jewish American Princess. As Prell documented in her chapter on the JAP in *Fighting to Become Americans*, the basis for the JAP stereotype lay in the Jewish rise to the middle class and Jewish struggles with consumerism and newfound affluence. Depictions of the young Jewish woman in the 1960s through the 1990s relied on this stereotype of the Jewish princess who was greedy, spoiled, whiney, a "Daddy's girl," and a tease who, when married, manipulated her husband into feeding her materialism. This image arose, as Prell argues, at a time of changing opportunities for women, as well as changing conditions in the Jewish community, for Jews no longer faced rampant anti-Semitism, and a majority of the community moved to the suburbs and pursued higher education and advanced career goals.[5] The JAP, then, embodied the community's anxieties over the changing roles of women in the wider society and its impact on the Jewish community, as well as the risk that Jewish women could present in disrupting Jews' ascent into the middle class and suburban, professional life.

While the JAP may have displayed some measure of intelligence and she often attended college, for pursuit of higher education went hand in hand with the ascent into the middle class, the JAP did not often harness this intelligence productively. As Prell argues, the JAP image in literature, film, and material culture produced mainly by Jews but marketed broadly reflected the anxiety of the community over women's changing role in education and economic pursuits; therefore, the JAP image served to demonstrate the dangers of the JAP's changing place in society.[6] The JAP's goals were to marry rich, Jewish men and consume. Certainly the

JAP was painted as ambitious, but this trait was more often countered by, as Prell notes, her dependence and passivity, which did not further her creativity or intelligence as in contemporary images, and left the JAP "unproductive."[7] Not only did the JAP fail to fill any useful role in society, she was also "unproductive" in the sense of not producing children, for she was often depicted as sexually manipulative with her male partner, withholding sex in order to get her way.[8] These tensions over middle-class affluence leading to education, careers, and consumption created the image of the JAP as ambitious yet dependent and manipulative in ways rejecting intellectual pursuits and career ambitions for herself, for they arose from the community's anxiety over women's advancement in these fields at that time.[9]

While the JAP stereotype served as the embodiment of the Jewish community's anxieties over the transition to the middle class, such concerns are no longer present for a majority of the Jewish community that is now firmly entrenched in the middle and upper middle class. Social status and class are not the driving force behind images of young Jewish women in television and film today as they were in the previous four decades, for these class characteristics are now often simply taken for granted. Instead, the current communal concerns result from trends in the broader American population that bear particular weight on the Jewish community. Cultural images of single, young Jewish women today may have arisen from the trend gaining traction in the 1980s and 1990s, and finding a place as a norm into the 2000s, for women, and Jewish women in particular, to increasingly pursue higher education and advanced degrees, and the impact of such educational pursuits on delaying marriage and family formation.

THE IMPACT OF DEMOGRAPHIC TRENDS

Education has long been a central concern in the Jewish community, especially as a facilitator of social and career advancement.[10] While the JAP reflected the beginnings of this advancement in Jewish women's educational and career attainment, therefore leading to an image that downplayed her intelligence and ambitions by focusing on dependence and consumption, the young Jewish woman today shows much more of an evolution in the trends toward education and career achievement. As scholar of the contemporary Jewish community Sylvia Barack Fishman argues, "Educational accomplishment for women became a coalesced American Jewish value decades ago, and now, occupational accomplishment for women is becoming a coalesced American Jewish value as well."[11] The effect of that valuing of men's and women's education is that Jewish women have started pursuing advanced degrees in higher numbers, and to such an extent that they are now rivaling Jewish men's attainment of higher degrees. Sociologists Harriet Hartman and Moshe Hartman analyzed the 2000–2001 National Jewish Population Survey (NJPS) in order to highlight key gendered differences in the Jewish community focused mainly on education, work, family, and involvement in the Jewish community. Hartman and Hartman found that "nearly two-thirds of men have earned at least a bachelor's degree, compared with slightly more than half of women; 30% of men have earned some graduate degree, compared with 22.5% of women, and 11% of men have earned a doctoral or professional degree, more than double the 5% of women." [12] However, the difference between the two groups in some cases is not great, and Hartman and Hartman argue it is narrowing. For example, Hartman and Hartman document that compared with 1990, the 2000–2001 statistics show that the proportion of Jewish women "completing doctoral and professional degrees increased, while the proportion of men completing such degrees actually decreased." [13] The greatest change in the number of Jewish women pursuing higher education is actually those completing some college, for compared with the NJPS data from 1990, "About four and a half times as many men completed some college in 2000–01 . . . and nearly five times as many women completed some college in 2000–01." [14] These statistics highlight the fact that Jewish women are pursuing higher education and advanced degrees in greater numbers, closing the gap between Jewish men's and women's educational accomplishments. As Prell documents, the JAP image reflected the trends Hartman and Hartman highlight in higher educational attainment by Jewish women, [15] but as these trends have evolved since the 1990s, so have the images of Jews in popular culture.

A related development that is important both in changing the dynamics of the Jewish community and for media representations of Jews is the trend toward delayed marriage. While this demographic change in delaying marriage is evident in the broader US population, this trend has particular consequences for the Jewish community. As Fishman states, "A congruence of religious values, economic necessities, and cultural and societal pressures within traditional Jewish cultures have promoted marriage as the preferable marriage status. . . . This belief or conviction makes married adults and their families central, while it marginalized the unmarried." [16] Yet, Jews have reflected broader societal trends in delaying marriage since the 1970s and "postponed marriage and childbirth are now phenomena that have been in place for several decades" in the American Jewish community. [17] Both Fishman and Hartman and Hartman find that Jews marry later than other white Americans, even when the later age at marriage of the broader population is taken into account. Using data from the 2000–2001 NJPS, Hartman and Hartman similarly document this trend by comparing the Jewish community with the broader, white, non-Hispanic American population. They found that "the marriage delay results in a higher average age of marriage for Jews than for those in the broader white population, in the total and in every age group for both men and women, especially noticeable up to age 45. . . . Up to age 55, in fact, Jewish women marry even later than do men in the broader population, on average."[18] There is a two-fold distinction here in the delay of marriage: (1) Jews marry later than the broader white population in the United States where delayed marriage is an established trend; and (2) Jewish women show a noticeable gap in delaying marriage to a greater extent even than non-Hispanic, white men.

This trend in delaying marriage may affect the broader US population, but both Jewish men and women are increasingly marrying later, and Jewish women display a greater delay compared with the broader population. Perhaps because of this gap between Jewish men and women and especially Jewish women and the broader population, contemporary media images bestow all of the consequences on Jewish women. Jewish women, in their pursuit of higher education and the careers that come with advanced degrees, are held accountable for the fact that "American Jewish women continue to have fewer children than do women in the broader U.S. population," and "a significantly higher proportion of American Jewish women appear to remain childless than among women in the broader U.S. population."[19] While Dashefsky and Levine note that having fewer children is a mark of the middle class and Jews followed such a trend as they gained middle class status,[20] scholar Elliot N. Dorff grounds this diminution in childbearing and the increase in childlessness on Jews' pursuit of education. He argues that

> American Jews in far higher percentages than the general American population go to college and graduate school. . . . As a result, Jews commonly do not marry until their late twenties, and they do not try to have children until their thirties. . . . As a result, Jews suffer from infertility more than other segments of the American population.[21]

While Dorff notes that the pursuit of higher education and the subsequent delay and reduction in childbearing affects both Jewish men and women, it is Jewish women who are the bearers of Jewish children and also more often subject to age-related childbearing difficulties. As both Jewish men and women pursue higher education and advanced degrees, and women in particular reach an age when childbearing becomes difficult or impossible, they exacerbate the Jewish "demographic crisis" by failing to meet replacement rates in childbearing.[22] The weight of Jewish continuity is therefore placed on young Jews, especially Jewish women who are the bearers of the next generation. The blame, then, is all on the shoulders of Jewish women who are increasingly closing the gap between Jewish men and women in their pursuit of higher education, and then are the bearers of the consequences of such educational accomplishments when the delay in childbearing results in a nonreplacement rate of progeny in the Jewish community.

EVOLVING IMAGES OF YOUNG JEWISH WOMEN

So how are these concerns in the Jewish community over delayed marriage and childbearing as a result of increasing educational attainment made manifest in popular culture? It is only around the turn of the twenty-first century and beyond that the combination of increasing involvement and achievement of Jewish women in higher education and the continuing postponement of marriage and family formation could create such stigmatized images of young Jewish women who choose to pursue educational and artistic achievements over healthy relationships. While the JAP dominated popular culture in the 1970s through the 1990s as a scapegoat of Jewish anxieties over their middle-class status and assimilation, today the ramifications of that middle-class status that emphasizes education, career achievement, and small family size as reflected in these cultural images again places blame on the Jewish woman.

In several popular and independent films and cable and premium network television shows premiering since 2000, images of single, never-married, young Jewish women under thirty-five years old exhibit similar traits that constitute a new and evolving image of Jewish women as a reflection of demographic and community changes. From those as young as high school students to characters in their late twenties, this image has become common, though perhaps not monolithic, in portrayals of young Jewish women on screen.[23] What distinguishes this characterization of young Jewish women is their intelligence and creativity, as well as their relationships with other people. This image draws on some of the characteristics of the JAP, such as feminine wile and ambition; however, the JAP's ambition was not often to advance her own intellectual concerns or artistic endeavors, but relied instead on pursuits of advantageous marriage and consumption.[24] Another evolution from the JAP is the fact that young Jewish women's attempts at romance in television and film today are failures both in heterosexual and same-sex relationships, a departure from the JAP who usually had a male partner to manipulate. In addition, the young Jewish woman's relationships with her peers on a platonic level are also an issue today.

One major divergence from the JAP is that the creativity and intelligence of contemporary, young Jewish women are the focus in recent television and film productions. In five examples of films and television shows since the year 2000, all of the young, Jewish female characters are highly creative, often portrayed as writers or artists, as well as highly intelligent, for they are good students or brainy intellectuals. The independent film *Kissing Jessica Stein* from 2001 focuses on the evolving love life of Jessica Stein as she attempts her first relationship with another woman while she manages her family's matchmaking and her relationship with her Jewish ex-boyfriend and boss, Josh. At the beginning of the film, Jessica's intelligence is highlighted as she is portrayed sitting alone in her book-strewn apartment marveling over a passage from turn-of-the-century writer Rainer Maria Rilke; this emphasis on Jessica's intelligence is the impetus for her cerebral connection with Helen, who connects with Jessica by placing the same Rilke quote in a singles' advertisement that catches Jessica's attention. Jessica also works as an editor at a local newspaper and she paints in her spare time, which later in the film leads to a showing of her work at an art gallery. The 2009 independent film *Adam* presents the relationship between young, Jewish woman Beth and her neighbor Adam, who has Asperger's syndrome. Beth works by day as an elementary school teacher while she works on her manuscript as an aspiring children's book writer. The Showtime network series *The L Word*, which aired from 2004 until 2009, presents an ensemble of lesbian and bisexual characters living in Los Angeles and the intricacies of their work, love lives, families, and friendships. In the pilot, Jenny Schecter is introduced as a college graduate who evolves from a focused creative writing student to an accomplished author, just as her relationships evolve from ending a relationship with her long-term boyfriend to a series of flings and relationships with women. Jenny's intelligence and creativity are apparent in her move from creative writer to Hollywood writer and producer for the film version of her published work.

The world of high school similarly presents highly creative, young Jewish women as exemplified in the Fox network television show *Glee*, which follows the experiences of members of a high school glee club in Ohio. All of the members of the glee club are marginalized in some way, for they are tormented by popular students at the school, as well as the cheerleading coach, yet they rally to work toward national glee club championships as well as acceptance in the school. *Glee* features Rachel Berry as the show-stopping vocal talent behind the glee club, who is portrayed as a hardworking student and ambitious performer. The low-budget 2009 film *Bart Got a Room* follows Florida high school student Danny Stein as he seeks out a prom date to rival his nerdy friend Bart, who is rumored to have a hotel room in expectation of a "hookup" after the prom. The film features Camille Goodson, a brainy high school student and Danny's best friend, who is involved in planning the school's prom with three other misfits, and her intelligence and creativity are underscored in her work as one of the two anchors on the school's morning news program. While these young Jewish women succeed in art, writing, singing, and event planning, they fail in their relationships with romantic partners, as well as often in their friendships.

Mitigating the prominence of these women's intelligence and creativity is the collapse of their platonic and romantic relationships. Jessica Stein's neuroses and logical intelligence ruin her romantic endeavors, for she overthinks her relationship with Helen—such as when Jessica brings pamphlets about lesbian sex on one of their dates—which ultimately leads to her lack of interest in sex, due in part to her discomfort with the same-sex relationship. Jessica sabotages the relationship when she puts her intellectual pursuits before her romantic relationship, as evident in a scene when Jessica refuses to stop reading a book in bed when Helen attempts to make the evening more intimate. Eventually Helen ends their relationship because she feels they have become "roommates," and Jessica is oblivious to the problems in their relationship. The film ends with Jessica at a crossroads between failed relationships as she meets ex-girlfriend Helen for lunch after bumping into ex-boyfriend Josh.

The relationship depicted in *Adam* similarly shows an intelligent young Jewish woman entering an ultimately doomed relationship with an unlikely partner as Beth is paired with Adam, a young man with Asperger's syndrome. As their relationship plays out, Beth is alienated from her friends and family due to her relationship with Adam, whom she defends and follows despite his difficulty with social norms, creating tension and ultimately leading to the demise of their relationship. Adam is seen as having the most growth in the film, for he is able to move out of New York and relate better to people in the end, due in large part to his relationship with Beth. But Beth is left unseen at the end of the film and her creative pursuits are seen to trump her relationship, for her only accomplishment is publishing a children's book based on Adam, the object of her doomed romantic relationship.

Jenny Schecter has perhaps the most dramatic failure in her relationships of all of these examples, for as columnist Gina Abelkop describes Jenny's trajectory in *The L Word*, Jenny "fucked over her friends . . . and was generally unpleasant and completely egomaniacal," and is the one character on the show who is "widely disliked."[25] While Jenny pursues many relationships over the six seasons of the show, first with a male partner and then with several female partners, she consistently ruins those relationships. One of Jenny's more dramatic failed relationships is with her doppelganger; in season 5, Jenny begins and ruins a relationship with the actress who plays the character based on herself in the film version of her autobiographical book. Additionally, Jenny is often shunned by her friends because of her selfish and condescending attitude. In the end, Jenny is "killed off," for she "must die for her sins."[26] Jenny's sins are her single-minded pursuit of her own intellectual and artistic endeavors in her writing and film work, as well as her self-centered motivations in her intimate relationships.

Teenagers Camille and Rachel similarly attempt to create or sustain questionable relationships and are punished socially, downplaying their intellectual and creative successes. Familial pressure and expectations fall on Camille to attend the prom with main character Danny Stein in *Bart Got a Room*, and she does make a desperate, though platonic, attempt to ask him to the prom, but he rejects her. Camille eventually gets ditched at the prom by her last-minute date, a friend whose girlfriend could not attend. Danny eventually reconnects with Camille, but it is an unsatisfying platonic reunion as he revels in spending prom night with his "oldest friend," along with his parents. Camille is left in the position of second best, condemned to a lonely prom night only partially assuaged by the friend who rejected her in the first place, and who does not seek any sort of romantic relationship with the homely, though intelligent and creative, Jewish girl.

Over the course of the show's first three seasons, Rachel Berry in *Glee* displays a much wider range in her relationships and failures. In the first season of the show, Rachel pines after high school football and glee club star Finn and attempts to seduce the glee club coach Mr. Schuester, and her short-lived relationship with football player and glee club member Noah "Puck" Puckerman fails because it was "built on a fantasy" due to their shared Jewish heritage.[27] In the third season, Rachel and Finn may be a couple, but Rachel's motives in the relationship are often questioned, such as Finn's rejection of Rachel when she tries to use sex to understand the character and prepare to audition for the role of Maria in *West Side Story*.[28] Even after Finn proposes to Rachel, the engagement is constantly called into question by the glee club members, Rachel's and Finn's parents, and even by Rachel and Finn. Most of the critiques of the engagement revolve around their age and Rachel's ambitions to pursue theater in New York City. With every twist in her path to gain acceptance to an elite theater school in New York, Rachel struggles to balance her engagement to Finn with her dreams for stardom. She may offer to defer her acceptance to the theater school, but only because her own dreams would not be complete if Finn could not join her in New York. Yet, Finn also recognizes Rachel's talent and ambition at the cost of their relationship, for he arranges for her to take a train to New York City to attend the elite theater college at the end of season 3, seemingly ending the relationship in order for her to pursue her career.[29]

Even beyond these typical high school flings and broken relationships, Rachel is often ostracized by the rest of the glee club members, further proof of her social failure. All of the glee club members, including the cheerleaders and football players who join the club, are ridiculed and rejected by the rest of the high school. While these characters also have relationships that sometimes fail, they remain a tight-knit group of friends, marking Rachel as the only true outcast, often made to sit apart from the other members of the glee club in the choir room when they are frustrated by her seemingly self-centered pursuit of her own talent. Even Rachel recognizes her precarious social place in the glee club for she states, "People just don't like me," to which Finn replies, "Yeah, you might wanna work on that."[30] In later seasons she manages to form tentative friendships with several of the glee club members, but these relationships are conditional, for one wrong move from Rachel leads her once again into rejection and isolation. She may be talented, but as a person she is not wanted.

ISOLATED, INTELLIGENT WOMEN VERSUS
SOCIABLE, SLACKER MEN

These images of young Jewish women who are creative, talented, and
intelligent but social self-saboteurs seem quite stark in comparison with
contemporary images of young Jewish men in the media. Demonstrating
another evolution from the JAP who was dependent on a father or husband figure—for as Prell notes, "there is no JAP without the Jewish male
partner"[31] —Jewish women in television and film today find an opposite
in portrayals of Jewish male characters. One important change in this
pairing is that for both images of Jewish women and men in television
and film, their characters are not limited to heterosexual relationships.
While the JAP was often depicted as "victimiz[ing] her husband," and
Jewish men were portrayed as "remain[ing] vigilant against the JAP,"[32]
young Jews on screen are now shown in interfaith and same-sex relationships, yet they still maintain important character traits that differentiate
images of Jewish women from Jewish men. These characters in same-sex
relationships may distance themselves from the pressure to marry and
procreate because of their sexuality, but the fact that these character traits
are consistent for Jewish women in comparison to those typical of Jewish
men despite their sexuality underscores the punishment of Jewish wom-
en for their pursuit of intellectual and creative success over relationships,
while Jewish men escape such admonishment.

However, the boundary between characteristics distinguishing images of Jewish women and men is blurred when comparing the images of
young Jewish women today with older versions of the image of Jewish
men long popularized by Woody Allen. In her article on several Jewish
films focused on Jewish women, including *Kissing Jessica Stein*, Ruth D.
Johnston notes, "A number of recent women's films . . . have resisted the
Jewish woman's systematic exclusion from representation by reclaiming
Woody Allen territory and swapping the roles of male schlemiel and JAP,
which . . . are actually reverse or mirror images of one another . . . both
are sexual neurotics."[33] Contemporary images of Jewish women are
blending both positive and negative Jewish male characteristics in their
incorporation of Woody Allen–esque features such as neurotic personalities and sexual failure, as well as highly intelligent characters who are
often involved in the arts. These images of young Jewish women, then,
are stunted by all of the drawbacks of this older image of Jewish men
with their sexual insecurity and self-centered loss of relationships, even
as they also benefit from following similar career paths and achieving
professional success.

While images of the young Jewish woman are adapting characteristics
from the Woody Allen realm of Jewish male stereotypes, compared with
contemporary images of young Jewish men, she is still losing out. As
Hartman and Hartman note, Jewish men and Jewish women both

achieve high levels of education, they are both "much more highly educated" than "the broader U.S. white population," and both Jewish men
and women exhibit the trend in delaying marriage.[34] So how do Jewish
women get saddled with a negative stereotype of young, unmarried
women with few or no friends and doomed relationships, while Jewish
men are spared such disparagement and rejection? Contemporary images of Jewish women seem to be paired with another evolving image of
the Jewish male that complements her in his contrasting characteristics as
he is often depicted as a slacker, pothead, or nerd.[35] In these images, the
young Jewish male is never friendless, he is constantly pursuing romantic
relationships, and even when these relationships fail, the Jewish male is
seen to triumph in the end. Daniel Itzkovitz describes this evolving image
of Jewish men as follows:

> Most of the "new schlemiels" are hardly "edgy new personas," but
> rather reprisals of old personas, somehow made more palatable for
> mass audiences. This becomes clear in the repetitive nature of many of
> the characterizations, whereby the Jewish man has become an ordi-
> nary, lovable, supremely unthreatening *mensch* who could use a little
> excitement and finds it in a pairing with a non-Jewish and often zanily
> extreme character.[36]

The "lovable" and "ordinary" personas of these young Jewish men in
television and film help them become "vaguely eccentric embodiments of
the middle-class American everyman" who can then "embody . . . [the]
status quo."[37] It is because in these images young Jewish men represent
nonthreatening averageness as "non-professional Jews, seemingly devot-
ing their lives to taking drugs, playing video games and *schtupping* . . .
rather than pursuing successful bourgeois goals such as careers and families"[38] that they can be accepted. An exact opposite of images of the
Jewish woman, the Jewish man has friends, achieves a mediocre level of
success in his work life, and is often successfully paired romantically
with a non-Jewish partner.

The opposing nature of these images produces a Jewish man on screen
who is welcomed socially because he is mediocre. While this image of
Jewish men does assume some level of intelligence and education, the
Jewish male does not experience the stigma of delayed marriage and
childbearing as a result of educational achievement, for these characters
are almost always rewarded with romantic, and often non-Jewish, partners. Their creativity and intelligence is tempered by their nonthreatening "schlemiel-ness," which enables them to stand in as an "everyman,"
avoiding any social condemnation or failure.

SEXUALITY AND IMAGES OF YOUNG JEWISH MEN AND WOMEN

Additionally, these images of Jewish men and women differ in their sexual interest. While contemporary images of young Jewish women often draw on the neuroses of Woody Allen characters who frequently exhibited sexual impotence, images of Jewish men in television and film again demonstrate opposite characteristics. Images of Jewish men in popular culture often show them as obsessed with sex, also a continuation of a Jewish male stereotype from the past.[39] On the contrary, Jewish women's sexuality is not often highlighted in these media representations, and in the case of Jessica Stein mentioned earlier, is often downplayed to friendship or a muted sexuality. Jenny Schecter exhibited the most explicit sexual relationships and encounters in *The L Word*, likely due in part to the conditions of the show's run on a subscription-based cable channel; however, her personality and sexuality are ultimately rejected through her demise at the end of the show. In these portrayals of young Jews' sexuality, it is clear that images of Jewish women, with their chaste, neurotic, or threatening sexuality, are bearing the blame for delayed marriage and childbearing. If they are doomed to delay marriage and produce fewer children, then the images drawn from those demographic changes must reflect such trends in young Jewish women's chastity and failure in relationships.

While the Jewish male succeeds with mediocrity, the Jewish woman refuses to accept the status quo and strives for intellectual, creative, or career success over her social connections. Images of Jewish men can rely on their comfortable averageness and portray them as sex-crazed young men, while Jewish women constitute the threat of ambition and achievement that overrides sexuality. Entrepreneurship and ambition are usually values espoused by the broader American culture as well as the Jewish community; however, because the Jewish woman delays marriage and childbearing in pursuit of her ambition, she is viewed as a threat to the community. Her talent alienates people, unlike the bumbling "antihero" that is the Jewish male;[40] therefore, she is ostracized and rejected for choosing education and career over pursuing relationships and family formation. It is made especially clear that the Jewish woman is bearing the burden of these trends in these media images because images of the Jewish male do not similarly bear the consequences of ambition in education and career. The Jewish woman is often left alone and unloved, while the Jewish male succeeds with a non-Jewish romantic partner, therefore, targeting the Jewish woman as the crux of the perceived problem with delayed marriage and childbearing in the community.

CONCLUSION

So why is the Jewish man the accepted everyman, and the Jewish woman is rejected and cannot be "palatable for mass audiences"? Images of Jewish men can rely on the fact that, despite the statistics on delayed marriage for Jewish men, for they may be complicit in delaying marriage and then producing later and fewer if any children, they are not the embodied cause of delayed and decreased childbearing. Instead, Jewish women are portrayed in a way that highlights their connection with a "decline . . . in the fertility level of American Jewish women,"[41] for they value achievement and creativity over their relationships and often lack an interest in sexual relations. Images of Jewish men are not burdened with the criticisms of delayed childbearing, for they are not portrayed as the direct cause, as their career attainments in these images are mediocre, and they are often paired with non-Jewish partners, hence distancing themselves from Jewish continuity in any case.

I have argued that contemporary images of young, single Jewish women in television and film echo demographic concerns in the United States in general, but are of particular concern in the Jewish community. Images of Jewish women in popular culture are not rewarded for their intelligence and creativity reflecting higher educational attainment, but instead are plagued with qualities that make it difficult for them to form and maintain romantic and platonic relationships, paralleling trends to delay marriage and childbearing in the community. These fictional images promote a vicious cycle for Jewish women, for if these characters do not demonstrate sustained relationships with friends or romantic partners, then delayed marriage and childbearing are further reinforced.

While the Jewish woman may be a scapegoat for such anxieties over demography and Jewish continuity through her media representations, such images hardly alleviate the community and gendered pressures she faces. Once again it is the Jewish woman who is painted as less likeable and unsuccessful in relationships, while the Jewish man is spared such rebuke. As seen in the demographic data, Jewish women, as a cohort, are achieving high levels of education and career success. In their representation on screen today, they are no longer depicted as unproductive princesses who use men to achieve their career goals. However, characterizations of young Jewish women are still plagued by the consequences of the JAP image as they are presented in narratives that punish them for their problematic characteristics of ambition, creativity, and intelligence, rather than rewarding them for signifying Jewish middle-class values of high educational and occupational achievement. Ironically, these images distort demographic realities in which American Jewish men and women share ambitions and achievements. It remains to be seen when images of young Jewish women will positively reflect the reality of a disappearing gender gap.

NOTES

1. *Glee*, "The Rhodes Not Taken," 2009.

2. Nathan Abrams, *The New Jew in Film* (New Brunswick, NJ: Rutgers University Press, 2012), 44.

3. See Abrams, *The New Jew in Film*, and Riv-Ellen Prell, *Fighting to Become Americans* (Boston: Beacon Press, 1999).

4. Prell, *Fighting to Become Americans*, 190.

5. Prell, *Fighting to Become Americans*, 189.

6. Prell, *Fighting to Become Americans*, 201, 204.

7. Prell, *Fighting to Become Americans*, 186, 188. Examples scholars cite of the JAP in film are Marjorie Morningstar in *Marjorie Morningstar*, Brenda Patimkin in *Goodbye, Columbus*, and Lila Kolodny in *The Heartbreak Kid*. See *The Modern Jewish Experience in World Cinema*, edited by Lawrence Baron (Waltham, MA: Brandeis University Press, 2011) for details.

8. Abrams, *The New Jew in Film*, 69; Prell, *Fighting to Become Americans*, 204.

9. Images that in some ways rejected the JAP image during this time and portrayed well-educated, productive, politically active young Jewish women are Katie Morosky in *The Way We Were* (1973) and Allison Porchnik in *Annie Hall* (1977). In different ways these women are rejected for their intelligence and political activism, but mostly because they are "too Jewish" for their non-Jewish and Jewish male partners, respectively. See Eric Goldman, *The American Jewish Story through Cinema* (Austin: University of Texas Press, 2013), 131–36; and Sylvia Barack Fishman, "When Chippewa Falls Meets Manhattan," in *The Modern Jewish Experience*, ed. Lawrence Baron (Waltham, MA: Brandeis University Press, 2011), 303–10.

10. William W. Brickman, "Education," in *Encyclopaedia Judaica*, 2nd ed., ed. Michael Berenbaum and Fred Skolnik (Detroit: Macmillan Reference, 2007), 6:159–61.

11. Sylvia Barack Fishman, "Choosing Lives: Evolving Gender Roles in American Jewish Families," in *The Cambridge Companion to American Judaism*, ed. Dana Evan Kaplan (Cambridge: Cambridge University Press, 2006), 249.

12. Harriet Hartman and Moshe Hartman, *Gender and American Jews* (Waltham, MA: Brandeis University Press, 2009), 15.

13. Hartman and Hartman, *Gender and American Jews*, 22.

14. Hartman and Hartman, *Gender and American Jews*, 22.

15. Prell, *Fighting to Become Americans*, 201.

16. Fishman, "Choosing Lives," 237.

17. Sylvia Barack Fishman, *Jewish Life and American Culture* (Albany: State University of New York Press, 2000), 97–98.

18. Hartman and Hartman, *Gender and American Jews*, 37.

19. Hartman and Hartman, *Gender and American Jews*, 26.

20. Arnold Dashefsky and Irving M. Levine, "The Jewish Family: Continuity and Change," in *Families and Religions: Conflict and Change in Modern Society*, ed. William V. D'Antonio and Joan Aldous (Beverly Hills, CA: Sage Publications, 1983), 163–90.

21. Elliot N. Dorff, "Judaism and Children in the United States," in *Children and Childhood in American Religions*, ed. Don S. Browning and Bonnie J. Miller-McLemore (New Brunswick, NJ: Rutgers University Press, 2009), 74.

22. Dorff, "Judaism and Children in the United States," 74.

23. While an analysis of the HBO series *Girls* is beyond the scope of this chapter, it is interesting to note that while the character of Shoshana, the only clearly distinguished Jewish woman among the four main characters, may represent the JAP in many ways, she is the only current student and the only virgin among the four girls at the start of the show.

24. Prell, *Fighting to Become Americans*, 186, 188.

25. Gina Abelkop, "R.I.P. Jenny Schecter: In Memory of a TV Lesbian," *Jewcy*, March 2, 2009. http://www.jewcy.com/arts-and-culture/rip_jenny_schecter_memory_tv_lesbian (accessed 6 April 2011).

26. Abelkop, "R.I.P. Jenny Schecter."
27. *Glee*, "Ballad," "Mash-Up," 2009.
28. *Glee*, "The First Time," 2011.
29. *Glee*, "Goodbye," 2012.
30. *Glee*, "Wheels," 2009.
31. Prell, *Fighting to Become Americans*, 194.
32. Prell, *Fighting to Become Americans*, 194.
33. Ruth D. Johnston, "Joke-Work: the Construction of Jewish Postmodern Identity in Contemporary Theory and American Film," in *You Should See Yourself*, ed. Vincent Brook (New Brunswick, NJ: Rutgers University Press, 2006), 216. A *schlemiel*, in Yiddish, is a "sort of cosmic fool combined with cosmic victim," as described by Abrams, *The New Jew in Film*, 6.
34. Hartman and Hartman, *Gender and American Jews*, 17. Recent data from the Pew Religion and Public Life Project on Jewish Americans similarly document this educational achievement of American Jews in 2013, finding that "nearly six-in-ten adult Jews are college graduates, including 28% who have obtained a post-graduate degree. By comparison, roughly three-in-ten U.S. adults overall are college graduates, including 10% who have a post-graduate degree." Pew Research Center, *A Portrait of Jewish Americans* (Washington, DC: Pew Research Center, 2013), 42, http://www.pewforum. org/2013/10/01/jewish-american-beliefs-attitudes-culture-survey (accessed 18 November 2013).
35. Examples of such Jewish male characters are Ben Stone in *Knocked Up* (2007), Howard Wolowitz in *The Big Bang Theory* (2007–2012), Noah "Puck" Puckerman in *Glee* (2009–2012), and Max Blum in *Happy Endings* (2011–2012).
36. Daniel Itzkovitz, "They All Are Jews," in *You Should See Yourself*, ed. Vincent Brook (New Brunswick, NJ: Rutgers University Press, 2006), 243–44. A *mensch*, in Yiddish, is "a decent, upstanding, ethical and responsible person with admirable characteristics," as described by Abrams, *The New Jew in Film*, 20.
37. Itzkovitz, "They All Are Jews," 241, 245.
38. Abrams, *The New Jew in Film*, 32. *Schtupping* in Yiddish means sexual intercourse.
39. As Abrams argues, these images reclaim Jewish male sexuality from negative images representing menacing sex-obsession in Jewish men in early anti-Semitic images. Abrams, *The New Jew in Film*, 68.
40. Itzkovitz, "They All Are Jews," 241.
41. Fishman, "Choosing Lives," 240.

BIBLIOGRAPHY

Abelkop, Gina. "R.I.P. Jenny Schecter: In Memory of a TV Lesbian." *Jewcy*, March 2, 2009.   http://www.jewcy.com/arts-and-culture/rip_jenny_schecter_memory_tv_ lesbian (accessed 6 April 2011).
Abrams, Nathan. *The New Jew in Film*. New Brunswick, NJ: Rutgers University Press, 2012.
Adam. Directed by Max Mayer. 2010. Los Angeles: 20th Century Fox Home Entertainment, 2010. DVD.
Baron Lawrence, ed. *The Modern Jewish Experience in World Cinema*. Waltham, MA: Brandeis University Press, 2011.
Bart Got a Room. Directed by Brian Hecker. 2009. Beverly Hills, CA: Anchor Bay Entertainment, 2009. DVD.
The Big Bang Theory. Directed by Mark Cendrowski. Written by Chuck Lorre, Bill Prady, and Steven Molaro. Performed by Johnny Galecki, Jim Parsons, Simon Helberg, Kunal Nayyar, Kaley Cuoco. Los Angeles: CBS, 2007–2012.
Brickman, William W. "Education." In *Encyclopaedia Judaica*, 2nd ed., edited by M. Berenbaum and F. Skolnik, vol. 6, 159–61. Detroit: Macmillan Reference, 2007.

Brook, Vincent. "Film." In *You Should See Yourself*, edited by Vincent Brook, 205–6. New Brunswick, NJ: Rutgers University Press, 2006.

Dashefsky, Arnold, and Irving M. Levine. "The Jewish Family: Continuity and Change." In *Families and Religions: Conflict and Change in Modern Society*, edited by W. V. D'Antonio and J. Aldous, 163–90. Beverly Hills, CA: Sage Publications, 1983.

Dorff, Elliot N. "Judaism and Children in the United States." In *Children and Childhood in American Religions*, edited by D. S. Browning and B. J. Miller-McLemore, 71–84. New Brunswick, NJ: Rutgers University Press, 2009.

Fishman, Sylvia Barack. *Jewish Life and American Culture*. Albany: State University of New York Press, 2000.

———. "Choosing Lives: Evolving Gender Roles in American Jewish Families." In *The Cambridge Companion to American Judaism*, edited by Dana Evan Kaplan, 237–52. Cambridge: Cambridge University Press, 2006.

———. "When Chippewa Falls Meets Manhattan." In *The Modern Jewish Experience in World Cinema*, edited by Lawrence Baron, 303–10. Waltham, MA: Brandeis University Press, 2011.

Glee. Directed by Brad Falchuk, Bradley Buecker, and Eric Stoltz. Written by Ian Brennan, Brad Falchuk, Ryan Murphy. Performed by Matthew Morrison, Jane Lynch, Lea Michele, Cory Monteith, Mark Salling. Los Angeles: 20th Century Fox Television, 2009–2012.

Goldman, Eric. *The American Jewish Story through Cinema*. Austin: University of Texas Press, 2013.

Happy Endings. Directed by Rob Greenberg, Jay Chandrasekhar, and Jeff Melman. Written by David Caspe, Daniel Libman, and Matthew Libman. Performed by Eliza Coupe, Elisha Cuthbert, Zachary Knighton, Adam Pally, and Damon Wayans Jr. Los Angeles: ABC, 2011–2012.

Hartman, Harriet, and Moshe Hartman. *Gender and American Jews*. Waltham, MA: Brandeis University Press, 2009.

Itzkovitz, Daniel. "They All Are Jews." In *You Should See Yourself*, edited by Vincent Brook, 230–51. New Brunswick, NJ: Rutgers University Press, 2006.

Johnston, Ruth D. "Joke-Work: the Construction of Jewish Postmodern Identity in Contemporary Theory and American Film." In *You Should See Yourself*, edited by Vincent Brook, 207–29 . New Brunswick, NJ: Rutgers University Press, 2006.

Kissing Jessica Stein. Directed by Charles Herman-Wurmfeld. 2002. Los Angeles: 20th Century Fox Home Entertainment, 2002. DVD.

Knocked Up. Directed by Judd Apatow. 2007. Los Angeles: Universal Studios Home Entertainment, 2007. DVD.

The L Word. Directed by Rose Troche, Angela Robinson, and Ilene Chaiken. Written by Michele Abbott, Ilene Chaiken, and Kathy Greenberg. Performed by Jennifer Beals, Laurel Holloman, Mia Kirshner, and Katherine Moennig. Los Angeles: Showtime, 2004–2009.

Pew Research Center. *A Portrait of Jewish Americans*. Religion and Public Life Project. Washington DC: Pew Research Center, 2013. http://www.pewforum.org/2013/10/01/jewish-american-beliefs-attitudes-culture-survey (accessed 18 November 2013).

Prell, Riv-Ellen. *Fighting to Become Americans*. Boston: Beacon Press, 1999.

Index

About the Editor

Laura Mattoon D'Amore is assistant professor of American studies at Roger Williams University. She received her PhD from the American and New England Studies program at Boston University. She was a former research scholar in the Women's, Gender, and Sexuality Studies program at Northeastern University. She regularly chairs presentation areas at the Film and History conference and has also presented at the Popular Culture/American Culture Association and the National Women's Studies Association. She is the editor of *Bound by Love: Familial Bonding in Film and Television Since 1950* (2009) and co-editor of *We Are What We Remember: The American Past through Commemoration* (2012). She has also published articles and chapters about comic book superheroines, supermoms, working motherhood, and historical memory. She is currently writing a book about the American supermom.

About the Contributors

Rachel S. Bernstein is a PhD student in the Departments of Near Eastern and Judaic Studies and Sociology at Brandeis University, where she received her MA in Near Eastern and Judaic studies and women's and gender studies. Her main research interests include representations of Jewish women in television and film; religious and cultural expression in emerging adulthood; and Jewish culture and the arts.

Sheri Chinen Biesen is associate professor of film history at Rowan University and author of *Blackout: World War II and the Origins of Film Noir* (Johns Hopkins University Press, 2005). She received her PhD at the University of Texas at Austin and her MA and BA at the University of Southern California School of Cinematic Arts, and she has taught film at USC, the University of California, and the University of Texas, as well as in England. She has contributed to *Film and History, Historical Journal of Film, Radio and Television, Quarterly Review of Film and Video, Literature/Film Quarterly, Film Noir: The Encyclopedia, Film Noir Reader 4, Gangster Film Reader, Film Noir: The Directors, Film and Literary Modernism, Popular Culture Review, The Historian, Television and Television History,* and *American Jewish History,* and she has edited *The Velvet Light Trap.* Her newest book, *Music in the Shadows: Noir Musical Films* was published in 2014.

Raewyn Campbell is a PhD candidate in the faculty of law, humanities, and the arts at the University of Wollongong in Australia. Her research is on shifting discursive regimes surrounding nerd/geek identity and the ripple effects these shifts have throughout culture. She is particularly interested in the intersection of nerd identity and gender in the realm of pop culture. This research has been a cunning way for Rae to combine her own nerdy interests with employment.

Stephen R. Duncan is associate professor of history at Bronx Community College–CUNY. His articles and research interests span from Civil War journalism to television satire as a transnational phenomenon in the 1970s. He is currently completing a study of American urban underground culture and its role in social liberation movements during the early Cold War.

Mikaela Feroli is a graduate student at the London School of Economics Gender Institute. Her research interests include feminist media representation and the cultural construction of sexual identity.

Helen Kang recently completed her PhD in sociology at Simon Fraser University. In her dissertation she examined the emergence of and shifts in the moral and scientific norms of medical doctors in Canada. Her research areas include health humanities, science and technology studies, and popular culture and the media. Her work has been published in *Mass Communication & Society* and the *Journal of Gay and Lesbian Social Service*.

Linda Levitt is an assistant professor in communication studies at Stephen F. Austin State University. Much of her research investigates the intersection of media and cultural memory, and she has published work on television studies, celebrity culture, and public acts of commemoration. Dr. Levitt's recent publications include "Death on Display: Reifying Stardom through Hollywood's Dark Tourism" in *Velvet Light Trap*, and "Speaking Memory, Building History: The Influence of Victims' Families at the World Trade Center Site" in *Radical History Review*.

Stefania Marghitu is a PhD student with the Division of Critical Studies at the University of Southern California. Her current research project focuses on women show runners in contemporary television, and her primary interests deal with post–network TV and production practices, feminist TV criticism, and authorship. You can find her paper on Lena Dunham's authorship in HBO's *Girls* in *Gender Forum* and her interview with the co-creator of HBO's *Family Tree* Jim Piddock in *Flow TV*.

Melissa Meade is associate professor of humanities at Colby-Sawyer College in New Hampshire, where she teaches courses in media and cultural history, and gender studies. She is working on a book-length manuscript investigating "all-girl" sonic culture in the mid-twentieth-century United States. She serves on the boards of the Third Wave Foundation and the New Hampshire Women's Caucus.

Natasha Patterson recently defended her PhD in women's studies at Simon Fraser University, exploring women's narratives of reality TV participation and the methodological implications such work poses for feminist cultural studies audience research. She teaches and publishes in the areas of gender and film, television, postfeminist media culture, and celebrity culture.

De Anna J. Reese is an assistant professor in the Department of History and the Africana Studies Program at California State University, Fresno. Originally from Los Angeles, Reese earned both an MA and PhD in US history from the University of Missouri–Columbia. Her areas of emphasis include twentieth-century African American, women's, social, cultural, and urban history. Within these areas, Reese examines the intersection of race, gender, class, culture, and identity. Her current research explores the relationship between black beauty culture, black female entrepreneurship, and the career of African American beauty pioneer and philanthropist Annie Turnbo Malone.

Amanda Stone is a graduate student at the Savannah College of Art and Design, studying gender and sexuality in various forms of media. She is currently writing two master's theses—one examining the visual culture of menstrual activism and the other an auteurist analysis of German filmmaker Rosa von Praunheim. Amanda received her BA from Middle Tennessee State University, concentrating in art history, American literature, and women's studies.

Margaret Tally is chair of the Policy Studies Program and professor of social policy in the School for Graduate Studies at the State University of New York, Empire State College. She is the author of "Television Culture and Women's Lives," the co-editor of "The Millennials on Film and Television," and "HBO's *Girls*: Questions of Gender, Politics, and Millennial Angst," and a contributor to collections including *MTV and Teen Pregnancy* and *Bound by Love: Familial Bonding in Film and Television Since 1950*. Tally has also written on the marketing of teens in Hollywood, on the representation of middle-aged women's sexuality in popular culture, and on changing gender roles as portrayed in television series from the 1960s to the 1990s.

Allison Whitney is an assistant professor of film and media studies in the Department of English at Texas Tech University. She holds a PhD in cinema and media studies from the University of Chicago, and her research interests include the history of film technologies, representations of space exploration, and studies of gender in film genre.